THE INCONVENIENT TRUTH

CHINOOK ZD576
CAUSE AND CULPABILITY

David Hill
with John Blakeley

The views expressed are those of the author alone and should not be taken to represent those of Her Majesty's Government, the Ministry of Defence, HM Armed Forces or any Government agency, unless quoted. The events outlined are real. Other participants may have their own views.

By its very nature, this book draws in part on the work of others. Unfortunately, some have passed away, others remain anonymous due to the subject nature. 'Fair use' is claimed, and only those who have placed their identity in the public domain, or have been identified by MoD, are named.

Other books by David Hill, in paperback and Kindle

Their Greatest Disgrace - The campaign to clear the Chinook ZD576 pilots
(2016)

Breaking the Military Covenant - Who speaks for the dead?
(2018)

Red 5 - An investigation into the death of Flight Lieutenant Sean Cunningham
(2019, updated 2023)

A Noble Anger - The manslaughter of Corporal Jonathan Bayliss
(2022)

All titles published by Nemesis Books
nemesisbooks@aol.com

The issues related in these books are ongoing, and they will be regularly updated. If you have purchased a previous edition, please contact the author for a free Kindle or pdf version.

https://sites.google.com/site/militaryairworthiness/home

All proceeds to St Richard's Hospice, Worcester
https://www.strichards.org.uk/raise-funds/

Dedicated to those who lost their lives on 2 June 1994

Major Richard Allen
Colonel Christopher Biles
Detective Inspector Dennis Bunting
Detective Chief Superintendent Desmond Conroy
Flight Lieutenant Richard Cook
Martin Dalton
Detective Superintendent Phillip Davidson
Detective Inspector Stephen Davidson
John Deverell
Major Christopher Dockerty
Assistant Chief Constable Brian Fitzsimons
Master Airloadmaster Graham Forbes
Detective Superintendent Robert Foster
Lieutenant Colonel Richard Gregory-Smith
Detective Superintendent William Gwilliam
Sergeant Kevin Hardie
John Haynes
Major Antony Hornby
Anne James
Detective Inspector Kevin Magee
Michael Maltby
Detective Chief Superintendent Maurice Neilly
Detective Superintendent Ian Phoenix
Major Roy Pugh
Stephen Rickard
Major Gary Sparks
Flight Lieutenant Jonathan Tapper
Lieutenant Colonel John Tobias
Lieutenant Colonel George Williams

David Hill and John Blakeley

As a civilian engineer and avionics/aircraft programme manager in MoD, David Hill led engineering and project teams, and gained experience of initiating, conducting and managing technical investigations, and implementing recommendations. His submissions to the Nimrod XV230 Coroner (2007) and the Nimrod Review (2007-9) precipitated the resetting of airworthiness management. His submission to the Mull of Kintyre Review (2010-11) demonstrated the RAF Chinook fleet was not airworthy on 2 June 1994.

Air Commodore John Blakeley has extensive leadership and front line experience. He has been the engineering member of both Unit Inquiries and Boards of Inquiry. On a *pro bono* basis, and at the behest of Michael Tapper, father of Flight Lieutenant Jonathan Tapper, in 2003 he wrote a paper, reproduced here, studying the airworthiness, engineering and maintenance aspects of the Chinook ZD576 Board of Inquiry. This complemented David's work by viewing matters from an In-Service perspective.

Both are retired, and continue to provide assistance to bereaved families and their legal teams, and Coroners in both military and civil accidents.

ZD576 as an HC Mk1 *(Crown Copyright)*

Acknowledgements

Robert Burke, test pilot

Tony Cable, Senior Inspector, Air Accidents Investigation Branch

Robin Cane, pilot

Tony Collins, journalist

Brian Dixon, former RAF medic and police officer

Andy Fairfield, pilot

Steve George, engineer

Simon 'Satori' Hendley, composer of 'ZD576'

Omar Malik, pilot and author

Malcolm Perks, software engineer

Niven Phoenix, pilot, son of Detective Superintendent Ian Phoenix, RUC, late Parachute Regiment

Dr Susan Phoenix, retired military nurse (Queen Alexandra's Royal Army Nursing Corps) and now author, who lost her husband Ian on ZD576

Dr Michael Powers QC

The late Mike Ramsden, engineer and aviation journalist

Chris Seal, pilot and author

Tim Slessor, author

David Walmsley, journalist

and...

the many, serving and retired, who helped but wish to remain anonymous. Thank you all.

ZD576

The isle is calling heroes
A green siren set apart
The flying men have landed with a start
In the corridors intelligence
Weave a shroud of negligence
The swords are rusted to a stain
And I don't know where to place the blame

The differential airspeed
The instruments and information feeds
The dossiers dosed and fixed
ZD576
A black mark, an unfound claim
And I don't know where to place the blame

A house rises from the brine
Cloaked in white somite and shine
The heroes come to rest at last
'Too late to climb, too young, too fast'
No accolades, no names, no fame
And I don't know where to place the blame

There's something wrong in Avalon. Once the future king, malfunction. Now the confidence has gone. ZD576

(The Ministry of Defence notes the Committee's report, but does not accept its conclusion).

<u>Simon 'Satori' Hendley, 2003. Reproduced with permission.</u>
<u>Performed by Rome Burns</u>

Contents

Foreword	1
Preface	3
PART 1 - GENERAL BACKGROUND	6
1. Beinn na Lice	7
2. The Inquiries	9
3. Evidence is a bridge to the truth	33
4. Double standards	36
PART 2 - ACCIDENT INVESTIGATION	43
5. Preventing recurrence	44
6. The lead anomaly	57
PART 3 - TECHNICAL	66
7. The Full Authority Digital Engine Control (FADEC)	67
8. Digital Electronic Control Units (DECU)	77
9. Communications System	85
10. Navigation System	94
PART 4 - AIRMANSHIP	110
11. Navigation	111
12. Incapacitation and fatigue	116
13. Flying too fast and too low	120
14. Air Commodore Carl Scott	125
PART 5 - RAIN UNRAVELLED TALES	131
15. A second aircraft	132
16. If there is no evidence, there is no logic	137
17. State sponsored murder	140
PART 6 - UNDEMANDED FLIGHT CONTROL MOVEMENTS	148
18. UFCM history 1994-2001	149
19. Known causes of UFCMs in Chinook	159
20. Four examples of UFCMs	169

PART 7 - THE END OF THE BEGINNING   176
21. Concealed evidence   177
22. Power destroys all reason   191
23. Conclusions   195

ANNEX A   199
Review of the Airworthiness, Engineering and Maintenance aspects of the Board of Inquiry into Chinook HC Mk2 ZD576

Author's note   226
Bibliography   227
Glossary of Terms and Abbreviations   229

Figures

1. Overview of intended route
2. Mull of Kintyre lighthouse
3. Orographic cloud over the Mull of Kintyre
4. Typical orographic cloud
5. Carnlough, looking north to the Mull of Kintyre
6. Slide 14 of Air Chief Marshal Day's evidence
7. Actual terrain profile
8. ZD576 SuperTANS
9. Aircraft sightings 1730-1755, 2 June 1994
10. Southern tip of the Kintyre Peninsula showing area of Tiree radar trace and impact site
11. AN/ALQ-157 Infra-Red Countermeasures System

Foreword

'Those who plead their cause in the absence of an opponent can invent to their heart's content, and can pontificate without taking into account the opposite point of view, for aggressors are always quick to attack those who have no means of defence'.

Christine de Pizan

Having watched this tragedy unfold, from standing on the Mull the morning after the accident, to the present day, I have always refrained from applying the all-too-easy tones of conspiracy to an accident that ended in mystery. The loss was too great and too important to encourage a growing cottage industry of theorists that developed over the years. Especially as there was apparently no evidence pointing to a cause, no eye-witnesses or survivors, an unanswered final radio call, and no cockpit or flight data recorders on board.

For too long amid this vacuum I gave the benefit of the doubt to the Ministry of Defence. I believe in government and I could not bring myself to believe those entrusted with the Sovereign duty to protect would simply blame pilots without evidence.

How wrong I was. As Dave Hill conveys, this was a cover-up from even before take-off. While MoD always maintained it was open-minded, keen to receive 'new evidence', it is striking that it accepted zero new discoveries in the intervening 17 years before finally being shamed into an apology to the families of the two blamed pilots.

Every time a fresh look was tabled, MoD ruled it out of order. None of this was new evidence, not to it, because MoD had the material all along. It just never released it. The Monty Python scriptwriters would have rejected the premise as too absurd.

It was into this circle of Hell that campaigners chased the lie, and understandably, it is only now, some 27 years later, that the story crystallizes.

This seminal book conveys the story the Ministry actively tried to stop. It is also something more than the story of one accident, albeit with enormous loss of life. It is a story about choices, and the damage an unaccountable government department acting in the name of both the State and the Queen can wreak.

The ministry was not used to its accidents being reviewed by third parties.

Chinook, in fact, was the very first open to such scrutiny. What else, I do wonder, has MoD got away with?

I was a young man, younger than the pilots, when I attended the four-week long Fatal Accident Inquiry in Paisley, Scotland into the crash. Even with the limited script put before him, Sheriff Sir Stephen Young concluded the findings against the pilots were unjust. Yet on MoD went, flogging its tale of dead men reckless at the controls.

I was slow to conclude Chinook was a cover-up. I knew, perhaps, what such a conclusion would mean. I didn't want to find it, but in these pages you will find the proof, and more.

And I take only sorrow from such findings. I cast my mind back to those pale blue painted rooms in the temporary courthouse at Paisley. I think of the relatives in the public gallery looking for answers. The widows of many of the passengers generously invited me one evening to join them at dinner during the Inquiry. I remember still their emotions about the limited evidence heard. They expressed anger, confusion, determination and distrust.

It turns out the questions they were asking did have answers. There was an abundance of evidence never presented, despite the Inquiry in Scotland and latterly in the House of Commons and House of Lords.

The whole process was treated by MoD with a cynicism; with contempt. To have looked in the eyes of the bereaved and to have offered nothing is a cardinal sin of omission and a morally bankrupt position. It was, simply, wrong.

I never met Flight Lieutenants Jon Tapper, forever just 28, or Rick Cook, 30. Neither did I know Master Air Loadmaster Graham Forbes, 36, nor Sergeant Kev Hardie, 30. But I grew to know them through their reputations. These were very different to the story peddled from the ministry shadows.

The official recalcitrance, and the cover-up illustrated in this book, provides the story with a timeless vigour to it. We know there remain secrets still beyond our reach. To those of you who have more parts of the puzzle, please consider doing the right thing, and get in touch with any one of us.

David Walmsley, journalist
Toronto, February 2021

Preface

To understand the cause of this tragedy is the Holy Grail of aircraft accident investigation. The ultimate cold case. The greatest obstacle is that the UK Government, the Ministry of Defence (MoD), and the organisations to which the deceased belonged, do not want it solved.

This book is a prequel to *Their Greatest Disgrace* (David Hill, 2016), which described the successful campaign to clear the deceased pilots of gross negligence but avoided the plethora of hypotheses as to cause. Discussing them in that context would have detracted from the primary aim.

Throughout the campaign MoD said it would study any *'new evidence'*, omitting that the standard of proof had not been met in the first place. But the true meaning of its words went unnoticed. New evidence is that which subsequently becomes available; whereas fresh evidence was available at the time of the initial Inquiry, but for various reasons was not put before it. Here, evidence of organisational failings, prior negligence and the probability of technical malfunction was ignored. Why?

By examining and explaining this fresh evidence I hope to stimulate debate about an unsolved accident in which 29 died, but about which their employers, government and legal authorities have shown no interest since MoD's position was proven to be unsustainable in 2011. The pilots have been cleared, but the case closed. Why?

This is not, as MoD would tell you, an isolated case. It took the loss of Nimrod XV230 in 2006, killing 14 servicemen, to finally bring long-known and tolerated systemic violations to the fore. The subsequent Nimrod Review reset aviation safety, worldwide. The same evidence was then presented to the Mull of Kintyre Review, headed by Lord Alexander Philip. Mindful that Government and MoD had already accepted it in the Nimrod case, he did not have to think too hard. There could only be one outcome - the pilots were exonerated. Yet the failings remained, killing more aircrew. Why?

These questions, and more, are answered in the following pages.

*

Please note. When using 'RAF' I am referring to just that Service. When using 'MoD' I am referring to the wider Department. This is important. You will learn of many examples where it is RAF practice to disregard formal MoD policy. Moreover, it introduced policies that were in direct conflict with legal obligations placed upon all MoD staff. Daily, they were faced with a choice - *Do I do my duty, or do I obey orders?* An impossible position when, either way, subject to sanction. This had a direct bearing on the loss of ZD576, and many other fatal accidents I will mention.

The established facts
A fact is established when it can be accurately and readily determined from sources whose accuracy cannot reasonably be questioned. Here, the primary source is MoD's own papers, which formed the basis of my submission to the Mull of Kintyre Review. That is, I did not indulge in conjecture - I exposed hitherto concealed evidence to scrutiny, and explained it to the Review.

There will always be naysayers who argue illogically against known facts. This is often brought about by the culture in which they operate. For example, in the military a senior officer is deemed correct by virtue of his or her rank. Even when proven wrong, the official record is never amended. So, for example, while the ZD576 pilots were exonerated in 2011 as a result of the evidence accepted by the Review, the findings of the Senior Reviewing Officers were never changed. If one asks MoD for the definitive document on apportionment of blame, it will supply the original findings. Similarly, when asked to review new or fresh evidence, legal authorities simply point to the Reviewing Officers' discredited findings, ambivalent to rampant perjury.

Here are the most important and relevant established facts of this case. I accept them without question, and will explain each as the book develops:

- On 2 June 1994 the status of the RAF's Chinook HC Mk2 fleet was that it was *not to be relied upon in any way whatsoever*. This was *mandated* upon the RAF, but concealed from aircrew.
- The Master Airworthiness Reference was signed by the Assistant Chief of the Air Staff assuring aircrew the Mk2 *was* airworthy.
- Chinook HC Mk2 ZD576 was *neither serviceable nor fit for purpose*.
- The above was known by the office of the Senior Reviewing Officer *before* the accident.
- MoD officials and military personnel *lied* by omission and commission about the above, causing Ministers to *mislead* Parliament.
- MoD *failed to disclose* exculpatory evidence, both to families and legal authorities, and denied its existence even after being submitted by members of the public.

The above are imprisonable offences. No action has been taken.

Despite all, MoD's position remained that the burden of proof lay with the deceased pilots. Your first reaction might be disbelief. It is an immoral, disreputable and venal stance. But it is true. Lord Philip, in his report:

'Sir John Day's approach places the onus of disproving negligence on the deceased, which is also wrong'.

But it wasn't just Day's approach. MoD, the RAF and Ministers fully endorsed it. Notably, on 18 March 2004 Minister for the Armed Forces Adam Ingram MP used a similar argument in the Sea King ASaC Mk7 mid-air collision of 22 March 2003, in which seven aircrew were killed. Andrew George MP asked the Secretary of State for Defence, Geoff Hoon:

'What assessment he has made of whether senior officers are satisfied that there was no malfunction of equipment?'

Mr Ingram replied that the deceased crews had not submitted a formal report about any malfunctions during the flight.[1] Did I say venal?

---

1 Letter D/Min(AF)/AI PQ 1067P (and 10 others), 18 March 2004.

PART 1 - GENERAL BACKGROUND

'My mother has been lied to by the MoD. It treated my family with utter contempt following the crash, and despicably tried to enact the Warsaw Air Carriage Act to limit payouts to the widows and families. Hardly the actions of a moral outfit.

Even after we overturned this obscene effort, it forced my mother to produce receipts for the clothes my father wore on the day of his death, and list how many potatoes he would eat in an average year as part of its quest to limit compensation. The callousness was breathtaking and displayed a complete lack of integrity.

Quite frankly we were treated like Irish peasants by uncaring, absentee feudal landlords, and the disdain was palpable'.

Captain Niven Phoenix, son of Detective Superintendent Ian Phoenix RUC (late Parachute Regiment).

1. Beinn na Lice

On the evening of 2 June 1994, Chinook HC Mk2 ZD576 crashed into the western slopes of Beinn na Lice (Hill of the Ledge) on the Mull of Kintyre, the southernmost part of the Kintyre Peninsula, in Scotland. All 29 on board were killed - the four RAF crew, and ten Royal Ulster Constabulary, nine Army, and six Security Service officers.

The passengers were en route from RAF Aldergrove, 18 miles north-west of Belfast, to Fort George, 11 miles north-east of Inverness, to attend the annual Northern Ireland security conference. Essentially, this was a bonding session for the Intelligence community, principally Army G2 (Intelligence and Security), Special Branch of the Royal Ulster Constabulary, and the Security Service, MI5. Thirty-two attendees were nominated, the list approved by John Deverell, head of MI5 in Northern Ireland, who was killed in the accident. Eight were stood down two days before, but one Army officer successfully argued for reinstatement, which Deverell approved at the behest of the Chief of Army G2 and also G3 (Operations), HQ Northern Ireland, Colonel Christopher Biles, who was also on the flight.

In previous years the conference had been held at RAF Machrihanish on the Kintyre Peninsula, but it was closing. The Fort George site reconnaissance and preparation was conducted by an Army G2 Major, who was to have attended but was one of those removed from the list. In winter the area can be cold and bleak, but summers are balmy. The Fort itself, built in the mid-1700s, is considered a secure garrison as it sits at the end of a small spit of land outside the village of Ardersier, with the sea on three sides and extensive underground facilities.

ZD576 took off at around 1742 hours, navigating the low Antrim Hills to the coastal town of Carnlough, continuing over the narrow North Passage of the Irish Sea to the Mull of Kintyre. It was to have turned slightly left near the Mull lighthouse and headed north to the next navigation waypoint at Corran, hugging the coastline, and thence up the Great Glen to its destination. As they approached the Mull at about 1800 hours the planned waypoint change to Corran was made, but the aircraft did not make the intended turn, climbed, and impacted Beinn na Lice 810 feet above sea level.

I seek to explain why that left turn was not made.

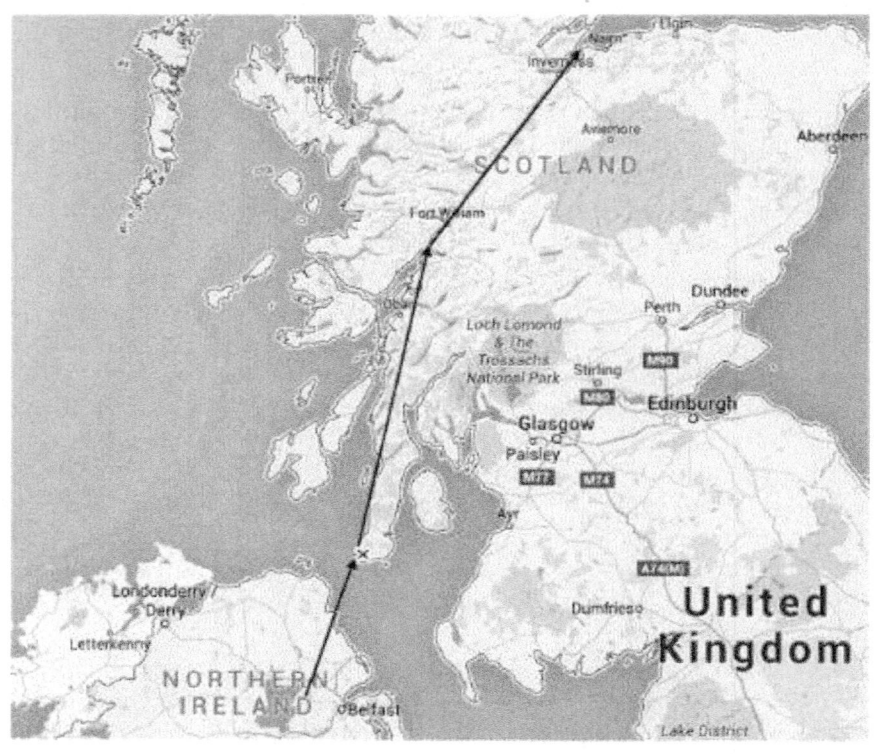

Figure 1: Overview of intended route. In practice, none of the legs would be straight lines. Actual route would be determined by terrain, weather and general Visual Flight Rules restrictions.

Figure 2: Mull of Kintyre Lighthouse, looking east. ZD576 approached from the right. Note: the wall of the compound slopes down towards the shore, making it more visible during a low-level approach. *(Stock)*

2. The Inquiries

It is essential to understand the link between the RAF Inquiry into the cause of the accident, and the Fatal Accident Inquiry into the cause of the deaths. A fundamental dependency of the latter is the accuracy of the RAF report. If it is wrong, or ignores known facts, then the Fatal Accident Inquiry is immediately hamstrung, with MoD effectively dictating its direction.

The RAF Board of Inquiry (1994/5)

The Board, comprising a Wing Commander and two Squadron Leaders, postulated that the pilots had departed from the planned route and selected an inappropriate rate of climb for an overflight of the Mull. The possibility (indeed, as I will show, probability) that this was not a conscious decision was barely considered. The legal test it had to apply if considering gross negligence was:

> *'Only in cases in which there is absolutely no doubt whatsoever should deceased aircrew be found negligent'.*[2]

The bar was set so high because the deceased cannot defend themselves.

The Board concluded, without offering evidence, that Flight Lieutenant Jonathan Tapper, the aircraft captain and non-handling pilot, made an error of judgment, but was not negligent. But that no failings could be attributed to the pilot, Flight Lieutenant Richard Cook. The Board's report was then reviewed by more senior officers.

Group Captain Roger Wedge, Officer Commanding RAF Aldergrove, was only required to remark on operations at Aldergrove, confirming *'the exact train of events can never be determined with absolute certainty'*.

Group Captain (later Air Commodore) Peter Crawford, Officer Commanding RAF Odiham, Hampshire, said the reasons for the accident were *'open to conjecture and, in the absence of hard evidence, I do not feel there is much to be gained by speculating'*. He then contradicted himself by concluding Flight Lieutenant Tapper failed in his duty to ensure the safety of the aircraft, its crew and passengers. He did not address whether the aircraft was safe in the first place, but did reflect on some dangerous shortcomings highlighted in the Release to Service (the Master

---

[2] AP3207, Annex G, Chapter 8 (RAF Manual of Flight Safety, 6th Edition, March 1993). Guide to the Consideration of Human Failings.

Airworthiness Reference, of which more later). There was no logical progression to his words, but he too stopped short of declaring negligence.

Air Vice Marshal John Day, Air Officer Commanding 1 Group, and the Convening Officer, disagreed. (At the time of the accident Air Vice Marshal Peter Squire held this position. Day took up post shortly after, when Squire was promoted and appointed Assistant Chief of the Air Staff). Taking no further evidence, he asserted *both* pilots were negligent to a gross degree. His words were seemingly written *before* Group Captain Crawford added his criticism of Flight Lieutenant Tapper, as he criticised Crawford for not finding blame.

Air Chief Marshal Sir William Wratten, Air Officer Commanding-in-Chief Strike Command, and Senior Reviewing Officer, agreed with Air Vice Marshal Day. The deceased pilots were found negligent to a gross degree, the equivalent of manslaughter. This illogical leap, from insufficient evidence to gross negligence by default, is normally unsustainable in law.

*

It is often said the Senior Reviewing Officers 'overruled' the Board. More accurately, the Board was required to give an opinion on human failings. Wratten and Day disagreed with that opinion. The very existence of differing opinions meant there was doubt, but no formal process existed to resolve the conflict. The gross negligence findings stood, despite the evidence not matching the conclusions.

On the other hand, the Board *was* required to determine cause, and *could* be overruled. Air Vice Marshal Day concluded that *'the actions of the crew were the direct cause of this crash'*. Air Chief Marshal Wratten agreed, but the two later differed on precisely when and where the alleged negligence occurred. Neither offered probative evidence.

Air Chief Marshal Sir Michael Graydon, Chief of the Air Staff and professional head of the RAF, reviewed the findings. He agreed the pilots were grossly negligent but offered a different opinion as to cause, claiming the aircraft was *'off course by some miles'*. This staggering claim only became known some years later, and is easily disproved by comparing the route planning map with the crash site. MoD has never commented on this, never mind tried to justify it. He also criticised as *'barely adequate'* the performance of the Board President, Wing Commander (later Air Chief Marshal Sir) Andrew Pulford. His reason was that Pulford had *'avoided any attribution of negligence to the pilots'*.[3]

---

3 Letter D/CAS/16/1/6(W0279f), 4 February 1997 to Marshal of the RAF Sir John Grandy.

Graydon's status in the process remains unclear, RAF Legal Services confirming on 22 April 2002 that:

'There are no prescribed reviewing procedures after completion of the remarks by Air Officer Commanding-in-Chief Strike Command'.

But his influence is clear, because it was he who briefed Secretary of State for Defence Malcolm Rifkind and Marshal of the RAF Sir John Grandy.

*

In his remarks, Air Chief Marshal Wratten began rationally:

'Without the irrefutable evidence which is provided by an Accident Data Recorder and a Cockpit Voice Recorder, there is inevitably a degree of speculation as to the precise detail of the sequence of events'.

Then, straying from the evidence and becoming ever more careless with the facts, he claimed the pilots flew *too fast and too low* towards high ground. That, Cook carried this out, and Tapper allowed it. He overlooked that Tapper, by selecting a new navigation waypoint, had signalled their intention to turn away from the high ground and continue on their planned route. He omitted that Cook was flying well within the Chinook's speed limits, and strictly prohibited from flying at the altitude mooted - a restriction directed by Graydon's Air Staff. Immediately, major conflicts of interest emerge.

The RAF, and later MoD, claimed the accident took place in thick fog, with low level cloud extending some distance out from the Mull and obscuring the approach. It used the evidence of lighthouse keeper David Murchie and hill-walkers who were in ground-hugging mist - none of whom saw the aircraft. In his evidence to the Board, Mr Murchie said the mist was *'patchy'*, with visibility ranging from *'15-20 metres'* to *'400-500 metres'*.[4]

This mist is a prevalent feature in the area and was well understood by the pilots - Tapper had flown the route before and even landed at the lighthouse. It tends to follow the height contour on the windward side, meaning the land below that height is normally plainly visible. This was confirmed in the evidence of Mark Holbrook, a yachtsman who sighted the aircraft around two miles from the lighthouse. He was the only eye-witness interviewed, reporting good visibility of the coastline and lighthouse compound.

---

4 Board of Inquiry report, Part 6. Witness statement of David Murchie.

Figure 3: Orographic cloud on the Mull of Kintyre, similar to the conditions described by eye-witness Mark Holbrook. *(Stock)*

Figure 4: Typical orographic cloud. The line of the coast and the landmass are easily distinguishable, and suitable for flight under Visual Flight Rules if the intention is to hug the coastline. *(Bernard Smith)*

Figure 5: Carnlough, Northern Ireland, looking north to the Mull of Kintyre. ZD576 approached from the bottom left, witnesses reporting the aircraft dipping down towards the harbour and heading slightly left of the Mull. *(Robert Ashby)*

On 13 April 1995 Malcolm Rifkind was informed of the gross negligence findings by the Air Staff. He sought a verbal briefing from Air Chief Marshal Graydon and Air Vice Marshal Day, the discussion focussing on the findings and the question of compensation. Shortly afterwards, on 9 May 1995 his private office informed him that, upon closer inspection of the Board's report, the Senior Reviewing Officers had disagreed with the Board. Graydon and Day had not mentioned this, nor that Graydon disagreed with both the Board and his senior officers.

Lord Philip in his 2011 Mull of Kintyre Review report:

'Sir Malcolm took the view it was not appropriate for him to second guess the professional judgment of the Reviewing Officers and that the correct course was for him to assume the matter had been dealt with according to the rules'.

But it had not. Rifkind had not been advised of the standard of proof, nor of the known facts I set out here. On 15 June 1995 he announced:

'After an exhaustive Inquiry into all the circumstances, the possibilities of major technical or structural failure, hostile action, or electro-magnetic interference with navigation equipment, were eliminated as possible causes. On all the evidence, it was concluded that the cause of the accident was that the two pilots had wrongly continued to fly towards the Mull of Kintyre, below a safe altitude in unsuitable weather conditions'.

None of these possibilities had been eliminated. In fact, the probability of major technical failure, especially in the flight control and fuel systems, was known by MoD and the RAF to be extremely high; evidenced by previous fatal accidents and the fault history of ZD576, with investigations still ongoing. Material evidence was actively concealed from investigators, and so there was no exhaustive Inquiry.

When later told the truth, Rifkind, Prime Minister of the day Sir John Major, and his Minister for the Armed Forces Sir Jeremy Hanley, had the integrity to distance themselves from the findings. Sir John Major:

'We owe justice to the dead. I am not persuaded they have had it'.

MoD persisted, demanding *'new evidence'* be presented before it would reconsider, constantly ignoring that it carried the burden of proof.

The Fatal Accident Inquiry (1996)

The Mull of Kintyre being remote and inaccessible, the Crown Office & Procurator Fiscal Service (hereinafter 'Crown Office') decided to hold the Fatal Accident Inquiry in Paisley Sheriff Court, just outside Glasgow. It was conducted by Sheriff Sir Stephen Young over 18 days, between 8 January and 2 February, and heard from 38 witnesses.

Relatives have an automatic right to participate at a Fatal Accident Inquiry. The Sheriff has broad discretion to allow any other person to be represented who has satisfied the court that he or she has a valid 'interest in the Inquiry'. Evidence is given under oath, and witnesses are led in chief and cross examined as they would be in a civil or criminal court.

Prior to commencement, MoD argued successfully that if the author of written evidence was not in court, then that evidence could not be heard. MoD exploited this legal device by refusing to allow those who made the accusation of gross negligence to appear as witnesses.

It is possible the Sheriff's hands were tied due to the Inquiry being into the deaths of the MI5 officers, not the military or police personnel. At the time, and until 2018, under Scots Law the latter were not covered by the law governing Fatal Accident Inquiries. Here, the Sheriff exercised his discretion and allowed evidence pertaining to the servicemen and police, but the legal point was made at the outset that the Inquiry was into the deaths of those who died *'in the course of their employment'*. Servicemen and police are not employees. They are Crown Servants. This case remains unique, the only Fatal Accident Inquiry held in Scotland following a military aircraft accident.

Exacerbating matters, MoD made a series of false claims, especially in the closing submission by Alistair Dunlop QC:

'Against that background can I now turn to a number of findings in fact which I would invite your lordship to make as part of your determination'.

These 'facts' included:

'Chinook ZD576 was airworthy and fully serviceable. There were no technical failures in relation to the aircraft relevant to the accident. In particular, there were no such failures prior to impact in the aircraft's structure, controls and instruments, power plant, flight controls, utility hydraulic system, electrical system, transmission or rotors'.

First, to claim anything is irrelevant one must first be certain of the cause. Mr Dunlop must have realised his words wholly contradicted the sworn evidence of many witnesses. And he either did not read the Air Accidents Investigation Branch and Board of Inquiry reports, or was instructed by MoD to avoid those parts inconvenient to its case.

Continuing in the same vein he made a series of increasingly baseless claims, presenting unverified data and speculation as *'hard fact'*. The worst example was his distortion of Air Accidents Investigation Branch Senior Inspector Tony Cable's evidence. As the lead technical investigator, it was his role to be lead narrator - but only on the physical evidence at the scene. The Board's engineering member should have undertaken the role for all other engineering aspects, but he was not called to <u>any</u> Inquiry. MoD withheld vital evidence from Mr Cable, who was unable to tell the full story. In fact, the lack of evidence, and contradictory nature of that which he was allowed to gather, prompted him to heavily caveat his report - something he emphasised in court; and again, 15 years later, to Lord Philip.

Mr Dunlop also claimed a precise time and place was known for key events. He supposed a continuous stream of data from the SuperTANS navigation computer, implying, as did the RAF, it was a data recorder. In fact the designer, Racal, had confirmed that no time could be attributed to any positional data. Moreover, while the data, which was merely a snapshot of the final second before impact, was retained in memory, that does not mean it was being displayed. (Discussed later).

He then alleged *'cloud and fog extended from <u>beneath</u> the lighthouse to at least the summit of Beinn na Lice'*, ignoring that the 'fog' was ground-hugging mist, and the extensive lighthouse compound was visible.

MoD was required to advise the Crown Office of these 'errors'. But that would reveal gross misconduct. It remained silent.

*

Mr Dunlop constantly attacked witness Flight Lieutenant Iain MacFarlane, later to become the RAF's most decorated pilot, who had proposed an Undemanded Flight Control Movement (UFCM) scenario:

> 'Flight Lieutenant MacFarlane was very insistent that the scenario fitted <u>all the facts</u>. Well, in my submission they neither fit all the facts nor does it present a probable scenario'.

He claimed that a simulation by the Chinook manufacturer, Boeing, was also *'hard fact'*, saying MacFarlane was wrong to criticise it. He ignored that the parameters used for the simulation, by a company with a vested interest in there being no technical fault, were selective, unverified assumptions. Had the court known this, and of concealed UFCM evidence, Mr Dunlop's position would have been untenable. Flight Lieutenant MacFarlane intuitively knew where the main problem lay, he just didn't have the final piece of the jigsaw. That only emerged in 2010.

During questioning of Flight Lieutenant (later Air Commodore) Carl Scott by Aidan O'Neill QC, representing the Tapper family, Mr Dunlop constantly interrupted, disrupted and objected whenever airworthiness was mentioned, revealing where his client was vulnerable and nervous.

In his closing submission, Mr Dunlop said:

> *'The aircraft was subject to a certificate of airworthiness provided it was flown in accordance with its terms'.*

Unknown to the crew and the court, the 'certificate' was a fabrication.

*

It is difficult to find <u>any</u> example where Mr Dunlop's 'facts' match the evidence. Sheriff Young saw through his argument:

> *'It has not been established to my satisfaction that the cause of the accident was that found by the Board of Inquiry'.*

Disdainfully, MoD denied the authority of the court. Neither it nor the Government saw any of the above as sufficient reason to question the findings. But keen observers instinctively knew it was palpably wrong, both morally and legally, to assume pilot negligence, or even error, while not considering the technical and legal evidence. Had the finding been 'cause unknown', there would have been no argument. Instead, the RAF concocted a scenario. Not surprising, then, that the families took exception to the pilots being accused of manslaughter.

Thus, Sheriff Young was unable to fulfil his obligations under the Fatal Accidents and Sudden Deaths Inquiry (Scotland) Act 1976, to consider:

- Precautions which may have avoided the deaths.

- Defects in the system of working which may have avoided the deaths.

When made aware of these facts after the event, the Crown Office ruled that all the deaths were now a matter for the Metropolitan Police in London, because the offences committed (by the Air Staff) occurred there.[5] How interesting. They must have given the matter some thought.

The Metropolitan Police did not reply to a complaint of 29 November 2016, a position sustainable only with higher approval of the Home Office and/or the Ministry of Justice. The latter is acutely aware of MoD having committed the same offences leading to other fatal accidents.[6]

Parliamentary debates and hearings

On 4 March 1998, to the House of Commons Defence Select Committee, Secretary of State Dr John Reid MP claimed the moment when the pilots *'elected'* to enter cloud was the moment they committed gross negligence. He did not say at what altitude or position he thought this occurred.

Neither the Board of Inquiry nor Reviewing Officers had stated this, but his words went unchallenged, the Committee taking evidence only from MoD. He either came to an independent conclusion that they were all wrong, or he was briefed to this effect by a third party. Either way, the (different) opinions of the Board, the Senior Reviewing Officers, and the Chief of the Air Staff had been replaced with this new account, without explanation. There were now <u>four</u> different official hypotheses, none supported by a shred of evidence.

The evidence to the Committee was so flawed, on 19 May 1998 Robert Key MP felt it necessary to issue a nine-page press notice detailing the errors. Dr Reid promptly issued a statement saying Key's words were a *'recycling of old theories which have already been investigated and discounted'*, and that the Committee had *'painstakingly examined the airworthiness of the Chinook Mk2 fleet'*.[7] This was an outright lie. MoD had concealed from both Reid and the Committee that the aircraft was <u>not</u> airworthy. Like the Board of Inquiry, the Committee had taken no evidence on the subject, and their reports did not even mention the word.

Typical of RAF briefings to Ministers was a letter prepared for the Earl Howe, Parliamentary Under-Secretary of State for Defence, on 9 April

---

5 Crown Office & Procurator Fiscal Service letter LP-4, 8 November 2016.

6 Notification to Rory Stewart MP, Minister of State for Courts and Justice, 27 January 2018; and reply SD/TO/Mar18, 5 March 2018 from HM Courts & Tribunal Service.

7 Ministry of Defence press release 129/98, 19 May 1998 11:34.

1997. This, in reply to questions put to Lord Williams of Elvel and Minister of State for the Armed Forces Nicholas Soames MP, by the late Captain Ralph Kohn via his MP Nick Hawkins.[8]

'The Board of Inquiry thoroughly examined all possible causes'.

It did not assess historical and ongoing malfunctions.

'The Air Accidents Investigation Branch positively confirmed that both engines were functioning normally at the point of impact, and were able to categorically rule out any structural or technical malfunction'.

The Air Accidents Investigation Branch (AAIB) said no such thing, specifically denying such claims in Paisley 15 months earlier.

'Data downloaded from the Tactical Navigation System allowed the Board to derive an accurate picture of the flight path, confirmed by two independently conducted flight path simulations. The data confirmed the navigation equipment was serviceable up to the point of impact'.

The AAIB confirmed the existence of both faults and defects in the Navigation System. The data was not *'downloaded'*. It was extracted using an unverified procedure, and primarily a snapshot of the GPS buffers which were flushed every second. At the time there had been a simulation conducted by Boeing, and one by the Defence Research Agency at Bedford. Neither used a model which included the Full Authority Digital Engine Control (FADEC) (and Bedford's did not use a Chinook), so were irrelevant. (In any case, simulations are more useful in preventing accidents than they are in analysing them). The second Boeing 'simulation' in 2002 - more a re-assessment following identification of the errors in the first - produced quite different results.[9] There were three major contradictions: previous assumptions regarding rotor speed, engine power, and an alleged last-second flare (pulling emergency power and trying to turn away) were now questioned. The Senior Reviewing Officers' case was based almost entirely on the first simulation, but they did not take stock after the re-assessment.

'Safety Altitude was under 2,800 feet and the crew should have climbed to it'.

It was 5,900 feet. The pilots were strictly prohibited from attaining it.

'Not less than 5km visibility was required'.

---

8 Letter D/USofS/FH1504/97/A, 9 April 1997. This reply was sent after Parliament was dissolved prior to the 1997 General Election; Mr Hawkins was elected to a different seat on 1 May 1997. Earl Howe was succeeded by John Spellar MP on 2 May 1997.

9 Boeing Review and Re-simulation report, Task 07A001ES, 19 June 2002.

When under 140 knots Indicated Airspeed, the requirement is 'clear of cloud and in sight of the surface'.[10] ZD576 was *believed* to be at 135 knots maximum, and was around 120 knots at initial impact - evidenced by the recovered Drift Angle Groundspeed Indicator. Yachtsman Mark Holbrook thought its altitude between 200 and 400 feet when two miles from the lighthouse, and general visibility at sea level was good, with haze, based on his ability to see Sanda Island 8 miles to the east and Rathlin Island 15 miles to the west.

'The aircraft was properly cleared for squadron flying, and there was no reason not to deploy the Mk2 to Northern Ireland'.

The aircraft was not properly cleared. A declaration had been made that it was airworthy, knowing it was not.

Separately, the Chief of the Air Staff, Air Chief Marshal Sir Michael Graydon, wrote to Captain Kohn confirming he *'fully agreed'* with the Earl Howe's reply.[11] His letter is dated 3 March 1997, but refers to Earl Howe's of 7 April 1997, suggesting his staff prepared the latter.

The Earl Howe repeated these words in a debate on 22 May 1997. Did he realise his briefing was a pack of lies? Unlikely.

The House of Lords Select Committee (2001/2)

The Committee was set up on 2 July 2001 to consider the justification for the findings. It comprised: the Lords Jauncey (Chairman), Brennan, Bowness, Hoosen and Tombs. This was the first time the families had an opportunity to hear from the Senior Reviewing Officers, primarily (the now Air Chief Marshal Sir) John Day. I wish to discuss two aspects of his evidence - visibility and visual illusion - interspersing it with related evidence from other witnesses to provide context. I also discuss more of Mark Holbrook's evidence, refuting that of Day and considered pivotal by the Lords. Detailed technical issues are discussed in later chapters.

*

Air Chief Marshal Day:

'Flight Lieutenant Cook was in the right-hand seat as the handling pilot, Flight Lieutenant Tapper, the aircraft captain, non-handling pilot on the port side and

---

10 Confirmed by *(inter alia)* the Directorate of Air Staff in letter D/DAS/58/1/5, 10 November 2005, paragraph 4e, to Lord Jacobs.

11 Letter D/CAS/9/18/3/1(0562), 3 March 1997, signed by Air Chief Marshal Sir Michael Graydon.

responsible for not only the captaincy of the aircraft but also the navigation. The two air loadmasters and the 25 passengers were in the cabin. We do not know exactly where the two air loadmasters were. Master Air Loadmaster Forbes was operating at the front of the aircraft and Sergeant Hardie was at the back'.

This seemingly innocuous opening statement exposed the predicament the Reviewing Officers had placed themselves in - what was MALM Forbes doing? Board President, the now Group Captain Pulford, had already stated to the Committee:

'I would certainly have expected, whether MALM Forbes was sitting in the jump seat or indeed down the back, him to have been following through on the navigation, and that would certainly have been Special Forces practice and non-Special Forces practice as well'.

Other aircrew confirmed this. Flight Sergeant John Coles at the Fatal Accident Inquiry, when questioned by Aidan O'Neill QC:

'Did you see Messrs Forbes or Hardie making any navigational preparations in relation to this flight and navigation?'

'Yes, Master Air Loadmaster Forbes was preparing a one to half million scale map of the route, which was a copy of the pilot's. He had copied down from the pilot's master map the intended route, then put track lines on between various turning points on the route'.

'Why would he be doing that?'

'As a back-up to the navigator pilot. If for instance the non-handling pilot was required to make a radio call in circumstances which required navigational assistance, he would then hand on responsibility to the crewman, who would take over for a short period'.

'Would he also be assisting in the navigation when the non-handling pilot was available for navigation as well? Would there be two navigators?'

'Yes, he would continuously monitor the progress along the track line'.

Mr O'Neill then asked Flight Sergeant Coles to comment on Air Chief Marshal Day's remarks in the Board of Inquiry report. He replied that he disagreed with them, whereupon Mr Dunlop immediately objected to the line of questioning. Mr O'Neill persisted:

'In a helicopter heading towards cloud apparently covering land at cruising speed, and there is no apparent avoiding action being taken by the pilots, what would you expect the crewmen to do?'

'I would have questioned the captain or the handling pilot as to their intentions, certainly making reference to the fact that if there was a known point of land approaching covering cloud, certainly what they intended to do'.

'You would seek clarification from the pilot as to what was the intention?'
'Yes'.
'In so doing would you be bringing the matter to the attention of the pilot?'
'Yes, it is entirely possible that the pilots might be doing something and had not noticed for a split second the fact that that situation was occurring, and I would bring it to their attention immediately'.

MALM Forbes was acquainted with the Kintyre Peninsula, having been brought up nearby and later training there. But MoD was not keen to reveal such a level of familiarity because, taken with Pulford's statement, it challenged the notion that the crew lost situational awareness. Forbes' presence served as a triple-check, making it unthinkable that he and the two pilots would commit the negligence claimed by the RAF at the same time, or that an error of judgment would go unnoticed.

Squadron Leader Robert Burke, former RAF Odiham Unit Test Pilot, in evidence to the House of Lords:

'Mr Forbes was the best crewman I flew with. He was very quick in emergency procedures when he was reacting. If I was flight testing, I would try and get him. If there was anything really serious, he was there'.[12]

As ever, what went unsaid is just as interesting. The upper-forward starboard door was closed at impact, evidenced by witness marks. This was not mentioned by the Board, a shocking omission. It was uncovered by the Cook family's technical advisor, Andy Fairfield:

'The "official" scenario being proposed at the time was that the aircraft was being flown in poor weather. I was very interested to know what Graham Forbes was doing in the moments leading up to the accident. I flew with him on a number of occasions. If poor weather might be a factor, he would navigate while looking out of the open upper-forward door. A skill he was extremely good at, and a crew position that had become Standard Operating Procedure for Special Forces crews'.[13]

This is strong evidence that Forbes was satisfied with the visibility and progress. Perhaps more than anything else, it points to Flight Lieutenant Cook experiencing a sudden problem the others could not help with.

<u>Visibility from the cockpit</u>
Internal factors can affect visibility. As every car driver knows, if

---
12 Evidence of Squadron Leader Robert Burke to the House of Lords, 16 October 2001.
13 Fairfield/Hill, 9 April 2021 18:41.

windscreen wipers or screenwash systems fail, even on a wet road after the rain has ceased, visibility is non-existent. But a car can be stopped at the side of the road. On 26 October 1993 MoD's airworthiness specialists at the renowned Aeroplane and Armament Experimental Establishment, Boscombe Down, reported that performance of the windscreen wipers/washers was *'disappointing'* compared to the Mk1:

> *'At speeds greater than 80 knots the port and starboard wipers tended to lift from the curved parts of the screens, leaving large uncleared areas; this significantly reduced visibility. Although the wipers were little used during the trial, two failures were experienced. One motor failed, causing the circuit breaker to activate, and the ON/OFF/SPEED switch become inoperable'.*[14]

Boscombe's concern was that a previous attempt to solve the problem in 1988 had been unsuccessful, the system deemed *'unreliable'* with quality variable between aircraft. The Air Accidents Investigation Branch report mentioned the system once, saying the switch position was *'not highly positive'*, meaning there was little evidence to show what mode it was in at impact. The Board made no mention at all. A strange omission, given they claimed the aircraft was flying in poor visibility.

The Boscombe report is comprehensive, listing many unresolved issues. This is often a lengthy process, and the follow-on trials it mentions were delayed until after the accident due to their trials aircraft being grounded, twice. Yet, the Air Staff directed that the aircraft be operated with these failures and defects - but without mentioning them to aircrew.

*

The Board thought the weather conditions over the Mull were conducive to spatial disorientation. It claimed the cloud base was ill-defined and broken, and the visibility below degraded. However, when asked about cloud height by Lord Tombs, Mr Holbrook was firm:

'The lowest part, 1,000 feet'.

Impact was at 810 feet. Three weeks later, Air Chief Marshal Day presented slides to the Lords depicting cloud extending out from the Mull, with a base at no more than 265 feet and obscuring the approach. He claimed the pilots wilfully entered cloud some distance from landfall, rendering land, sea and waypoint invisible. While of poor quality, it can be seen the slide at Figure 6 is not to scale, in either axis. The reader is clearly meant to infer the pilots flew at an almost vertical cliff face rising over 650 feet above them, and that the summit of Beinn na Lice was to their front, when it was

---

14 Boscombe Down Letter Report E1109, paragraph 12g, 26 October 1993.

over half a mile to the right.

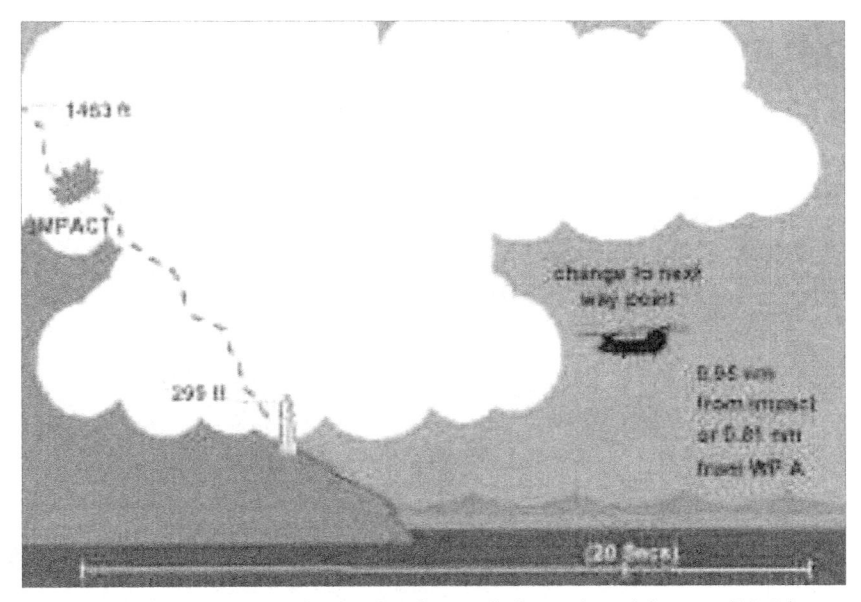

Figure 6: Slide 14 of Air Chief Marshal Day's evidence. *(MoD)*

The Air Accidents Investigation Branch had reproduced the <u>actual</u> terrain profile in their report. I have adapted it to show the cloud base according to Mr Holbrook's evidence, the ground-hugging mist described by ear-witnesses, and the terrain height shortly after final impact...

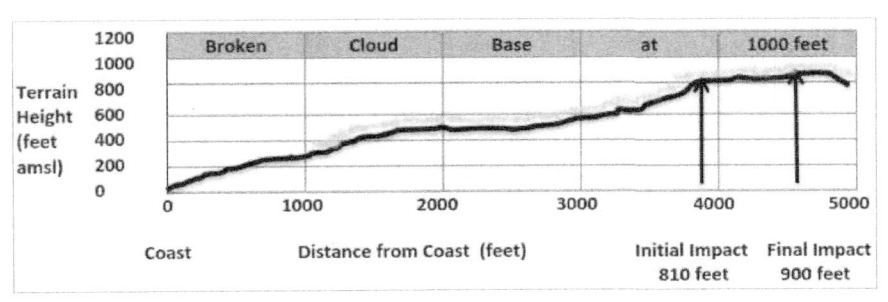

Figure 7: Terrain profile from coast to final impact. *(AAIB & author)*

Mr Holbrook later wrote:

> *'I was faced by a rather formidable array of five Lords. The Air Marshal had given evidence before me, and in the corner on a flipchart I recognised the infamous drawing showing fog all around the Mull - including the position where I had been and where I knew for a fact that there was no fog'.*

The correct terrain profile was available to Day when he produced his presentation to the Lords. Surely, in the intervening three weeks, his staff realised he was about to wholly contradict Mr Holbrook? Perhaps he thought the Lords, like MoD, would prefer his version by virtue of his rank. They didn't, instead saying Mr Holbrook's evidence was of *'considerable importance'*. Drawing on it, they concluded:

> *'The Air Marshals were not justified in concluding the pilots were in control four seconds before impact, or at any time after waypoint change. It has not been established to the required standard of proof that it was the voluntary action of the pilots which caused the aircraft to fly into the hill'.* [15]

Moreover, they rejected the RAF's claim that Mr Holbrook had changed his evidence between his initial interview and appearing at the Fatal Accident Inquiry, criticising the standard of questioning.

Please refer to Figures 3 and 4. The only eye-witness evidence suggests these are more representative. It was by no means perfect weather, but it was not nearly as bad as the RAF made out. Of course, I cannot prove Figure 7 is 100% accurate. But it is based entirely on eye-witness evidence; whereas Day's slide is a complete fabrication, the sole purpose being to suggest poor airmanship. In fact, the evidence suggests cloud played no part in the causal sequence. The Lords preferred Mr Holbrook's evidence:

> *'It seems more than probable that the breakers would be readily visible from a low-flying aircraft out at sea'.* [16]

And were condemning of Air Chief Marshal Day:

> *'Sir John Day's conclusions on this matter must be weakened by his reliance on matters which he treated as facts, but which have been demonstrated to our satisfaction to be not facts but merely hypotheses and assumptions'.* [17]

Extraordinarily, six weeks later Air Chief Marshal Wratten claimed:

> *'The assumption that the cloud extended out to render visibility very poor has*

---

15 House of Lords report, paragraphs 172 and 173.
16 House of Lords Select Committee Report, 5 February 2002, paragraph 145.
17 House of Lords Select Committee Report, 5 February 2002, paragraph 148.

never been made'.[18]

Three years later, Defence Minister Lord Bach was forced to admit:

'Unfortunately, we are not able to say, even approximately, how far the cloud extended over the sea'.[19]

In 2011 Lord Philip was pitiless, almost mocking:

'Sir William maintained that the perspective of the witnesses who were on the Mull at the time of the crash (in the ground-hugging mist) *was exactly the same as the perspective from the aircraft'.*[20]

The Mull of Kintyre Group's response

The Group was headed by the fathers of the two pilots, John Cook and Michael Tapper. It was chaired at various times by Lord Martin O'Neill, the late Lord Chalfont (Alun Jones MC), and James Arbuthnot MP. Dr Michael Powers QC provided *pro bono* legal advice.

As the Group's stance was entirely consistent - the standard of proof had not been met - one could offer almost any of its statements and reports. But as Air Chief Marshal Day's evidence to the Lords is used, here is an extract from the response by Mr Cook. It is worth pointing out he was a former Concorde pilot of some renown, and campaigned successfully for Voice and Data Recorders to become standard fit to airliners.

John Cook's reaction after listening to the evidence offered by the two Air Marshals

MoD claims that none of the witnesses noticed any change of engine noise. But if the aircraft were flying towards them, they would only have heard the slap of the rotors. One only hears the engine noise as they go overhead - odd that not one of the witnesses heard the very loud increase in noise generated by a flare manoeuvre! Nobody, of course, was viewing the weather from the same point as the crew.

Rick would have been watching out for the coastline under the lighthouse. He would have wanted to turn immediately left, and fly with the coastline down to his right-hand side. Had any cloud or precipitation blocked his view then he would have turned immediately hard left and away from the Mull. Over the Intercom the crew would have been discussing the progress of the flight, remarking on the weather in the Mull area and what they were approaching and passing e.g. fishing

---

18 Letter from Air Chief Marshal Wratten to author Tim Slessor, 21 December 2001.
19 Lord Bach, Minister for Defence Procurement, 19 May 2004.
20 Mull of Kintyre Review, paragraph 6.2.2.

boats, yachts, etc.

To rely on the navigation systems for proof of negligence requires one to accept Sir William's assumption that 'they had deliberately entered cloud below safety height':

- Not for one moment would Rick have done that.
- Neither would he have allowed anyone else to do it to him.
- Neither would he have deliberately crossed the coast. Neither would Jonathan or the two crewmen.

By blaming the pilots, the Air Marshals closed the matter to further investigation, thereby also compromising safety. Who or what were they protecting?

What proof is there of a continuous 1,000 foot/minute climb from the waypoint change to the (alleged flare? How can one know that the aircraft was not upside down, going sideways, or otherwise out of control? Look at the case in 1997 of the US CH-47 that miraculously returned to a wheels-down attitude at 250 feet after rolling out of control. After two years of intensive investigation no fault could be found - on an intact aircraft.

Sir John Day states: 'Therefore, I am satisfied that inadequacies in supervision, training or flying standards did not contribute to this accident'. Having been the Training Manager on the Concorde Fleet for five years, I find this statement to be totally incomprehensible and, dare I say, arrogant. Training is never static. It is forever being finely tuned. Of course, one cannot deny that a potential maverick might slip through the selection and training programme. But a whole crew? That would prove a serious flaw in the selection and training process.

<u>Scenario</u>

Having reached the point off the coast where he wanted to turn left, Rick applies left cyclic, but finds that this causes the nose to pitch down and right yaw, because, unknown to him, an Upper Boost Actuator has stuck. Not necessarily at that moment, it could have happened before, but would not have been apparent due to the small control inputs whilst flying straight and level in the cruise. He then applies back cyclic to flare but found this caused right roll and yaw. He then applies UP Collective and finds that increases right roll, yaw and pitches the nose down. He is forced to centralise the controls for a few seconds to avoid loss of control but he has already got an increase of speed and rate of climb. Jam clears and he starts an emergency climb - alas too late.

Captain J D Cook

9 October 2001

Analysis

MoD denied the failure mooted by Mr Cook could occur. But in 1992 an accident to a US Army Chinook in Alaska was caused by a screw in one of the Upper Boost Actuators failing from Hydrogen embrittlement. This restricted the movement of the pilot valve in the actuator, reducing controllability. To correct the problem, the material, plating and locking mechanism of the screws was changed, and a suffix 'A' added to the part number. A Safety of Flight signal was issued 30 October 1992, and US Chinooks were grounded until the actuators were replaced.

On 6 December 1994, a further Safety of Flight signal was issued. Despite Boeing apparently resolving the issue in 1992, units were still receiving pre-modification actuators brand new from suppliers. (Another cause of actuator failure is hydraulic fluid contamination, discussed later).

Significantly, Mr Cook's scenario was deduced without knowledge of Special Flying Instruction/Chinook/12, signed on 28 February 1994 but not distributed to aircrew at either Odiham or Aldergrove:

> 'Undemanded Flight Control Movement. There have been a number of incidents of yaw kicks on Chinook HC Mk2 ZA718 during recent flight trials at Boscombe Down. The characteristic is manifested by _very sharp uncommanded inputs to the yaw axis which result in a rapid 3-4 degree change in aircraft heading, in both the hover and when in forward flight, when the aircraft is subject to high levels of vibration_'.

How was he able to paint such an accurate scenario? Because experienced Chinook pilots were telling him of such occurrences, and he had listened to his son. I return to this Instruction later.

Air Chief Marshal Day based his case on unverified data the pilots were not permitted to rely on. This explains MoD's refusal to allow he and Air Chief Marshal Wratten to appear at the Fatal Accident Inquiry, where to repeat their claims would have constituted perjury. Mindful of Section 20(6) of the Fatal Accident Inquiry (Scotland) Act *('A person is not required at an Inquiry to answer a question tending to show that the person is guilty of an offence')*, perhaps MoD thought it would be unwise for these officers to spend their time in the witness stand repeatedly stating that legal advice was not to answer the question?

Evidence of Mark Holbrook

To change waypoints the pilots would have to identify Waypoint A. The large distinctive wall of the lighthouse compound, or the coastline below, would suffice. Having done so, they would know without reference to instruments that a slight left turn was needed, keeping land to the right. Mr Holbrook saw them in *'watery sunshine'*, with glimpses of sunlight breaking through and reflecting off the aircraft, around 600-800 feet below cloud. He was also able to see the compound, confirming the mist was above and behind it:

> *'I remember the aircraft being in level attitude and well below cloud level. At no time whilst I observed it did it move into cloud cover'.*

This was approximately two miles from the lighthouse, and he opined that the crew would also be able to see the compound and shore. I make the point again that the compound wall extends down a slope towards the shore. The lighthouse itself may be in mist, yet a very large a part of the large compound clearly visible.

The evidence of Mr Holbrook, and those in Carnlough in bright sunshine, suggests the pilots had a direct view of the ground-hugging mist throughout the transit across the North Channel, and were able to discern the Mull massif, compound and the coastline. Taken with Lord Bach's admission, the only reasonable conclusion is that when they entered the mist something had already happened to prevent the planned turn. And it cannot be known when and where they did so, nor what the condition, altitude, height, speed or attitude of the aircraft was. If at any time Flight Lieutenant Cook lost visual reference, he would have turned away from the high ground, immediately, instinctively and without discussion. That he did not, does not mean he did not try.

Asked by the Board at what speed he thought the aircraft was travelling, Mr Holbrook replied his only reference point was (RN) Sea Kings operating from HMS Gannet (Prestwick), saying it *'was somewhat faster than Sea Kings in level flight'*. The RAF translated this as *'high speed'*, despite the maximum cruise speed of a Sea King at sea level being 112 knots. He was aware this was of limited value. In that area Sea Kings hovered while conducting passive and active sonar training, transited north and south to underwater test and evaluation areas (near the Sound of Raasay and the Mull of Galloway), and conducted Search and Rescue operations; their speed depending on role. He asked if he could be shown a Chinook at various heights and speeds. It was a fair question. A Sea King's fuselage is longer than a Chinook's, but the shape of the Chinook makes it look nearer. The Board declined.

To the RAF, Mr Holbrook was an inconvenient witness. He presented himself voluntarily but the Board misrepresented his evidence, and did not take corroborating evidence. Notably, his statement to Strathclyde Police was not provided to the Board, nor mentioned in its report. Moreover, his statement to the Board was altered after the event by MoD. This later prompted Mr Holbrook to publish his full account.[21]

*

Mr Holbrook's colleague Ian MacLeod, and nearby fishermen, were not interviewed by the Board. Wing Commander Pulford, the Board President, to the House of Lords Committee:

'From what I recall, Mr Holbrook was deemed to have the best evidence from the vessel, and his friend would have merely provided duplication of what Mr Holbrook had to say'.[22]

This makes no sense. If Mr Holbrook had the *'best'* evidence, that implies Mr MacLeod was interviewed and their statements compared. But *'would have'* implies he was not. It makes even less sense given the Board reproduced evidence from 10 ear-witnesses who were together in pairs.

Mr MacLeod was also best placed to speak about timing. He had gone below deck to listen to the shipping forecast. The reception was poor, but he was able to decipher enough to learn of a coming Force 7. When he came up to report this, Mr Holbrook pointed to the passing helicopter; at around 200-400 feet, 300 yards to the west, in level flight.

How long this was before impact depends on speed, which is why the timing of this sighting is crucial. It would have been a simple task to ask Mr MacLeod *when* he came on deck (e.g. as soon as the Force 7 was announced), and compare that with the BBC's timed recording of the broadcast. Later, I discuss timing discrepancies in the Navigation System. Mr MacLeod may have been able to provide valuable corroborating (or contradicting) evidence.

When asked about the fishermen, the President struggled:

'From what I recall, we tracked down the fishing vessels to Northern Ireland and the RUC were asked if they could find anybody from the fishing fleet that had anything to add. From what I recall they had nothing to add, they had either not seen the aircraft or the boats could not be traced'.

The Lords were not satisfied:

'Do you mean they were aware of Mr Holbrook's evidence and concurred with it,

---

21 'Chinook Crash: The Yachtsman's Evidence' (Mark Holbrook, 2011).
22 House of Lords Select Committee Minutes of Evidence, 27 September 2001, paragraph 11. (Evidence of Group Captain Andrew Pulford).

or that they did not want to give evidence at all?'

'I cannot recall. We were working through the RUC as an intermediary...'

'Nothing to add implies nothing to add to what Mr Holbrook said'.

'Correct. Or, indeed, they had not seen the aircraft'.

'Do you mean they had nothing to add, or they did not wish to give evidence?'

'I do not know. It could have been either'.

Mr Holbrook's evidence was that (Scottish) Saltires and Lions Rampant were emblazoned on the hulls. The President did not say how he tracked the vessels to Northern Ireland, or at what stage he handed over to the RUC. The Police Service of Northern Ireland (PSNI) claims it has no records.[23] Mindful of the government's assurance that all records would be retained for 25 years, and the 2019 decision to retain them further, there are a number of possibilities.[24] One, the RUC did not seek out the witnesses. Two, it ascertained the vessels were Scottish-based and passed the matter back to the President. Three, the evidence has been destroyed. The President's response was unsatisfactory. The PSNI's is shameful.

Why did Wing Commander Pulford not pursue the matter? What investigator does not report that he was actively denied evidence? What investigation immediately treats an eye-witness as hostile, impounding his vessel, charts and logbook, and never returning the latter? Why have legal authorities in both Scotland and Northern Ireland been permitted to ignore the Government's 25-year edict? And why has it taken members of the public to expose all this?

The Board (and police) abandoned all investigative protocols, ignoring corroborating witnesses. This last is especially important in Scotland as, uniquely, Scots Law requires two independent sources of evidence in support of each crucial fact. It could be said fairly that a higher standard of investigation is required there.

Moreover, an investigator must identify any crime scene. The RAF considered it the cockpit. The police avoided the issue, by not conducting an investigation. The Crown Office correctly identified it as Main Building in London.

---

23 Undated letter from Police Service of Northern Ireland, F-2015-03280, received 6 December 2015, in reply to Freedom of Information request of 14 October 2015.

24 https://hansard.parliament.uk/Lords/2000-06-26/debates/9af08624-4406-454a-a895-2e2b9c490faa/ChinookHelicopterAccidentRetentionOfDocuments

The Mull of Kintyre Review (2010/11)

After a long and acrimonious campaign, the Mull of Kintyre Review was set up in 2010 under The Right Honourable Lord Alexander Philip, a retired Judge of the Court of Session and High Court. Required to review 'all the evidence', like the Board he was kept unaware of what existed. That was for campaigners to uncover, acquire, analyse and submit. Which they did, to such an extent he sought a 6-month extension to his deadline.

In his evidence to the Review, the now Air Marshal Andrew Pulford expressed regret over his criticism of Flight Lieutenant Tapper, saying the degree of doubt was such that it was unsafe to go into the question of human failings, or to try to quantify the degree of any error. Did he belatedly realise that, if one cannot determine cause, and there exist possibilities, probabilities and certainties not of the pilots' making, then natural justice dictates one cannot criticise without addressing the failures of others - who in this case happened to be those who sat in judgment? Perhaps, due to his now senior rank, he felt free of the shackles or direction imposed by his former superiors? It is unclear if he voiced these thoughts to superiors between 1994 and 2011, but it is well-known he regarded the findings as unacceptable.

In 2013 the now Air Chief Marshal Sir Andrew Pulford became the first helicopter pilot to be appointed Chief of the Air Staff. From the standpoint of this case, the most significant event of his tenure was a letter he wrote on 4 August 2014 praising *'those who have campaigned'* on flight safety issues and who *'gave evidence to committees, Reviews and Inquiries'*. That, without their work, these official bodies would *'not have been able to reach detailed conclusions'*. He was referring, primarily, to the Nimrod and Mull of Kintyre Reviews. He remains the only person in authority to admit the central and extraordinary role of these members of the public. His words may, in part, have been a rejoinder to a recent statement by Air Vice Marshal Martin Clark, Technical Director of the Military Aviation Authority:

'We've asked some difficult questions. That's why we were created'.[25]

I cannot say why anyone in MoD would make such a claim. MoD didn't ask difficult questions. The public did, submitted them (with the answers) to the Nimrod XV230 Coroner, Andrew Walker, who agreed MoD had failed. The Nimrod Review was set up, and Charles Haddon-Cave QC took evidence from the same civilians. He recommended the establishment of a Military Airworthiness Authority. MoD's input was limited to changing

---

25 Aviation International News, 13 July 2014.

the title to 'Aviation', deflecting attention from the root failure - despite the Air Officer Commanding-in-Chief Strike Command, Air Chief Marshal Sir Clive Loader, repeating long-standing warnings in the Board of Inquiry report:

> 'The loss of XV230 and, far more importantly, the 14 Service personnel who were aboard, resulted from shortcomings in the application of the processes for assuring airworthiness and safe operation of the Nimrod'.

It is widely held his penchant for the truth led to him being passed over for the top job. This was reinforced in January 2010 when the Chinook's *'positively dangerous'* engine control software implementation was reported in the media. The incumbent, Air Chief Marshal Sir Stephen Dalton, wrote to the Guardian supporting the gross negligence findings. An extraordinary degree of interference in the legal process, and an unlikely move without more senior (political) approval. I dissected and demolished his letter in a reply I drafted for Fellows of the Royal Aeronautical Society, and which was published in the Guardian, Times and Daily Telegraph.[26]

What would have prevented the accident?

While there were many factors and events, the stand out root cause is the refusal to implement Defence Standard 05-125/2 with respect to the safety critical fuel computer software, despite being mandated in all aviation contracts. Entitled 'Technical Procedures for Post Design Services' (defined as 'Maintaining the Build Standard'), 05-125/2 is the bible for anyone with airworthiness delegation. The subject includes maintaining Safety Cases, a pre-requisite to a valid Master Airworthiness Reference. Properly applied, the failures would have been fixed, or the Mk2 would not have been in service on 2 June 1994. In which case the pilots would have been allotted an aircraft they trusted, or another mode of transport used. Implementation and oversight of this process ceased in June 1991, leading directly to other fatalities with the same root cause - which can be summarised as gross negligence, lack of leadership, and manslaughter.

MoD will reply that it is easy for me to say the aircraft should not have been flown. But I merely repeat what was formally declared by Boscombe Down, who were properly exercising legal obligations; and which was then mandated upon the RAF by MoD's Controller Aircraft, Sir Donald Spiers.

One can only speculate what would happen to the chief executive of an airline who ignored such a mandate, killing his employees and passengers.

---

26 'Their Greatest Disgrace' (David Hill, 2016), Chapter 18.

3. Evidence is a bridge to the truth

'Politicians tell brazen lies and lying is common in public life' [27]
Sir Malcolm Bruce MP, member of the Mull of Kintyre Review.

Credibility of evidence and witnesses

In Scotland, a credible witness is one *'whose credibility commends itself to the presiding magistrate* (and) *the trustworthiness of whom is good'*.[28] In England it is one who is *'not speaking from hearsay'*, which is far from the same thing.[29] A witness may have more or less credibility, or none at all.

Credibility is not the same as honesty. Two witnesses can give honest accounts of the same events, and one or both can be totally wrong. Equally, a witness who is deemed credible based solely on rank or position can be a pathological liar.

When giving evidence, MoD bore false witness to Ministers, bereaved families, legal authorities and the public about almost every aspect of the accident. Ultimately it was exposed, Lord Philip having to seek current policy documents from the public, upon which he then based his recommendations. MoD was neither credible nor trustworthy.

While Ministers can plead they were briefed by their officials, that defence only holds good until they are shown the truth. If they then repeat the untruth, that is a lie and a breach of the Ministerial Code. When Sir John Major and Sir Malcolm Rifkind spoke up, both complained of the same thing - being misled by lies of omission.

The decisive suppressed evidence

One must always look for what is not there. All Inquiries were defined by the evidence concealed from them, and the exclusion of witnesses who could speak to that evidence. Primarily:

- Boscombe Down, who had reported in September 1993 that the Chinook HC Mk2 was not airworthy - and that matters had deteriorated by 2 June 1994.
- Directorate of Helicopter Projects, to whom Boscombe reported this.

---

27 Upon taking his seat in the House of Lords as Lord Bruce of Bennachie, 19 October 2015.
28 Manson v. Macleod (1918).
29 R. v. Noakes (1917).

- The RAF Inspectorate of Flight Safety, who had warned the RAF Chief Engineer and the Air Staff of systemic airworthiness failings.

The foregoing was the crucial fresh evidence to the Mull of Kintyre Review, and that this had been concealed from aircrew. Lord Philip made this the key point of his report.[30] The only real decision he had to make was the extent to which he would explain the offences committed. In the event he restrained himself, merely signposting the reader towards serious breaches of the Air Force Act (1955) - primarily the making of false record.

On 13 July 2011 the findings of gross negligence were overturned by Secretary of State for Defence, Dr Liam Fox MP. That evening the now Sir Malcolm Rifkind wrote to me:

'There remain unresolved matters. It is right that these issues should continue to be pressed'.[31]

And press I do. The principal unresolved matters are cause and culpability. If one asks MoD today what the findings of the Senior Reviewing Officers have been replaced with, the answer is nothing. Similarly, and in the face of 29 unexplained deaths, the Crown Office has declared itself content that Sheriff Young was misled and even lied to.

*

There is no reason to withhold unclassified evidence, or deny its existence. Classified evidence should be reviewed by someone with the relevant clearances, and their findings noted. That way, a Judge or head of a legal Review will be aware that there are issues to be addressed *in-camera*.

One piece of unclassified evidence was utterly crucial to clearing the pilots. On 25 May 1994, one week before the accident, a meeting was held at Boscombe Down to discuss various technical reports relating to the engines and their controls. It was chaired by Captain Mike Brougham RN, Assistant Director Helicopter Projects 1. (In charge of all Chinook and Lynx programmes). The minutes were published on 31 May, Captain Brougham concluding:

'DHP was aiming to review the position of the Assistant Chief of the Air Staff's request to a <u>further INTERIM Controller Aircraft Release</u> within the next two weeks. The 10 June 1994 was declared as an end date for this decision making process'.[32]

---

30 Mull of Kintyre Review, paragraph 2.2.8.
31 Rifkind/Hill, 13 July 2011 22:47.
32 D/DHP/57/4/1, 31 May 1994. 'Notes of a T55-L-712F Engine FADEC meeting held at A&AEE Boscombe Down on 25 May 1994', paragraph 8.

'INTERIM' is not a temporal term, it is a type of clearance; the others being 'Limited', 'Full' and 'Installation Only'. Its meaning was well-known to all concerned, and had been reiterated by Boscombe in their trials reports:

> *'Cannot be relied upon to function correctly, which may include incorrect functioning of any failure indications. The aircraft must not be operated in any way that places any reliance whatsoever on the proper functioning of this equipment'.*[33]

Two RAF Group Captains were present; as well as the Boscombe Down senior engineering staff responsible for validating and verifying the safety critical software for the fuel computers, and the aircraft itself. All were acutely aware of this INTERIM status, and the definition. The minutes also make it clear that an exchange of correspondence took place between the Air Staff and MoD(PE), something MoD has consistently denied when these papers were sought under Freedom of Information.[34]

INTERIM is usually applied to, for example, new equipment that has been fitted for assessment. It is permitted to be switched-on, but if a problem occurs the installation design must ensure that when switched off the aircraft reverts to a safe state. To apply INTERIM to a whole aircraft, which is rare indeed, means it cannot be flown. It merely permits ground training and familiarisation (a formal project phase) - something later admitted by MoD.[35]

Lord Philip confirmed this was *'mandated'* upon the Air Staff.[36] That mandate forms the baseline for much of this book. To ignore this fact is to proceed with a closed mind.

---

33 Boscombe Down AMS 8H/05, Letter Report AMS 107/93, 15 October 1993; and JSP 553 Military Airworthiness Regulations, Chapter J.27.2.
34 *Inter alia*, MoD letter 25-11-2010-164322-004, 22 December 2010.
35 Defence Equipment & Support letter 19-01-2012-163711-002, 28 February 2012.
36 Mull of Kintyre Review, paragraph 2.2.8.

4. Double standards

Jaguar GR1B XX733

In the book *'Lightning Boys'* (Richard Pike, 2011), the now retired Sir William Wratten contributed an anecdote from the 1960s, when he flew English Electric Lightning interceptors. It is an interesting window into his thought processes. He had experienced an emergency, indicated by an audio warning. Looking down, he saw that the cover of his Standard Warning Panel was missing. He could see lights, but there was nothing to tell him what each referred to.

> *'Unless I could figure out from memory the aircraft system represented by each bulb, especially the one that now glowed, the information on the warning panel was <u>meaningless</u>'.*

He was able to conclude that he had an engine fire warning. He put out a call, and received permission for an emergency landing. The cover was found lying loose on the cockpit floor. He had not noticed that this *'large piece of solid metal was rattling around in front of my very eyes'* during his pre-flight checks, or during the flight. When interviewed by his superior, he admitted that he simply hadn't noticed:

> *'The matter was as straightforward and as unsatisfactory as that. I am sure that it was only the good rapport that had developed between us which allowed him to accept this. I was off the hook'.*

He goes on to relate how, as Senior Reviewing Officer in a later fatal accident (Flight Lieutenant Gregory Noble, Jaguar GR1B XX733, 23 January 1996) he recalled this incident and decided the deceased pilot should not be found at fault as the *'concurrent demands of the moment'* may have become *'too many'*. He further confirmed he understood the definition of negligence, something later denied by the Government.

Let us compare his decisions:

- He did not notice that a Warning Panel cover, in his line of sight, was missing. In ZD576 a bracket in the Thrust/Yaw Pallet had recently become detached three times, including on the delivery flight to Aldergrove two days before. The pilots could not see into the Control Closet or if anything was jamming the controls in that area.

- The information on his Warning Panel was *'meaningless'*. So too were GPS 'Error' messages in the Chinook HC Mk2. The crew of ZD576 did not have the benefit of training that would help identify the reason for the error message, because no-one had yet worked out what it meant,

never mind written and verified a procedure to deal with it.
- He was able to tell his boss what had happened. He was *'cleared'* because they enjoyed a good relationship. Lucky him. The crew of ZD576 did not live to tell their tale or defend themselves. Nor, presumably, had they known their accusers well enough.
- If the *'demands of the moment'* becoming too many was an acceptable finding on Jaguar XX733, why did he not apply the same principle to ZD576? That, the demands of flying an immature and unairworthy aircraft, with numerous faults and defects, may have overwhelmed the crew. Wratten dismissed as impossible the notion of a major emergency just before impact. He knew his Lightning was flying normally - until he had a major emergency.

Published the same month the Chinook pilots were cleared - July 2011 - one can only assume he didn't relate his tale to Lord Philip. He certainly didn't when before the House of Lords Committee in 2001.

Why one rule for the late Flight Lieutenant Noble, but another for Flight Lieutenants Tapper and Cook? It wasn't the first time...

Tornado GR1A ZG708

Concurrently with ZD576, Air Chief Marshal Wratten and Air Vice Marshal Day were reviewing another Board of Inquiry. On 1 September 1994, Tornado ZG708 from 13 Squadron, RAF Marham, was tasked for a low-level reconnaissance training flight. The aircraft was being flown up Glen Ogle, above Lochearnhead, Scotland at close to 430knots (500mph) by Flight Lieutenants Patrick Harrison and Peter Mosley.

The glen rises sharply from south-east to north-west. To either side are a series of irregular steep ridges, with distinct sheer rock faces and craggy outcrops leading to the uneven glen floor. The aircraft was nearing the top of the glen, visibility was excellent, and the pilot would see Glen Dochart and the higher Breadalbane massif running across his front, south-west to north-east. A turn to the left or right would take them towards higher ground of almost 4,000 feet. The aircraft impacted at 918 feet; below, to the left, and just past the highest point of the glen, Beinn Leabhain (2,326 feet). It was destroyed, and both crew killed.

But this time the aircraft had both Accident Data and Cockpit Voice Recorders, meaning the Board of Inquiry knew <u>exactly</u> what happened:

> *'The aircraft commenced a turn to the right, using 70-80° angle of bank, in order to follow the line of the valley. At three seconds to impact, full right aileron was*

applied, almost coincident with a significant rearwards stick input and with the selection of reheat on both engines. The aircraft completed a further 180° of roll, through the inverted position, before striking the ground, left wingtip first, at a point three miles south of Killin'.

Analysis showed the aircraft responded correctly to control inputs. The following is a summary of the findings.

Board of Inquiry (December 1994)

'There was little doubt that the control inputs immediately prior to the crash had been made, either voluntarily or otherwise, by the aircraft pilot. Since the pilot's control inputs led directly to the loss of the aircraft, the Board concluded that his actions constituted an Error of Judgment and therefore the Board recommends that he be absolved from blame'.

Station Commander's Comments (December 1994)

'The fact remains that, albeit for understandable reasons, the Board has been unable to establish beyond doubt what caused ZG708 to crash. The term "Error of Judgment" involves a finding of an honest mistake accompanied with no lack of zeal where a person, through no fault of his own, and whilst exercising the degree of skill which could reasonably be expected, makes an inappropriate response. Given that we do not know exactly what happened...I believe that it would be unwise to draw any conclusions as to human failings - there is too much scope for conjecture. I do not accept, therefore, the Board's conclusions, and I recommend that there should be no finding regarding human failings'.

Air Vice Marshal John Day, Air Officer Commanding 1 Group (March 1995)

'Error of Judgment by the pilot should be qualified as having been the most likely cause of the accident, rather than the definitive cause'.

Air Chief Marshal Sir William Wratten, Air Officer Commanding-in-Chief, Headquarters Strike Command (April 1995)

'Notwithstanding a thorough investigation and the availability of evidence revealing the precise activities of the crew up to the point of impact, there is no explanation for the final manoeuvre. I find any consideration of human failings to be academic and fruitless'.

Let us again compare and contrast:
- Both aircraft hit visible high ground. The Tornado Board knew what caused this, the Chinook Board did not.
- The Tornado Board suggested three possible causes: an unconsidered response to a *'startling event'*, a control restriction, and medical incapacitation. They chose the first, saying the pilot made an *'error of judgment'* - a slap on the wrist to a living pilot. The Chinook Board also proposed three possibilities, guessing inappropriate rate of climb.
- Despite the certainty of who did and said what, Wratten and Day found no fault with the Tornado pilot. Lacking any such evidence, and despite the same standard of proof applying, they found the Chinook pilots negligent to a gross degree.

The findings of Air Vice Marshal Day

Throughout the Mull of Kintyre case, and to the frustration of the families and their legal teams, MoD and Ministers consistently conflated *absence of evidence* and *evidence of absence*. For example, Day said in his Chinook remarks *'I note that the Inquiry found no evidence of a technical failure'* (which was untrue), but used that as *'factual'* evidence that there was no technical failure. When judging the Tornado case, he stated *'there was no evidence of a control restriction'*, and later concluded, correctly, that *'the possibility of a control restriction...could not be discounted'*.

On Tornado, he stated *'the possibility of medical incapacitation could not be discounted'*. On Chinook, medical incapacitation was completely discounted, despite there being no Cockpit Voice Recorder and no medical evidence one way or the other.

On Tornado, he commented:

'Overwhelming evidence indicates that the aircraft responded, both directly and appropriately, to control inputs, either voluntary or otherwise, which were initiated by the pilot and led ultimately to the loss of the aircraft. I accept the Board's conclusion that the aircraft crashed as a direct result of control inputs which manoeuvred it into a perilous attitude with respect to the ground'.

On Chinook, he did not have the luxury of *'overwhelming evidence'*, or indeed *any* evidence as to control inputs. He admitted that he speculated as to what might have happened, maintaining this satisfied the 'no doubt' standard of proof.

On Tornado, he concluded:

'I agree with the Board that Flight Lieutenant Mosley's unconsidered response to

a "startling event" is the most plausible cause. It would not be unreasonable to suppose that the late sighting of a large bird might have prompted him to initiate a rapid roll away from the hazard, and this manoeuvre would have caused him instinctively to select full power'.

In other words, he was guessing that a large bird flew in front of the Tornado. Yet is certain, with absolutely no doubt whatsoever, that nothing similar happened to the Chinook. How does this Big Bird hypothesis advance MoD's Safety Management System?[37] In 1999 MoD claimed such a distraction had been considered by the Reviewing Officers in the Chinook case, and even if it had occurred would not have been sufficient *'to prevent an experienced crew from maintaining safe flight'*.[38] The Board had indeed considered distraction - but not by birds. But it *had* considered and rejected bird strike. And unlike the Chinook Board, their Tornado counterparts tried (with some success) to assess what species of birds would be in the Scottish glens on 1 September.

Finally:

'Regardless of the circumstances of this particular accident, I agree that Flight Lieutenant Mosley should be absolved from blame'.

What does *'regardless of the circumstances'* allude to? Given the plethora of known facts, might he be referring to evidence that has not been revealed, the voice recording being an obvious candidate? Only the final five seconds of audio was made available for analysis.

The findings of Air Chief Marshal Wratten

The Senior Reviewing Officer, Air Chief Marshal Wratten, began his remarks:

'Notwithstanding a thorough investigation and the <u>availability of evidence revealing the precise activities</u> of the crew up to the point of impact, there is no explanation for the final manoeuvre'.

Similarly, on Chinook he began:

'<u>Without the irrefutable evidence</u> which is provided by an Accident Data Recorder and a Cockpit Voice Recorder, there is inevitably a degree of <u>speculation</u> as to the precise detail of the sequence of events in the minutes and seconds immediately prior to impact'.

---

37 I acknowledge that Air Vice Marshal Day did not claim the bird was an eight-foot two-inch tall bright yellow anthropomorphic canary.

38 Lord Gilbert, House of Lords 22 May 1997.

Now contrast his findings. Despite having to speculate, he had no doubt as to the gross negligence of the Chinook pilots. But with infinitely more to go on, he harboured doubt on Tornado.

He then evaded the issue of human failings when dealing with Tornado:

'Despite the wealth of detailed evidence, we are confounded and under these particular circumstances I consider it futile to indulge in hypothesis'.

Yet, his entire case against the Chinook pilots was based on hypothesis.

Remember, these reviews were taking place at the same time. Any reasonable person would be concerned over the disparity between what counts as evidence in each case. How is it that the overwhelming detailed evidence from the Tornado accident, and the lack of evidence in the Chinook accident, brought about such inconsistent findings? It is bewildering that Ministers did not recognise this capriciousness.

More double standards

I mentioned earlier Air Chief Marshal Sir Stephen Dalton, when Chief of the Air Staff, writing to the press in support of the Mull of Kintyre findings. Here, as RAF Marham Station Commander, he was a Reviewing Officer:

'I believe it would be unwise to draw any conclusions as to human failings because there is too much scope for conjecture'.[39]

Hypocrisy

On 16 February 1995, two months before ruling on the Tornado and Chinook cases, Air Chief Marshal Wratten had issued a directive 'Disciplinary Proceedings in Aircraft Accidents', in which he demanded subordinate commanders rigorously apply disciplinary proceedings in any case of pilot *'negligence, indiscipline or incompetence'*. Also, that he would *'not tolerate shortcomings of concentration'*. In a letter to the House of Lords Select Committee, MoD later explained the directive:

'Sir William took up appointment on 1 September 1994. Against the background of a peak of accidents and disastrous loss of life, he determined that flight safety demanded renewed emphasis. Sir William was also concerned that there was an inconsistent approach across the Command to the disciplinary requirements of Queen's Regulations of the time. Against such a background it is entirely reasonable for a Commander in Chief to make certain that those in his Command chain are aware of the importance of adopting a consistent approach to such

---

39 Remarks of RAF Marham Station Commander, 19 December 1994.

issues; and of the emphasis he personally attaches to flight safety'.

No reasonable person would disagree with this sentiment. Except... Wratten breached his own directive.

Conclusion

I conclude that Wratten and Day (and Dalton) were fair to the Tornado pilot, but desperately sought a way to find *against* the Chinook pilots. Plainly, there was a higher political imperative. These murky waters cleared slightly upon Day's retirement in July 2003. The Advisory Committee on Business Appointments recommended he wait the statutory 12 months before taking up a senior position with British Aerospace. Prime Minister Tony Blair personally intervened, overruling the watchdog. Since leaving the RAF Day has never spoken publicly about the accident.

PART 2 - ACCIDENT INVESTIGATION

'Wherever there is a departure from proper practice, this should be regarded as a miscarriage of justice irrespective of its effect on the outcome of the case'.
Professor Andrew Ashworth QC - 'The Criminal Process: An Evaluative Study'

5. Preventing recurrence

Accident investigations attempt to uncover safety deficiencies, so that they may be eliminated. Even if such a deficiency is subsequently found to be unconnected to cause, it *must* be reported and resolved. The investigation must determine the actions, inactions, events, conditions or failures that led to the accident. This is achieved by gathering, recording and analysing *all* available evidence. Recommendations are then made to avoid recurrence. Underpinning this are three fundamentals: independence, autonomy and technical excellence.

In 1944, the Convention on International Civil Aviation (the 'Chicago Convention') established the International Civil Aviation Organisation (ICAO). About Aircraft Accident and Incident Investigation, it says:

'The investigation authority shall have independence in the conduct of the investigation and unrestricted authority over its conduct, must be strictly objective and totally impartial, and perceived to be so. It should be established in such a way that it can withstand political or other interference or pressure'.

This does not sit well within MoD. Uppermost in the Convening Authority's mind are the operational and political imperatives. To sustain both it is always convenient for the cause of the accident to be human error. In risk terms, the military prefers 'acceptable risk' whereby personnel and equipment are expendable, over the legal requirement to reduce risk to 'As Low As Reasonably Practicable and tolerable'. While MoD will not discuss the issue, in this case it is clear the Air Staff leaned too far toward the former, to the point where they not only ignored obligations but made false declarations that they had been met.

In 1986 Minister for Defence Support Lord Trefgarne appointed William Tench, former head of the (then) Accidents Investigation Branch, to conduct a study of military accident investigation procedures. He reported in January 1987, but senior military commanders succeeded in having the government suppress the report. In a 2009 interview Lord Trefgarne described his feelings as those of *'despair'*. He confirmed that the primary pressure came from the Chief of the Air Staff, Air Chief Marshal Sir David Craig; who, as Lord Craig, later supported the findings against the ZD576 pilots.[40] (Notably, in his previous post, Air Officer Commanding-in-Chief Strike Command, Craig had disagreed with the introduction of the *'absolutely no doubt whatsoever'* standard of proof, so possible motive

---

40 Lord Trefgarne, BBC Radio 4 'Today', 2 September 2009.

emerges). The report only became widely available in 2009, during the Nimrod Review.[41] However, campaigners were well aware of it because Messrs Tench and Cook had worked closely together when seeking to introduce Flight Data Recorders into commercial airliners.

Mr Tench confirmed *'mediocre standards where investigations are conducted by complete novices'*. Harsh but true. He cited accidents where the wrong causes were identified, and where investigators missed recurrences. His main criticism, however, was reserved for senior officers:

'A disturbing feature is the influence senior officers seek to exert on the investigation process, particularly in the RAF. The pervasive nature of the involvement of some Station Commanders, senior Staff Officers, and even Commanders-in-Chief, is an unwelcome intrusion upon what should be the complete independence of the Board. The opportunities for Staff Officers to influence the Board's interpretation of evidence, or their findings, must throw doubt on the complete freedom of the Board to draw its own conclusions. It must, of course, always be possible to have reservations about the findings of an Inquiry, but to assume superior insight on a basis of rank must be more doubtful. It is my considered view that Boards of Inquiry have outlived their usefulness as instruments of efficient aircraft accident investigation'.

The central tenet, he declared, was the need for independent, impartial investigation. That, a unit comprising trained professional investigators be established to take over investigation of all serious aircraft accidents. The following month, February 1987, Chinook HC Mk1 ZA721 crashed in the Falkland Islands, killing all seven onboard. The President of the Board of Inquiry had the findings dictated to him. Mr Tench was vindicated.

Mr Tench had been seconded to Man S(Org), an administrative branch of MoD. At the time of the accident, it was investigating a complaint about the RAF's *savings at the expense of safety* policy. This followed a submission from the avionic Deputy Directorate comprising former MoD(PE) staff recently transferred to the RAF's Air Member Supply and Organisation (AMSO). That is, they were challenging their new superiors. On 22 July 1994 Man S(Org) sided with AMSO's replacement, Air Member Logistics, headed by Air Chief Marshal Sir Michael Alcock - also a vocal proponent of the negligence findings. Fraud and waste were to be ignored.[42]

Man S(Org) were asked to review their findings. A full account of the policy

---

41 Sec(as)/366/00 - 'Report of a Study of Aircraft Accident Investigation Procedures in the Armed Services', W.H. Tench, January 1987.
42 Letter DD/AV4D1/PF, 15 June 1993, and reply D/Man S(Org)/69/2/2924, 22 July 1994.

and its effect was submitted, enclosing supporting evidence dating back to June 1987. [43] They did not reply. Another opportunity to prevent recurrence was lost.

My investigative approach

The truth in military accidents usually lies in what is missing or omitted. Here, MoD systematically destroyed much of the evidence trail, making it impossible to uncover all the facts. This led to much conjecture, most of it well-intentioned but uninformed. Nevertheless, sufficient remains to point any investigation in the right direction. Not least because most of MoD's failings are systemic; so the information, while fragmented, exists in the files of other accidents and with witnesses unconnected to Chinook. Where to look is helped by knowledge of these prior failures. In this the Board of Inquiry was disadvantaged.

My main reference point is the aforementioned loss of ZA721 in 1987. That accident bears directly on why the Chinook HC Mk2 fleet was not airworthy on 2 June 1994, and assists in understanding the most likely cause. To that end, I am grateful for the advice offered by Senior Air Accidents Investigation Branch Inspector Tony Cable. He led the investigations into both ZA721 and ZD576, and is internationally acclaimed for his Pan-Am Lockerbie and Air France Concorde investigations.

On matters of airworthiness, which is an engineering discipline, I use my own work, and that of John's. It has been peer reviewed, published, and accepted by the Nimrod and Mull of Kintyre Reviews, and various Coroners' Inquests. It is based entirely on mandated policy. I believe this should be implemented. MoD ceased doing so before the accident.

As to general airmanship, flying the Chinook, and understanding the difficulties pilots faced when transitioning from Mk1 to Mk2, I have been assisted by a cross-section of experienced Chinook pilots and aircrewmen, past and present. But one man stands out...

Squadron Leader Robert Burke

In a lengthy, multi-faceted case like this, contributors inevitably drift in and out of the story. Many held views honestly, but evidence proved them wrong. Most who knew the truth remained silent.

---

43 Letters D/DHP SKAV1/PF, 1 August 1994 and D/DDSS11(RAF)/24/1, 8 June 1987.

Robert Burke was different. In 1994 he was the RAF Odiham Unit Test Pilot, and had been for over a decade. His job was to identify problems before aircraft entered or were returned to service. Importantly, he did not waver from evidence he had presented as part of these duties before the accident. He postulated three main scenarios:

- Engine runaway up, whereby a malfunctioning Full Authority Digital Engine Control (FADEC) causes an engine to overspeed, often to the point of failure. This takes time to diagnose, as a run-up on one engine can be indistinguishable from a run-down on the other. On 26 October 1993 Boscombe Down warned of *'inadequate standard of FADEC software and the lack of integrity of the overspeed protection systems'*.[44] MoD denied the problem, but later quietly modified the safety critical software.

- Automatic Flight Control System fault, manifesting as violent bouncing ('porpoising') and lateral movement, which he characterised as a *'constant occurrence'*. This was confirmed by Flight Lieutenant Iain MacFarlane to the House of Lords Select Committee in 2001, who stated *'in one case over a period of days an aircraft bounced vertically every time it was turned right'*.

- Control Pallet Balance Spring Bracket insert bonding failure, manifesting as control jams. MoD omitted 'jams', merely talking of a *'stiffening'* of the Collective (thrust) lever. It claimed the problem would have to occur in all four channels (thrust, roll, pitch and yaw). But, as the controls are linked, if one goes, all may be affected.

The first two fall into the category 'Undemanded Flight Control Movement'. The last 'Control Restriction', which may cause the former.

*

While still at the crash site, Tony Cable called Squadron Leader Burke seeking his assistance. He and two technicians from RAF Odiham then commenced work on a Chinook in the 240 Operational Conversion Unit hangar, trying to replicate fault conditions. On the verge of a breakthrough, the Acting Station Commander at Odiham, Wing Commander John Cooke, sent his clerk, a Senior Aircraftman, to inform Burke his presence was required. He was ordered to desist.

Burke was asked about this by Lord Jauncey on 16 October 2001:

'You were given instructions not to discuss the matter further?'

'Yes, my Lord. I can be very specific about this. (We) had the aircraft on jacks with

---

44 Boscombe Down Letter Report E1109, 26 October 1993, paragraph 12b (8).

the gyros disconnected so you could wobble the aircraft's main gyro to simulate what we thought the condition of the aircraft might have been when it crashed. There was a very strange DASH (Differential Airspeed Hold) extension on the aircraft and nobody could work it out.

At midday, I got a message to go and see the Acting Station Commander, Wing Commander John Cooke. He called me into his office, sat me down and said, "I have had instructions that you are not to continue to help in this investigation in any way". Before I left the office, I stood up by the door and I said very formally, "Wing Commander Cooke, is this a direct order or is this a request?" And he put it in exactly these words, "This is a direct order Bob, you are not to discuss this crash with anyone. You are not to approach anyone. If anybody asks for information do not give it". I said, "Can I speak to my oppos about it?", and he said, "No, you are to speak to no-one about it and that is a direct order". From that moment I did not talk to anyone about it until I left the Service'.

'As a result, you did not give evidence to the Board?'

'I gave evidence to neither the Fatal Accident Inquiry nor the Board of Inquiry. I gave evidence to the National Audit Office when they asked me'.[45]

He added:

'There were also two nearly identical accidents, one of which involved me and half my test crew; the other involved the other half of my test crew and another pilot in the Falklands. There were massive gearbox failures, and my helicopter came down in two large parts. The front rotor flew off somewhere else and the rest of the aircraft landed with me and the crew in it. There was a fire in the Auxiliary Power Unit, and the aircraft caught fire internally'.

Wing Commander Cooke was not asked who told him to stand Squadron Leader Burke down. Instead, he provided a written statement via MoD saying *'I have no recollection of the meeting'*.[46] Nobody else was interviewed. His orders came from (at least) 1 Group HQ, headed by Air Vice Marshal Peter Squire, the Convening Officer. Perhaps, at this senior level, the RAF was being mindful that Burke, embarrassingly, had uncovered the most likely cause of ZA721 in 1987.

Whether or not Squadron Leader Burke's experiences explain the accident (and I believe they go a very long way), they represent serious problems which MoD did not address prior to the Mk2 entering service, and actively sought to conceal. It was, and still is, allowed to judge its own case, with no right of appeal. This is also the formal position of the police, Crown Office

---

45 Evidence of Squadron Leader Robert Burke to the House of Lords, 16 October 2001.
46 Written evidence of Wing Commander John Cooke to House of Lords, 5 November 2001.

(Scotland) and Crown Prosecution Service (England and Wales). Moreover, MoD and these legal authorities maintain that military investigations remove the need for Fatal Accident Inquiries (and Inquests elsewhere in the UK), despite them having different aims.[47]

The honourable exception was Sheriff Young, who rejected MoD's stated cause. He confirmed that the Senior Reviewing Officers, far from meeting the *beyond any doubt whatsoever* standard of proof, did not meet that of a civil case, *balance of probability* (more likely than not). They did not achieve 51%, when the pass mark was 100%.

Whenever Robert Burke gave evidence it was tested against the claims of the Senior Reviewing Officers. Not once was he found wanting. MoD accused him of lying and denigrated him at every turn, threatening legal action. I have no hesitation in accepting his evidence.

Hypothesis or theory? Fact or fiction?

Wing Commander Pulford confirmed he had:

'Hypothesised that the crew had decided to make a controlled climb over the Mull of Kintyre. Having found the most probable cause the Board were then required to look for any evidence associated with that most probable cause'.[48]

A hypothesis is a tentative explanation or assumption made before any investigation has been completed. A theory on the other hand is an explanation based on supported data. An inability to disprove a hypothesis does not make it true. If one part of a hypothesis turns out to be true, that does not mean the whole is true. A theory or hypothesis might have holes which are not always evident, due to hidden facts and incomplete evidence. Equally, new or fresh evidence might turn a hypothesis into fact.

When studying MoD investigations, deeper examination is always necessary to fact-check its claims. Only then can the known facts be identified; and from them the lead anomaly derived, any follow-on anomalies, and the lead event that led to them. Only then can theories be offered, which *must* match *all* the known facts.

Here, the investigation was chronologically and procedurally wrong. Basic protocols were violated. Instead of seeking out known facts and the lead

---

47 *Inter alia*, 'Supplementary written submission from the Crown Office & Procurator Fiscal Service' to the Justice Committee reviewing the Inquiries into Fatal Accidents and Sudden Deaths (Scotland) Bill, 18 June 2015.
48 Fatal Accident Inquiry, 24 January 1996, evidence of Wing Commander Andrew Pulford under questioning by Mr Aidan O'Neill QC, for the Tapper family.

anomaly, an incorrect hypothesis became the primary influence over investigative decision-making. The President's statement invalidates his entire investigation.

*

Investigators must have access to a maintained database of anomalies and previous recommendations. Additionally, the study of Hazard Logs and Safety Cases will reveal if past lessons have been learned. Deficiencies, primarily failure to take action, are indicative of serious failings in the organisation's Safety Management System. Here, we are concerned with systemic failures.

To assist in this, MoD must provide a single, named, point of contact for any given equipment, aircraft system or aircraft type - termed the Technical Agency on equipment and systems, and the Type Airworthiness Authority on aircraft. His job is to maintain the build standard and Safety Cases underpinning the airworthiness certification. However, as part of the RAF's policy to run down airworthiness management, from 1991 the Technical Agency posts were gradually disbanded. This created an even greater degree of complex multi-stranded issues for the (relatively) junior officers of the Board of Inquiry to deal with, which they were ill-equipped to identify.

Also, Risk Registers will reveal if predicted risks can be linked to known facts. At best, in 1994 this data was fragmented. At worst, simply not there. MoD's risk management policy was, and to a large extent remains - *wait to see if the risk occurs, then consider doing something*. A proactive approach is positively discouraged, by the simple expedient of withholding resources. Here, the most obvious risks, in fact certainties, were (a) it was not policy to maintain airworthiness (a policy remains an aspiration until resourced), and (b) the Chinook HC Mk2 was not airworthy. Both were known <u>before</u> the accident, and had been the subject of condemning audit reports.

A good example of this process breaking down can be found in the mid-air collision between two RN Sea King ASaC Mk7s on 22 March 2003, killing all seven crew. The Board of Inquiry's three main contributory factors were recorded as major risks eight years before the accident, and plans drawn up to mitigate them. However, the RN asked for one not to be implemented, and an administrator cancelled the other two contracts without considering impact or consulting with the RN or the programme manager. All had one thing in common - situational awareness. It was inevitable that, sooner or later, crews would find themselves in darkness with no idea they were on a collision course. While the Board identified the factors, it was kept unaware of this background so was unable to identify the real failures. Instead, it criticised those who had identified and sought to mitigate the risks. Not dissimilar from ZD576.[49]

*

Recommendations must be linked to evidence, to ensure relevance. The Board's Terms of Reference said *'make appropriate recommendations'*. It made only three: fit a Cockpit Voice Recorder, fit an Accident Data Recorder (both repeated *ad infinitum* in other reports), and develop instrument climb procedures for the Support Helicopter Force. This implies there was no evidence to justify further recommendations. Or perhaps it did make more, but they were removed?

The procedural recommendation was implemented shortly afterwards, although it would be some time before a suitable simulator was available. In 1999 MoD stated that the requirement for recorders was satisfied by the forthcoming Helicopter Health and Usage Monitoring System (HUMS) programme. This was misleading. At the time, those responsible were still actively resisting the recording of audio; and in any case Chinook had an unsuitable Intercom. The RAF, and the HUMS project office (in the same Directorate as Chinook), had rejected several calls for the aircraft to be suitably modified.

The ZD576 investigation

By agreement between nations, in civil accidents there are two independent investigations - safety (technical) and criminal. Pending agreement of the known facts they may proceed in parallel.

In the military there is one, and it is not independent. It is required to study Legal (and hence, Illegal), Technical and Airmanship perspectives. (This book is structured accordingly). But it never adheres to one basic rule - always ask if this has happened before. If this can be proven, then it cannot be said - as MoD did - that an event such as equipment malfunction is improbable. Instead, it compartmentalises, always dismissing accidents as one-offs. But if one does not ask if the accident is a recurrence, that is a poor starting point if the principal aim is to prevent recurrence.

While not mandated, Boards may engage the services of the Air Accidents Investigation Branch, at the time part of the Department of the Environment, Transport and the Regions. However, its role is extremely limited in military accidents. It is not an investigating authority. It is purely

---

49 'Breaking the Military Covenant' (David Hill, 2019).

there to support the Board of Inquiry, who determine the scope and direction of the investigation. Prohibited from looking at Legal and Airmanship, or the airworthiness aspects of Technical, it must confine itself to reporting on the physical evidence at the scene. Here, denied key parts of that evidence, its report was inconclusive. This was partly corrected when some of the evidence offered here was shown to the Senior Inspector many years later, he assimilated it, and presented his conclusions to the Mull of Kintyre Review.

*

Prime Minister John Major immediately spoke of the allegedly poor weather, the implication being poor decision-making to fly in that weather. Who would feed him this? The list of senior officers invited to brief a Prime Minister is very short - on RAF matters, the Chief of the Air Staff. But there is another route. It is the role of the Government's Defence spokesman in the House of Lords to engage with retired senior defence personnel. In 2011 the incumbent, Lord Astor of Hever, blithely repeated the RAF line following the announcement that the gross negligence findings had been set aside. The lines of communication between the current Air Staff, their predecessors and Ministers remained intact.

More fundamentally, one of the most basic principles of accident investigation was broken. Conclusions were drawn before all evidence had been gathered, categorised, examined and compared. Selected evidence was tailored, and worse, invented, to fit the preferred scenario, while probative evidence of prior negligence was neglected.

Critically, there had been a series of previous fatal Chinook accidents with, in some cases, identical root causes. (A root cause is a factor that, if removed from the problem-fault sequence, would have prevented the accident). This is why I believe the Board was directed away from proven technical and legal deficiencies, towards imaginary airmanship failings.

*

Despite only 80% of the aircraft surviving, and much of that in no condition to be examined properly, the Board confirmed its immediate focus was pilot error. This was the first indication it was being directed. In fact, the evidence showed technical failure was highly likely to be the primary cause, if not quite a certainty. Legal was not mentioned, and the Board offered only unsubstantiated criticism of Flight Lieutenant Tapper's airmanship.

Yet, on 27 September 2001 the Board President (the now) Group Captain Pulford confirmed to the House of Lords he had spoken to Boscombe on

10 June and 30 September 1994:

'Did they provide you with a report about their conclusions?'

'No, we did not take a formal report. We already had the Controller Aircraft Release'.

But what he actually had was a reproduction of a *'document in the form of an INTERIM Controller Aircraft Release'*, with a covering letter stating it <u>had</u> to be read in conjunction with reports articulating why the aircraft was not airworthy. Pulford had already used the term 'INTERIM' in reply to a previous question. It is possible that before the accident he did not fully understand its meaning - *not to be relied upon in any way*. But it is highly unlikely he remained unaware after 10 June 1994.

These would be rather one-sided conversations, Pulford told the facts in no uncertain terms. There would be no point beating about the bush with a Wing Commander, when the establishment's Superintendent, directly accountable to the Secretary of State for Defence, had already stated this. Repeatedly. Even if directed towards pilot error, and even if ordered not to listen to Squadron Leader Burke, these conversations should have been the turning point in his investigation. He might perhaps apply different weight to certain evidence, but being told that the aircraft is not airworthy leaves no room for argument. It should immediately become the focus of the investigation.

I concede all this may have been in an early draft of the Board's report, but removed during review. Either way, the President and another Board member were Chinook pilots, and all too aware of what had caused previous fatal accidents. If they had no direct experience, their own Unit Test Pilot at RAF Odiham had - in fact, an alarming amount.

*

A word about Boards of Inquiry. Their conduct is dominated by the requirements of Statutory Instruments. As such, they tend to concentrate on satisfying these rules, with the more important work - the resolving of cause - secondary. Senior Reviewing Officers are more concerned that the Board has satisfied its Terms of Reference, irrespective of the quality of the Inquiry. In fact, these Terms of Reference are often so restrictive, it is impossible for a Board to uncover cause. This formalised approach wastes time and is inefficient. For example, the rules require that a witness may only give evidence orally, and to all three Board members. This diverts the engineering member from his main role - working alongside (in this case) the Air Accidents Investigation Branch to assess physical evidence at the scene. Also, aspects he has sole responsibility for, such as airworthiness.

To be clear - this is a demanding and upsetting job, and in cases such as this it can seem, with justification, that the eyes of the world are upon you. Those anticipating what you conclude, and those determined to dictate what you conclude. Moreover, there is little incentive to learn from mistakes, as members seldom sit on a second Board. This is a deliberate control mechanism.

The rules were changed shortly after this accident, Boards renamed 'Service Inquiries'. Most of the above still applied, the main difference being Senior Reviewing Officers are no longer permitted to attribute blame. A further change has seen only one set of remarks, from the Convening Authority. Blame is still attributed, just not in so many words. On Nimrod XV230, for example, Mr Haddon-Cave QC was guided by MoD towards a number of named accused. Legal action commenced - and was swiftly abandoned when the Crown Prosecution Service and Thames Valley Police were advised of the seniority of those really to blame.[50] This inequality of treatment of one group over another is illegal, but unfortunately all too common.

Professionalism and an inquiring mind should have ensured the Board fully understood why the Mk2 was in service, and why ZD576 was declared serviceable and fit for purpose. It was the first Mk2 in theatre, arriving at Aldergrove two days earlier, unserviceable and with an already appalling record. In its short life it had exhibited a disturbing number of faults, mainly relating to the Navigation System, fuel computers and flight controls. It would not be going too far to ask why the aircraft had not been declared rogue. By avoiding this, and organisational failures that allowed it, the Senior Reviewing Officers and Air Staff ensured this prior negligence was overlooked.

<u>The main anomalies in each domain</u>
While it is possible, I do not think there was an <u>airmanship</u> anomaly, or any adverse event at all caused by the crew. However, there *were* contributory Human Factors hazards, not least that the pilots did not trust the aircraft. That was an organisational failure, not a personal one.

The fabricated Release to Service, and the active concealment of this from aircrew, were illegal acts rooted in a culture that, to this day, encourages and condones maladministration. This should have added to the

---

[50] *Inter alia*, notification to Thames Valley Police, 6 July 2010, and reply from Assistant Chief Constable Helen Ball, 11 October 2010.

confidence level of there being a technical failure.

The primary technical anomalies - airworthiness status, persistent Undemanded Flight Control Movements, and uncertified engine control software - are inextricably linked. To each other, and to the legal and Human Factors anomalies.

All this was known to the Air Staff.

The lead event

The lead event that caused the technical and legal anomalies, and Human Factors hazards, was the RAF's *savings at the expense of safety* policy. In May 1997 the late Baroness Park of Monmouth (Daphne Park, a former senior controller in the Secret Intelligence Service, MI6), said in a House of Lords debate:

'MoD's commitment to saving money and contractorising has very dangerous long-term implications both for the safety of the aircraft and the crews. Are too many corners being cut in the sacred name of value for money? Could the cause of this accident been in some way the result of poor maintenance, inadequate training, pressure on inadequate staff, the financial pressures of the budget and too severe cuts in service manpower at the support end?'

An accurate assessment, and good questions. The answer to each is *'Yes'*.

Summary
- The published version of the Board of Inquiry report is almost entirely without merit. However, I stress my enquiries reveal that the reports of the engineering member, at least, were returned for 're-write'.
- The Air Accidents Investigation Branch conducted its limited role satisfactorily, but was impeded by MoD's concealment of evidence, and the removal of physical evidence from the scene by others with MoD's agreement.
- Strathclyde Police and the Royal Ulster Constabulary abrogated their responsibilities. Now Police Scotland and Police Service of Northern Ireland (PSNI), they remain uninterested. The former say they are *'not in receipt of any instruction from the Crown Office to reinvestigate this accident'*; implying Strathclyde Police carried out a prior investigation, which they did not.[51] The PSNI simply point to the Board of Inquiry

---

51 Letter IM-FOI-2915-2431, 25 November 2015, from Sir Stephen House, Chief Constable of Police Scotland.

report as the official record and cause, despite its findings being overturned following the Mull of Kintyre Review (which they also cite).[52] This is particularly sad when 10 of their colleagues died.

Police Scotland was formed in 2013, merging eight regional police forces. The Police Service of Northern Ireland (incorporating the Royal Ulster Constabulary George Cross) was formed in 2001 under the Police Northern Ireland Act (2000) *'to allow for the body of constables known as the Royal Ulster Constabulary to continue in being'*.

*

Those who sought to control the flow of information had an easy job - they were already in control. They had rank and power, using this to control the actions of subordinates. This allowed them to conceal organisational failures and illegal acts, ensuring both their own and the RAF's reputations were not questioned. The constant turnover of staff in MoD, and the ethos, supported by military discipline, that senior officers can never be wrong, gave them ample opportunity. Add to that ego, and you have a potent and wicked brew.

There must be a clear start and end to evidence, and the conclusions must match that evidence. Here, they did not.

---

52 Letter F-2015-03280, 7 December 2015, from C. Morris.

6. The lead anomaly

It is beyond the scope of this book, and in any case unnecessary, to rehearse the detailed evidence that Chinook HC Mk2 was not airworthy on 2 June 1994. Instead, this chapter summarises important points, with an Annex at the rear written by John offering an in-service perspective.

Airworthiness

Airworthiness is both a technical and legal aspect, due to the enduring obligations of those with formal delegation. This applies to servicemen and civilians, without time or geographical limit. At the time, RAF personnel were subject to the Air Force Act (1955), which lists several relevant offences such as making false record in aircraft documentation. But Ministers and Heads of the Civil Service have consistently ruled this is not an offence in MoD. Interestingly, the case most often cited involved a decision by the Director General in charge of...Chinook.[53][54]

Airworthiness of an aircraft type is governed by simple but strict rules. One attains it, then maintains it. ('Continuing airworthiness' applies to individual aircraft). The foundations are: a Statement of Operating Intent and Usage, an agreed and maintained build standard, and maintained Safety Cases. Lacking any of these, airworthiness cannot be verified. In turn, compromising the ability to declare serviceability or conduct Service regulated flying.

One might think airworthiness *is* maintained. After all, it is mandated by the Secretary of State. But at the time of the accident it was RAF policy not to. Primary funding had been slashed. Particularly on avionics, which are central to this case. It had been given to the RAF, but diverted to compensate for conscious waste. This maladministration was a contributory factor in this and many other fatal accidents.

One Defence Standard was dedicated to the subject, the aforementioned 05-125/2. It relates to all Air, Land and Sea electronic systems, but sets out principles for use in any technical domain (so much so, no other domain needs or has an equivalent). Primarily, it ensures functional safety. The RAF stopped updating it in 1992, eventually cancelling it without

---

[53] *Inter alia*, Loose Minute XD1(304) from Ian Fauset, Executive Director 1, Defence Procurement Agency, 10 January 2001.

[54] *Inter alia*, unreferenced letter from the late Sir Jeremy Heywood, Cabinet Secretary and Head of the Civil Service, 28 October 2014.

replacement. Yet, intriguingly, it remains the basis of the Army's flagship Integrated Soldier System programme, whose sole purpose is to reduce casualties. This programme updated relevant content in 2001-2, but as updating the Standard itself was prohibited these revisions were issued in separate Army plans.[55]

The Board did not mention airworthiness. Yet, it is the most basic question. If the aircraft was not airworthy, that is the obvious starting point. The overall lead anomaly.

The overlap between the campaign to clear the pilots, and the desire to uncover cause, will be apparent. But one must be careful not to conflate the two, while still noting that the campaign uncovered known facts that pointed towards potential cause. Some of these are central to both issues. For example, the aircraft being unairworthy meant one could not blame the pilots, and also pointed towards potential cause and culpability.

The known facts

The RAF's investigative shortcomings, and the complexity of the case, means questions will always remain. But most are side roads or lay-bys. The main path is still clear. The known facts permit valid conclusions. The RAF's claims do not stand the test of these facts, chief among them:

- In August 1992 the RAF Director of Flight Safety (Air Commodore Martin Abbott) had warned the RAF Chief Engineer (Air Chief Marshal Sir Michael Alcock) and Assistant Chief of the Air Staff (Air Vice Marshal Anthony Bagnall) of serious concerns over the airworthiness of the Chinook HC Mk1, and the forthcoming Mk2.[56]

- MoD's Independent Safety Assurance Authority, Boscombe Down, confirmed the Mk2 was not airworthy - due primarily to FADEC safety critical software implementation that was *'positively dangerous'* and needed re-writing, and the need for essential safety modifications that were not yet developed.[57]

- On 15 October 1993 Boscombe confirmed *'INTERIM (Switch-On Only)*

---

55 DCC2/21/03/0001, 13 December 2001 - 'Establishment of a Core Soldier System Co-ordinating Design Authority', and DCC2/21/01/0001, 12 February 2002 - 'Soldier System Integration & Interoperability Management Plan', Issue 2. ('Interoperability' was later deleted, as that would exceed MoD policy).
56 Loose Minute D/IFS(RAF)/125/30/2/1, 14 August 1992.
57 Boscombe Down letter AEN/58/119(H), 30 September 1993, and Report TM 2210, paragraphs 2 & 3, October 1993.

clearance was requested by the Sponsor.[58]

- Consequently, on 9 November 1993 Air Vice Marshal Bagnall was placed under mandate by Controller Aircraft, Sir Donald Spiers, that the Mk2 was not to be relied upon *in any way whatsoever*.[59] The mandate was still in force on 2 June 1994; yet on 22 November 1993 Bagnall had authorised Service regulated flying. The reality was that the aircraft had a Ground Training and Familiarisation clearance only. MoD finally conceded this in 2012.[60] On 2 June 1994, aircrew *thought* the Chinook HC Mk2 was airworthy - but only because the Assistant Chief of the Air Staff made a false declaration to them that it was.
- This INTERIM status was to be renewed two weeks *after* the accident, further proof that the Air Staff had already accepted *before* the accident that the Mk2 was not airworthy.[61]
- The office of the Senior Reviewing Officer knew the aircraft was unairworthy. When his findings of gross negligence were issued on 3 April 1995, this was not mentioned. I discuss this later in the chapter.

These known facts run counter to the controlling thesis of the Reviewing Officers, and mean the allegation that the accident was caused solely by pilot error is unsustainable. Their concealment from all onboard robbed them of the opportunity for survival.

The sheer weight of this factual evidence forced the setting up of the Mull of Kintyre Review in 2010. Additionally, the same evidence that had succeeded during the Nimrod Review (2007-09) was submitted, Lord Philip accepting it as fact. To reject it would be to reject the Nimrod Review, which both Government and MoD had recently accepted in full. Something he was all too aware of.[62]

In its desperation, MoD dumbfounded families and the Review by claiming some of the evidence did not exist. The implication was that the hard copies submitted by campaigners were forgeries. Two key examples were the Master Airworthiness Reference and the policy directive defining safety critical software, both of which I supplied to Lord Philip.

---

58 Boscombe Down Letter Report AMS 107/93, paragraph 1, 15 October 1993.
59 Mull of Kintyre Review report, paragraph 2.2.8.
60 Defence Equipment & Support letter 19-01-2012-163711-002, 28 February 2012.
61 Minutes of meeting held to discuss status of FADEC software, 25 May 1994.
62 'Submission for consideration by the Mull of Kintyre Review' (David Hill, June 2011).

Safety Cases

There are three levels of Safety Case, each relating to a specific build standard. In turn, each is associated with a different stage of the Aircraft Release process, and can be viewed as a 3-tiered layered defence:

- *As Built* (by Boeing), owned by the company and subsuming subsidiary Safety Cases.
- *As Trialled* (by Boscombe), which will include UK-specific modifications, and owned by the Aircraft Project Director and reflected in the Controller Aircraft Release.
- *In-Use* (by the RAF), which may include, for example, classified equipment and Service Engineered Modifications, owned by the Air Staff and reflected in the Release to Service.

Hence, the Release to Service is the Master Airworthiness Reference. And why, when discussing Service aircraft, one must always refer to *it*, not the Controller Aircraft Release. Post-accident, the RAF's persistent and inappropriate use of the latter was *the* clue what it was anxious about. The Release to Service states what equipment is permitted in the aircraft, and its level of clearance. On 2 June 1994, what little that was listed was *not to be relied upon in any way*.

The importance of maintaining the build standard, and with it Safety Cases, is self-evident. The responsibility lies with the aforementioned Technical Agencies and Type Airworthiness Authorities; the former, uniquely, named in the contract. Otherwise, the outputs become disconnected and progressively invalid, with Service regulated flying increasingly difficult to justify. The oversight committees chaired by senior Technical Agencies were shutdown in June 1991, and by January 1993 implementation was dangerously fragmented. On 2 June 1994 there could be no realistic expectation that Chinook was airworthy, and it wasn't.

The effect of funding cuts on trials

From 1991-1994 a ~28% per annum cut was applied to support funding, ostensibly as part of 'Options for Change' following the end of the Cold War. (To the RN, this was on top of a 33% cut in 1988). There is a rule of thumb in aircraft support. Stop flying when the support budget per aircraft has been cut in half. That point was reached on Chinook by 1992 at the latest. These were the biggest ever cuts in the Air Systems budget. Worse, they were applied across the board, even to domains that were not volume-related. Airworthiness management is (or was) structured in such a way. A simple example. The cost of preparing a given amendment to an Air Publication is a one-off, no matter how many books are to be amended. Printing is funded from a separate budget, which is based on volume. Similarly, the upkeep of Safety Cases. This is why these and other components of maintaining the build standard are grouped together, and procedurally controlled by Defence Standard 05-125/2. It can be seen attaining and maintaining airworthiness trials fall into the same category. The same work is required whether you have one, or one thousand aircraft. The variable comes with Continuing Airworthiness Management.

These *savings at the expense of safety* inevitably caused the Safety Management System to collapse - the thrust of the 2009 Nimrod Review.

*

By July 1993 some preliminary flight assessments had been carried out by Boscombe. While generally positive, progress was hindered because they didn't yet have a representative Mk2. Problems in FADEC Reversionary Mode were noted, such as torque splits during rapid power changes, engine starting at altitude, and control ergonomics (e.g. engine control switches in the wrong place):

> 'The recommendations and comments were forwarded in late 1990, via H/C (the head of MoD(PE)'s Chinook section) *to the UK Chinook Liaison Office at Boeing, in order that they may be considered for incorporation in the design*'.[63]

A polite way of saying *We were ignored*.

Initial Mk2 flight trials commenced on 30 September 1993, but the trials aircraft was still not at the required build standard. Regression testing would be inevitable. Trials were then suspended twice, on airworthiness grounds, and remained so on the day of the accident.

Boscombe's reports clearly set out why the aircraft was not airworthy. It is vital to grasp their significance. They are generated after each phase of testing or trials, to set a baseline for the next phase. They facilitate the gradual exploration of the flight envelope by test pilots in the trials aircraft. Recommendations are made on performance and safety, based on the specified use. The Aircraft Project Office, which manages the entire process, is <u>required</u> to address any concerns. If any are rejected, or perhaps waived, it must state why, in writing.

On the day of the accident, Officer Commanding Boscombe Down's Rotary Wing Test Squadron, manned in part by RAF pilots, <u>reiterated</u>

---

[63] For example, Boscombe Down Letter Report PE/Chinook/40, July 1993. 'Chinook HC <u>Mk1</u> - Assessment of T55-L-712F FADEC'.

their position, especially regarding FADEC, in an internal letter to the Chinook Project Manager responsible for the trials:[64]

- Safety critical software was unverifiable. It contained *'illegal'* code, the effects of which were unknown, and should be re-written.
- Hence, the risks associated with operating FADEC were unquantifiable, and it must be assumed it would act unpredictably at some point.
- Therefore, the aircraft was still not considered airworthy.

On 6 June 1994 this was passed to the Aircraft Project Director and RAF, Boscombe confirming they had again suspended all flying and recommending again the RAF do likewise.[65] In practice, no meaningful flying had taken place for some time, as the software issue prevented flight above 5,000 feet, when the clearance required was 15,000 feet. For example, this had been notified to the Project Director at a meeting on 25 May 1993.[66]

The response of Air Officer Commanding-in-Chief Strike Command was to draft a letter to the Assistant Chief of the Air Staff, Air Vice Marshal Bagnall, urging him to ensure trials would resume by September, only six weeks hence. What Strike Command were saying was, *Get on with it and declare the aircraft airworthy, even though we know it isn't.* The author failed to grasp Boscombe were highlighting, not creating, serious problems. They were implementing mandatory safety regulations, and reiterating known facts. Not what the project office or RAF wanted to hear, but what they fully expected to hear.

Later, at the House of Lords Select Committee in November 2001, MoD succeeded in having this correspondence suppressed. The only mention was when Air Chief Marshal Wratten was asked if he was the author. He replied that he had not seen it, as he did not take up his appointment until September 1994. He did not say if he had been briefed about the contents, claiming it had been prepared by Air Chief Marshal Sir John Thomson, his predecessor twice removed (who had passed away on 10 July 1994). Dead men can't speak, as he well knew. Thomson's deputy, Air Marshal Sir Richard Johns, who had been promoted to Air Chief Marshal and briefly appointed Air Officer Commanding-in-Chief on 30 June 1994, was not asked. The Lords went no further. But someone thought it wise to keep a

---

64 Boscombe Down Rotary Wing Test Squadron AFW/R/127/04, 2 June 1994.
65 Boscombe Down letter, ADD/308/04, 6 June 1994.
66 D/DHP/57/4/1, 31 May 1993. Minutes of T55-L-712F Engine FADEC meeting, 25 May 1993.

copy of the draft, and then leak it to the pilots' families. That would not be Johns, who later campaigned against the pilots.

Given Boscombe had been voicing these FADEC concerns for over four years, and for over seven on other safety issues relating to flight controls, this 6-week 'deadline' was unrealistic. In any case, Bagnall had no control over Boscombe, having to conduct his business through the Aircraft Project Office - at his level, Air Vice Marshal Peter Norriss. The events of 2 June would be uppermost in their minds. Was the accident a manifestation of Boscombe's prior warnings? The precise final acts were unknown, but there were known certainties. The aircraft was not airworthy. It was unserviceable. It was not fit for purpose. All concerned were fully aware of these inconvenient truths.

The focus on pilot error was self-serving to the Air Staff. Technical or organisational failures would immediately highlight the mandate they were under, and give Boscombe a voice in the investigation. The immediate concern was to exclude them at all costs.

A key player

It was another 19 months before Bagnall's successor, Air Vice Marshal Peter Squire, (legally) authorised Service regulated flying for the first time. You will recall he was the original Convening Officer, later becoming Air Officer Commanding-in-Chief Strike Command and then Chief of the Air Staff. From 1993-2003 he held four senior posts with Chinook on his slop chit, and in each would have been acutely aware of the problems associated with its introduction. The fine detail would be a nuisance to him - that is what his staff were for - but nonetheless he had a significant conflict of interests. His later support for the gross negligence findings, and in particular his advice to Secretary of State Geoff Hoon to reject the findings of the House of Lords Inquiry, must be viewed in this light.

That does not exonerate Hoon. As a barrister and lecturer in law he would understand the burden and standard of proof issues. While certainly misled on technical and airmanship matters, he ignored legal obligations. Likewise, Prime Minister Tony Blair, another barrister.

On 22 June 2005 the now retired Sir Peter Squire recorded an interview for the Imperial War Museum, of which he was chairman of the Board of Trustees. He revealed that one motivation behind the findings was to *'avoid any claim of whitewash'*. He did not mention the converse - blaming pilots who could not defend themselves, while concealing exculpatory evidence and protecting the guilty, was itself a whitewash. Nor did he mention that there should be no motivation other than truth, justice and preventing recurrence.

Special Trials Fits (STF)

I will mention these often, so they need explaining. The Services are given authority to design, manufacture and fit Service Engineered Modifications (SEMs). The relevant Design Authorities must appraise them for physical and functional safety. They are short-term measures, to be followed-up by a submission to the relevant HQ Modifications Committee, or cancelled. But these Committees had been disbanded in June 1991.

The technical procedures are mandated in two Defence Standards. Briefly in 05-123, with the full version in the aforementioned 05-125/2, in Specification PDS/8. This partial duplication is confusing to the untrained user. The essential problem is that 123 was written by staff who would seldom have to implement it; whereas 125/2 was written by experienced, current practitioners. That is, the Technical Agencies. One can always tell which was implemented.

However, and correctly, neither mentioned STFs. Therefore, they could have no contractual status and Aircraft Design Authorities (ADA) were permitted to ignore them. It is not uncommon for an ADA to refuse an MoD aircraft permission to land on its property with certain SEMs or STFs fitted (because they have never been proven safe). If they do allow them, and they interfere with their subsequent work, they are removed and discarded unless otherwise agreed in the contract. Often, when the Service later tries to refit them, the real estate is taken up. By definition, these contracts are drawn up by the Aircraft Project Office, whose involvement the STFs are intended to bypass in the first place. So, they often have no knowledge of them.

On 2 June 1994 the Chinook HC Mk1 Release to Service listed 39 STFs. There was no indication in the Mk2 Release that any had been superseded by formal modification, yet plainly many remained. And we will see later that the Mk2 publications for the Navigation System continued to describe a crucial STF that had been completely changed, with equipment and functionality removed.

I mentioned before that Boscombe's Chinook was not at the Mk2 build standard. They did not know what it was meant to be, or what was required by the RAF. It follows that the Project Director's Safety Case could not be validated. From the RAF's viewpoint, an aircraft lacking the STFs would not be fit for purpose. A moot point to the project office and Boscombe, as the aircraft was not permitted to be flown anyway. In other words, the predicted and inevitable outcome of the RAF policy to run down airworthiness management had come to pass.

For the purposes of this book, it is important to appreciate that STFs are not subject to normal fault reporting procedures. The primary reason is that the design is neither Under Contractor Control nor Under Ministry Control. ('Ministry' in this sense being the appointed Technical Agency or Type Airworthiness Authority). The Board criticised Flight Lieutenant Tapper and his ground crew for not reporting faults on (e.g.) the SuperTANS navigation computer. As it was an STF in Mk1, this criticism was unsafe. More so, because Aldergrove had a Mk1 and a Mk2, each subject to very different rules.

PART 3 - TECHNICAL

'Anomalies in testing should bring your organisation to a standstill. They are a violation of requirements. They are a clue something worse may happen'.

Dr Sheila Widnall (US Secretary of the Air Force and investigator of the Space Shuttle Columbia disaster)

'The current organisational structure for tasking and fleet management, and the lack of resources, is not a healthy recipe for the future sound airworthiness of the Chinook. Since entering service in 1980...the Chinook has been regarded by maintenance staff as the 'Cinderella' of the RAF fleet'.

Air Commodore Martin Abbott, RAF Director of Flight Safety, August 1992

7. The Full Authority Digital Engine Control (FADEC)

'The software contains <u>illegal code</u> and the structure of some parts is so intricate it is <u>impossible to determine the effect</u>. At some stage the FADEC <u>will act in an unpredictable manner</u>. The standard of software is of such <u>poor quality</u> that in our opinion it cannot be independently verified. <u>Engine overspeed/runaway is a major concern</u>. An undemanded acceleration of the engine by the FADEC can cause the rotor speed to increase above the required datum. In this event, failure of the overspeed limiter will result in <u>catastrophic damage to the rotors</u>. The limiter also has the ability to reduce the engine speed to ground idle, <u>undemanded</u>. An assessment of the integrity of the overspeed limiters revealed a number of <u>dormant failures</u>. There is very little meaningful evidence to support the clearance of the software used in the UK FADEC. We can go no further with any integrity/safety studies'.

Boscombe Down Superintendent of Engineering Systems, August 1993.

'The hazard analysis of the Chinook HC Mk2 conducted by Boeing identifies the software in the engine FADEC as <u>Safety Critical</u> and states that "any malfunctions or design errors could have <u>catastrophic results</u>". Investigations at Boscombe Down have not cast any doubt on that'.

Boscombe Down T55 Engine FADEC Software report, September 1993.

'FADEC is not flight safety critical'.

John Spellar MP, Parliamentary Under Secretary for Defence, to the House of Commons Defence Select Committee, April 1999.

With his permission, this chapter draws on the work of Mr Malcolm Perks, former Head of Technology at Rolls Royce Aerospace Group and one of the world's leading authorities on FADECs.[67]

Introduction

The purpose of a FADEC is to allow the engine to perform at maximum efficiency for a given condition. 'Full Authority' means FADEC controls fuel flow over the entire range, from shut-off to maximum. A true FADEC has no manual override available, placing full authority over the operating

---

67 Perks/Hill, 11 April 2020 17:15.

parameters of the engine in the hands of software. There is usually at least one reversionary (backup) software lane. If there is one lane, and a mechanical backup, the system is not considered to be a FADEC, but merely to have an electronic engine control unit.

A FADEC permits the use of a simpler and more reliable hydro-mechanical control system, the trade-off being the complexity of the safety critical software. The primary risk is associated with software development, which must be carried out against rigorous standards, and independently verified. Once in flight FADEC is 'hands-off', but the pilot is always conscious of his dependence on it.

Background

Textron, the engine manufacturer, were awarded the FADEC contract. Neither they nor Boeing had developed a helicopter FADEC before. With MoD's agreement, and without competition, they sub-contracted to Chandler Evans Corporation (CECO), who sub-sub-contracted the Digital Electronic Control Units (DECUs) and their safety critical software to Hawker Siddeley Dynamics Engineering (HSDE). In turn, HSDE sub-sub-sub-contracted much of the work to software houses. This sounds convoluted, and it is. MoD was too remote from the developer of the safety critical part of the system. It paid Textron, but to gain wider business CECO and HSDE worked free of charge. The problem was, they designed what they wanted to, ignoring industry and MoD standards.

The easy bit is the engine control. More difficult is getting the fault management aspect of the software to do what is required, to assure safety. Even more difficult is the necessary disciplined and structured design and development of the software, to minimise errors. This is labour intensive and costly. But HSDE were doing it for 'free'. Shortcuts became inevitable.

Design control was non-existent from the beginning. Textron and CECO were in the US, HSDE in the UK, each lacking the necessary experience. While CECO audited HSDE, they did not identify fundamental shortcomings. As prime, Textron were required to conduct Design Reviews, but did not. Irregularities were largely invisible to MoD.

CECO and HSDE claimed the programme was low risk, the design based on the Rolls Royce Gem engine FADEC (fitted to Lynx), so were left to their own devices. But the Chinook FADEC had few of the Gem's non-digital safety features. In fact, in areas that mattered it had little similarity to Gem at all. Primarily, its safety depended entirely on the software.

The danger in such a situation is that the false assurance (and acceptance by MoD) of low risk means few resources are allocated. Here, mechanical specialists managed a programme whose highest technical risk was an electronic device hosting safety critical software, with the regulations governing oversight by electronic specialists disregarded. When it became apparent the programme was in serious trouble, there was too much of MoD's credibility at stake to stop. Up to a certain point it could have cancelled and retained the Mk1 system, or at least a manual reversionary mode (which is what Boscombe recommended), explaining it away as a valiant attempt at something technically demanding, but not quite a success. But the delays meant FADEC was no longer a stand-alone Mk1 modification. It now had to be incorporated into the Mid-Life Upgrade. From that point on, cancellation, or a software re-write, became infinitely more expensive and embarrassing.

The 'Wilmington Incident'

Following an incident at Wilmington, Delaware, USA on 20 January 1989, in 1994 Mr Perks was engaged by MoD to act as its expert witness in legal action against Textron, for negligence in the development of FADEC.

Textron had certified the software was compliant with its specification without actually knowing this. When trialled, it failed catastrophically. During tethered testing to confirm the management of failure modes, an engine runaway up occurred taking the rotor speed to over 140%. The aircraft was severely damaged. MoD claimed $5,815,350 damages, and after arbitration was awarded $3M. Textron blamed their sub-contractor. MoD, correctly, said Textron was responsible. The very fact this had to be argued should have forced a review of Textron's suitability, and the entire programme. Starting afresh should have been a serious consideration.

The Board of Inquiry was fully aware.[68] Had a similar FADEC runaway occurred on ZD576, that would fit perfectly with the known facts. To contain the rotor rpm the pilot *must* apply a large amount of collective pitch, which *will* result in a climb. This makes it all the more astonishing that the Board did not call Mr Perks or Boscombe as witnesses. The potential link is so obvious, this can only have been directed.

*

Prior to arbitration, and for the consideration of $500,000, in 1994 the UK Government released Boeing from all claims related to the incident. John

---

68 Evidence of Group Captain Andrew Pulford to the House of Lords Select Committee, 27 September 2001.

Dougherty III of Boeing, in a 2002 interview with David Walmsley:

'We and MoD never really came to an agreeable conclusion, but we reached an agreeable settlement'.

The company were not asked to accept liability, nor did they offer to. Yet they cut a deal to extricate themselves from the mess. This might seem odd to the layman, and needs explaining.

MoD had contracted Textron to deliver FADEC to a specification agreed between Textron, Boeing and MoD. Boeing would (or should) witness the rig testing and co-sign (along with MoD) the Test Schedule results, establishing the baseline for their own work. Textron would sign the Certificate of Design and Performance, which in this case *had* to be accompanied by Safety Critical Software Certificate signed by Boscombe. Additionally, safety critical software *had* to be coded to the satisfaction of the Defence Research Agency at Malvern. When certifying, both are confirming the *'Requirement, Hazard Analysis, Design, methods employed and standard of work carried out, with specific regard to safety, meet* (their) *satisfaction'*. Only then could MoD accept FADEC off-contract, and give it to Boeing to integrate into the aircraft. But, as we have seen, Boscombe declared the software implementation *'positively dangerous'*, so there was no such certification. It follows that MoD was wrong to accept FADEC off-contract, as the necessary maturity had not been achieved. A key question is who agreed to this. I cannot say, but no deviation is allowed from this procedure without the express approval of the Treasury Solicitor.

Furthermore, Boeing were required to deliver a Certificate of Design and Performance for the aircraft, and a Whole Aircraft Safety Case. Both are pre-requisites to declaring airworthiness. How did the Safety Case deal with *'positively dangerous'* implementation? On 2 June 1994 the software was not permitted in RAF Chinooks. In October 2000, the government refused to release details of the faulty procedures used by Textron.

Context

At the same time as the Wilmington proceedings, the Directorate's Sea King section was investigating a case of suspected fraud. This related to two contracts to upgrade Active Dipping Sonar winches to take a longer cable, part of a 'deep water' enhancement package. The contract documentation had recently been transferred from Directorate General Underwater Weapons - a paper transfer, after (alleged) completion and all monies being paid.

Almost immediately, MoD's Bill Paying Branch in Liverpool asked the Sea King avionics programme manager (myself) to approve further expenditure of over £1M

- money I didn't have, at least not for that purpose. I conducted an investigation and uncovered fifteen instances of double-billing, one of triple-billing, five of claiming and receiving payment for work not carried out, and five lost winches; over a five-year period. I submitted a report to my Assistant Director on 7 November 1994.[69]

MoD's auditors came down on the side of administrative error. Our Director, Dr David Hughes, was furious. The company was merely required to issue credit notes against future contracts, meaning there would be no guarantee that Sea King would benefit. And it did not.

Safety criticality

When speaking in the House of Lords on 1 November 1999, Lord Norton of Louth hit the nail on the head:

'The whole problem stems from the fact that the judge and jury are also the defendants. It is a situation that the civilian world of flying would not tolerate. MoD released into service an aircraft whose engines were controlled by <u>flight safety critical software that was flawed</u>'.

To every Inquiry, MoD claimed the FADEC software was <u>not</u> safety critical. It was, and all contracts were let on that basis. The lie was repeated to the House of Commons Defence Select Committee on 4 March 1998, who reported:

'Boeing did not consider the FADEC to be flight safety critical because the engines on the Chinook are not considered to be safety critical'.

Contrast this with Boscombe's statement:

'The hazard analysis of the Chinook HC Mk2 conducted by Boeing identifies the software in the engine FADEC as <u>Safety Critical</u> and states that "any malfunctions or design errors could have <u>catastrophic results</u>".

And an MoD document prepared for the arbitration proceedings, but concealed from all Inquiries:

'FADEC...had few safety features that did not depend on the software. The software was <u>truly critical in maintaining safe flight</u>'.

The Defence Committee reported:

'Flight-safety critical is defined as "a failure of a component which <u>would - not could</u> - prevent the safe continued flight and landing of an aircraft". Within that carefully drawn definition, therefore, FADEC software was not regarded as

---

69 Letter report D/DHP 48/5/7, 7 November 1994.

flight-safety critical, because in the event of a total failure the aircraft would be able to land safely'.

In fact, the true definition of safety critical was laid down in a policy directive, and reflected in JSP 188, Edition 4, Chapter 1:

'Components whose failure <u>could</u> result in loss of life or serious damage to the environment, where there is <u>no possibility of reversion to manual control</u>'. [70]

This lie over the use of a modal verb rendered the Committee's report meaningless. Boeing and the MoD project office had correctly classified FADEC and the engines as safety critical; not least because it had a software Reversionary Mode. The lie diverted questioning away from false certification. I sent the MoD policy directive to Lord Philip.

Moreover, MoD claimed there had been no safety critical FADEC incidents in the US Army. Another lie. The US did not use the RAF's unique FADEC, rendering comparison worthless.[71]

Aircrew were less confident. Lieutenant Ian Kingston RN expressed his misgivings over:

'The uncertainty of how FADEC would perform during operational sorties in Northern Ireland, and what sort of emergencies or situations the present amount of spurious and unexplained incidents would lead to'.

Concerned over the severe operational limitations imposed on the Mk2, Flight Lieutenant Tapper suggested to Squadron Leader David Prowse that a second Mk1 be retained in theatre. Prowse was second-in-command of 7 Squadron at RAF Odiham, and took this to his superiors. The suggestion was rejected. But out of this a later conflict of interest arose. Station Commander Group Captain Peter Crawford did not mention Tapper's concerns or suggestion in his remarks, making it easier for Day and Wratten to condemn the pilots. However, and as noted elsewhere, his remarks were contradictory, and it is entirely possible his original comments *did* mention this. Later, to the House of Lords, he confirmed:

'There was a degree of professional concern about some of the problems, yes, and there was a high degree of frustration that the aeroplane could not be used to its full operational capabilities'.

The RAF officer responsible for developing the syllabus to 'train the

---

70 DUS(DP)/924/11/2/9, 14 December 1989 - Joint MoD(PE) / Industry Computing Policy for Military Operational Systems.

71 On 18 February 2007, a US Army Chinook crashed in Afghanistan, killing 8 and injuring 14. The investigation concluded an engine suddenly flamed out. It suggested a DECU had shut down, causing engine failure, due to an 'electrical anomaly'.

trainers' confirmed that he and his team travelled to Philadelphia in 1992 to receive a briefing from Boeing on FADEC, only to discover the Boeing engineers waiting for <u>him</u> to give the briefing. As he couldn't, the information provided to MoD staff was negligible.

*

In December 1994 MoD completed its reports for the Arbitration Tribunal, claiming faulty logic in the design of FADEC software was the immediate cause of the incident, and that it was not airworthy. Other issues were listed, among them:

- The design did not comply with RTCA/DO-178A or JSP 188.[72][73]
- Textron did not adequately respond to warnings of design flaws, or supervise work adequately. They had adopted an unnecessarily high-risk strategy, and took short cuts with safety.
- The program was unverified and inadequately documented. (Software is not just the program, it is the documentation as well. If there is no documentation, there is no software).
- The Hazard Analysis failed to cover possible critical failures.

RTCA/DO-178A does not say how to write the software. It lays down an orderly process and the documents to be produced. Failure to follow this means the product is unverifiable and hence unfit for purpose - and so it proved on Chinook. Withholding this evidence meant Sheriff Young was unaware that FADEC was capable of causing a fatal accident. And that it had already caused a number of serious incidents.

*

In 1998 the Defence Select Committee was told that the litigation against Textron was *'nothing to do with software'*, only negligent testing procedures. Also, that FADEC problems prior to the accident were *'trivial'* and related only to *'soft'* faults. That, Boscombe's concerns did not relate to safety, only their inability to read the FADEC software and therefore inability to verify it. But if software cannot be verified, its implementation cannot be certified as safe.

MoD insisted that Boscombe were trying to test the code using a method of testing - static code analysis - that was not widely used, apart from in

---

72 RTCA/DO-178A 'Software Considerations in Airborne Systems and Equipment Certification' (1991); since superseded by DO-178B and then C.

73 Joint Service Publication 188 'Requirements for the Documentation of Software in Military Operational Real Time Computer Systems'.

the nuclear industry. In fact, Defence Standard 00-55 called up static code analysis and Boscombe were provided with the tools to carry it out; including SPADE and MALPAS, the latter developed by MoD. Using these, Boscombe had read the software, declaring it unacceptable.

Having been serially lied to, the Defence Committee concluded:

> *'We are concerned by the failure of Boscombe Down to give final approval to the FADEC software. We conclude, however, that this is a management failure, and are persuaded by the evidence that this absence of approval raises no safety-critical questions. We have not found evidence to suggest that RAF safety procedures subject personnel to unnecessary risk'.*

Most inferred the management failure was by Boscombe, and that is who the Committee meant. In fact, Captain Brougham had implored his superiors to heed Boscombe. They did not; and later MoD would not accept the possibility of a FADEC failure, despite ongoing problems. To the House of Lords in 1999, Minister of State Baroness Symons of Vernham Dean repeated MoD's lie:

> *'FADEC had been ruled out as a possible cause at an early stage'.*

If software is unverifiable, how can one rule out malfunction? In fact, the decision to fit it despite the software being uncertified was a root cause.

Engine compressor surge or stall

A combination of high pressure altitude, high ambient temperature, and dirty or damaged compressors, tends to reduce compressor efficiency - resulting in reduced airflow within the compressor. If these conditions become sufficiently severe, engine surge and/or stall occurs. A sharp rumble or series of loud reports emanating from the engine can be heard or felt, along with abnormal vibration, rapid fluctuations in critical engine parameters, and noticeable loss of power and rotor rpm.

While it cannot be proven that any of this occurred in ZD576, it becomes more relevant when considering Boscombe's concerns over the effects of blockages in the engine inlet screens on the surge margins of the engines, in icing conditions. Consequently, the Icing Limit was restrictive, with flight prohibited in precipitating or recirculating snow, and in airframe and engine icing conditions.[74]

I mentioned earlier the meeting at Boscombe Down on 25 May 1994, a week before the accident, at which the Aircraft Project Director reaffirmed

---

74 Boscombe Down Letter Report E1109, paragraph 13b, 26 October 1993.

Chinook HC Mk2 held an INTERIM clearance - *not to be relied upon in any way*. Among discussion points was engine surging and stalling during trials and in-service use. It was noted that Boeing were:

> 'Progressing with a revised procedure (and) there was a need to review periodicity of the test requirement. Further testing of engine serial number 79131 at Textron will investigate this <u>surge prone</u> area further. The meeting noted Boscombe's decision to abandon further high altitude flights in reversionary mode'.

The minutes are damning. Six months after the Assistant Chief of the Air Staff (ACAS) declared to aircrew that the FADEC safety critical software had been certified, the project office remained in the invidious position of not being able to certify it *to any level*. Here is evidence that the long-term problem of engine overspeeds which had almost destroyed the Wilmington Chinook was, five years later, still the subject of ongoing engine tests. This does not describe a product that meets the Secretary of State's Technical and Systems Integration maturity requirements for entering production, never mind Service use - precisely Boscombe's point.

As further background, in December 1993, during flight testing in Philadelphia, an RAF Chinook experienced an undemanded engine overspeed, coming close to the critical limit. After examination the aircraft was flown again and the overspeed recurred, observed by Boeing and the UK's Chinook Liaison Officer. When Squadron Leader Robert Burke, the co-pilot, later offered this evidence, MoD dismissed his claim implying he was a liar. His written reports were later uncovered in Boeing's records. He received no apology.

Was FADEC acceptable?

No. Boscombe pronounced it unairworthy, and it remained so after the accident. They recommended an engineering solution, but did not have the authority to implement it. Their findings should have been a complete showstopper. Until software can be verified, it must be considered unpredictable. It can do almost anything - cause an engine to be lost, run-up, run-down, or cause spurious warnings. FADEC, in those early days of RAF use, was doing all of these things. It must be a distinct possibility that this unpredictability was a factor in the accident, with or without accompanying aircraft power problems.

The National Audit Office later concluded FADEC was within budget and on time, implying it as a success. How could it be on time if delivery was delayed by four years, and a further four years passed before the most severe restrictions were lifted (1998)? It added there were *'no significant impacts on the acceptance to service'*.[75] Well, one impact was it never saw service in the Mk1, as intended.

Aircrew trust that if something does not meet its specification or safety standards, they will be consulted over a Concession or Production Permit. They certainly do not want anything their own assessors describe as *'positively dangerous'* and *'unairworthy'*. They want the aircraft to be airworthy, serviceable and fit for purpose. (Three different things). And they expect their superiors to be honest about the risks they are expected to take if the operational or political imperative prevails.

The programme took 13 years from start to finish, in which time at least one aircraft was severely damaged and a plethora of FADEC-related faults forced front line aircraft into deep maintenance. At introduction to service the Mk2 had a load-carrying capability some 40% less than hoped for, and 25% cent less than where it started. Its maximum operating altitude was 5,000 feet instead of 15,000. Only a complete fool or someone with something to hide would call that a success.

And conveniently overlooked was the fact that serious offences had been committed, primarily the making of false record. Perhaps the National *Audit* Office did not look at the *audit trail*?

*

After many years of denial, in 2011 MoD admitted the FADEC software was modified in 1996.[76] *Inter alia*, these changes addressed:

- False Engine Out indications
- Engine Runaway Up and Runaway Down
- Reversionary Mode power interrupt faults

Despite this, problems continued. Eventually, in 2010 a new type Digital Electronic Control Unit was introduced as part of an upgrade to a new engine. It had a new Central Processing Unit, the basis of Boscombe's *'positively dangerous'* statement in 1993. Once again, they and Squadron Leader Burke were proven correct.

---

75 National Audit Office report 'Accepting equipment off-contract and into service', 11 February 2000, page 36.
76 Defence Equipment & Support letter 09-05-2011-121318-007, 30 June 2011. (List of Block 1 software changes to FADEC DECUs).

8. Digital Electronic Control Units (DECU)

The DECUs are best thought of as fuel computers. They read all the sensors (i.e. what the pilot has commanded and what the aircraft is doing), calculate the fuel needed by the engines, and then control the hydro-mechanicals to achieve the required condition. They are located in the cabin, one on either side, continually checking both themselves and the connected parts to ensure that developing malfunctions do not cause the engines to go out of control. As with any computer, they only do what the software tells them to do.

The norm is for identical primary and reversionary lanes. Here, the reversionary lane was simpler, most of the safety features depending on the primary lane remaining in control. Although the DECUs exchanged information, if one failed the other was not designed to record faults from the first engine. One of ZD576's DECUs was destroyed, so it cannot be known what fault codes it held. Yet MoD stated there were none.

If either DECU lane failed, its reversionary lane automatically took over; but reversionary mode could also be demanded by the pilot. As the reversionary lane could not automatically govern rotor rpm, a degree of manual control over fuel flow was provided when making Collective lever inputs, by means of a rocker 'increase/decrease' switch on the hand grip. From the pilot's viewpoint, reversionary mode was not dissimilar to the way Mk1 worked. However, in the background it was very different.

No Fault Found

This is the bane of a maintenance engineer's existence. The effect on front line is enormous. MoD measures reliability by Mean Time Between Faults, and that figure is used to determine spares holdings. But the actual demand for spares is determined by Mean Time Between Removals, whether or not a fault is later found. Plainly, if a given item has a significant No Fault Found rate - as was the case with DECUs - then there will quickly be a spares shortage, necessitating robbery from other aircraft. This became the norm soon after Chinook Mk2 deliveries commenced. Typical aggravating factors are lack of training, poor publications and inadequate test equipment. Chinook suffered badly from all of these.

Within reason, it is the role of the Service HQ Provisioning Authority to prevent this in the first place. If it occurs, he must identify the cause and mitigate the effect. He is the designated 'owner' of a range of equipment (for example, one person might manage all airborne radars) and responsible for, *inter alia,* availability, reliability, maintainability, managing modification programmes, and making materiel and financial provision. He is the single point of contact for in-service support problems. If more resources are required, it is he who makes the case and provides management oversight, to the point when an endorsed requirement is handed to procurers.

In March 1992 the former MoD(PE) Assistant Directorate that, by default, had taken up the reins on avionics after the above Service HQ posts were stood down, was also disbanded, having been taken over by the RAF. By June 1994 there could be no expectation, within any Service, that support would be adequate. And it wasn't.

Not in time

A word about the so-called 'just in time' logistics concept. Few, even in MoD, know that in 1990 the RAF introduced a 'not in time' policy. Instead of having sufficient stock on the shelf to satisfy demands 'just in time', requisitions to procure or repair would only be raised when there was an outstanding demand. That is, after depot stock, Contingency (16% of depot stock) and War Reserves ran out. Military spares are seldom mass produced. Suppliers don't hold stock on the off-chance an MoD contract will come along. Lead-times can be up to two years. Potentially, that's two years of aircraft robbery. It only needs to be one critical spare to ground an aircraft. And it doesn't have to be an aircraft component...

This policy was uncovered in October 1990 when faulty test equipment caused Sea King radar repair work to be suspended at RNAY Fleetlands. Only upon receipt of a demand from the workshop was a requisition raised to initiate a repair contract or procure a spare. Two months before, Iraq had invaded Kuwait. Much was made of apparent equipment shortages. But it went unsaid that serviceable equipment sitting on a shelf was seen as an unwanted addition to the Debit column in a balance sheet, so routinely scrapped.

Loose connectors, intermittent faults

It was not only the FADEC software implementation that was dangerous. From the House of Lords Select Committee proceedings:

'Squadron Leader Burke...also spoke to problems with the multi-point connectors which went from the engines to the DECU. These were of bad design and liable

to be displaced by vibration, which then produced a power interruption. On two or three occasions pilots had lost control of the Engine Condition Lever. As a result, <u>squadrons introduced</u> a procedure whereby <u>crewmen</u> every quarter of an hour checked the connections had not been displaced in flight. <u>At the time of the accident DECUs still presented recurring problems</u>. They were removed from the aircraft when something had gone wrong and returned to the makers who on many occasions <u>could find no fault</u>'.

(The *connectors* were not of bad design. It was the installation design, Boeing failing to route and secure cable assemblies correctly).

When Boscombe and RAF Odiham experienced this *in-flight*, a 2-part Servicing Instruction was raised: (1) the application, involving painting witness marks on the connectors which would reveal any movement, and (2) subsequent checks for movement. The Instruction required the checks to be made *before* and *after* flight.[77] The RAF Engineering Authority warned:

'The connector loosened sufficiently to affect the functioning of the FADEC system. The potential for DECU connectors to work loose is the subject of a Boeing investigation'.[78]

The Instruction concluded by saying that operation, handling and Electro-Magnetic Interference (EMI) were *'not affected'*. A remarkably brave statement when the DECU hosted unverified safety critical software, the outcome could be catastrophic, and the investigation had only just begun. Moreover, loose connectors and, for example, chafed wiring looms, are typical entry points for EMI.

Why was this not identified before acceptance off-contract, and why was a Servicing Instruction deemed a satisfactory response to a safety-critical defect? What would happen if a DECU went off-line? The other DECU is designed to take over, but this is not instantaneous and by no means guaranteed - the uncertainty made worse by the unverified software. The aircraft might yaw. It might drop. It might recover, but at what attitude and altitude? The recovery action might take too long.

A pre-flight check might be temporary mitigation for an operationally imperative flight, but is not the engineering solution. The reason for this Servicing Instruction should have precluded <u>any</u> flight. Given the Engineering Authority knew all this, the implication is they were rebuffed

---

77 Servicing Instruction/Chinook/57.
78 Priority Signal D/GH/105/9/4/389 from SM(Hels)28D1(RAF) (Harrogate), 18 November 1993. (Application of witness marks to DECU connectors).

in their attempt to seek proper resolution. Perhaps - and I am not being facetious, because it happened many times - they followed the mandated regulations and submitted their concerns to the correct department, but no action was taken because it had been disbanded in March 1992.

Faced with numerous DECUs being replaced due to erratic behaviour, yet the majority later declared No Fault Found, and unable to get a response from the correct quarter, RAF Odiham extended the Instruction to include 15-minute checks, in-flight. Servicing Instruction regulations do not cover such a concept, as one is not permitted to write procedures on the assumption regulations will be ignored. The failure of others more senior to do their duty exposed the Senior Engineering Officer at Odiham to the risk of prosecution - one reason why Boards of Inquiry do not 'go there'.

But to cap it all, Annex B to the Board of Inquiry report ('Details of Aircraft') states:

'Serial Numbers and classes of relevant modifications embodied, and of SIs and STIs complied with; NONE'. (MoD's emphasis).

Why was this Servicing Instruction not applied pre-flight? One assumes the Board double-checked before making such an emphatic statement relating to a possible cause. And how did it know it had not been applied *during* the flight? The Board of Inquiry should have been suspended immediately, pending full investigation by MoD police.

*

On 21 December 2011 a Freedom of Information request sought:

- The Boeing report following its investigation.
- Details of reported instances of connectors coming loose between November 1993 and August 2004.
- Details of current instructions in the Aircraft Maintenance Manual.

MoD replied on 15 February 2012, refusing to provide the report on the grounds that the content would *'prejudice relations between the UK and US Governments'*.[79] Once again, Boeing were being shielded. Nevertheless, MoD listed five cases of DECUs or connectors being the cause of a fault (in a period when there were few Mk2s). It admitted the Maintenance Manual had not been amended. But the reply omitted that, in 1992, a directive had been issued to Engineering Authorities not to submit such reports individually. To save money, they were to be saved up and submitted as an 'omnibus'. Subsequent investigations often grouped similar faults

---

79 Defence Equipment & Support letter 22-12-2011-121642-005, 15 February 2012.

together and only reported on one example. Five is unlikely to be anywhere near the real figure.

But the greatest irregularity is MoD's claim that the Boeing report was an *'Interface Memorandum'* between Boeing and Textron, dated 28 February 1994. This hides a multitude of sins. The DECU is an electronic device. Therefore, a Radio Installation Memorandum (RIM) is required. (In this sense 'radio' means all electronics). It must be supplied to the Aircraft Design Authority (Boeing) by MoD *before* the aircraft installation design commences. It sets out, for example, compass safe distances and other protective measures against Electro-Magnetic Interference. In many cases it also acts as the Interface Control Document, describing pin-to-pin connections, type and level of signals carried, and what they do. In turn, this dictates the composition of the aircraft wiring looms to/from the DECUs, and their routing.

For a modification, the relevant HQ Modifications Committee oversees this. (Remember, FADEC was a modification). If the Service sponsor cannot table the RIM, the chairman will defer approval. In June 1991, as part of the decision to disband these oversight committees, RAF suppliers decreed that RIMs were no longer required. But many hundreds remained and had to be maintained because, regardless of the ruling, only an idiot would attempt the installation design and integration without one. No opinion was offered on where the information would come from in future, or how it was to be managed or controlled. If there was no RIM, or a flawed one, that would explain many of the issues later reported - and not only in this accident.

Is this what MoD meant by the report being an *'Interface Memorandum'*? Or did it mean Interface Control Document? Or the even more fundamental Interface Definition Document? Either way, anything discussing the FADEC *interfaces* in February 1994 was far too late in the day. The aircraft was already in-service.

*

Shortly after the rundown of airworthiness management commenced, the RN attempted to fit an inboard Magnetic Anomaly Detector (MAD) system to Sea King HAS Mk6 (to detect submarines), without Design Authority support.

During trials, the system indicated a target was in the aircraft. The device had been located too close to the radar Transmitter/Receiver's magnetron which, when it started to vibrate with the aircraft, excited the MAD. The radar RIM, dictating safe distances, had been ignored, and MAD didn't have one. Compensating magnets had to be fitted to the Transmitter/Receiver Tray.

All very amusing, until one realises a two-aircraft deployment for two weeks of trials cost £25k an hour, plus the hire of a ship, and were only able to be re-arranged two years later. Whereupon, the ship (the Colonel Templar) broke down and was docked in Liverpool for repairs. A local fisherman at Kyle of Lochalsh was enticed with single malt to hang an Echo Repeater over the side of his vessel each day while he was sitting in the Inner Sound and Sound of Raasay, meaning the time spent wasn't entirely wasted. (Sláinte!).

*

The Servicing Instruction ignores that it arose from an uncorrected design defect. As it related to the integrity of a safety critical system, and given the known history (the software implementation being *positively dangerous*), the RAF Handling Squadron would be unlikely to comment without mentioning this. The correct process was followed, up to a point. But the output from a Fault Investigation is not an *'Interface Memorandum'* between Design Authorities. It must be a formal report to the MoD Technical Agency; via MoD's Quality Assurance Representative (QAR) at Boeing, who must oversee the investigation and countersign the report.

The issue is then 'sentenced'. MoD will usually fund rectification of a random fault. If a modification is necessary sometimes the cost will be shared, without prejudice. There are no rules governing this - the Technical Agency is empowered to enter into an agreement without resorting to lengthy negotiations. Much depends on his experience and engineering judgment.

Here, the installation design was, frankly, appalling. The sentencing would be 'defect', and a Defect Investigation required to determine what happened, and prevent recurrence. As MoD might seek damages, this is essentially a contractual/legal procedure (because the engineering solution is generally already known from the Fault Investigation), under advisement from the Technical Agency.

*

The Servicing Instruction states *15 minutes* are required to check the DECU connectors. This would have to be verified before promulgation in order to reconcile crew duties, and update technical publications.

The Board President, Wing Commander Pulford, opined MALM Graham Forbes was *'following through on the navigation'*; implying Sergeant Kevin Hardie, in the rear of the cabin, had to check both DECUs. Experienced Chinook operators concurred.

There were other duties placed upon the crewmen, which the Reviewing Officers were keen to avoid. For example:

'Inspect the Transmission Debris Screen magnetic indicators on the maintenance panel at least every five minutes during flight'.

The aircraft has Debris Detection Screens for each of the three main gearboxes. (Fore, Aft, Combiner). The Maintenance Panel, at the rear near the ramp, has a number of gauges allowing the aircrewman to monitor the status of a (e.g.) transmission and hydraulic oil pressures and temperatures. Sergeant Hardie would also have carried out that inspection. But which was conducted first when DECU and Debris Screen checks coincided? The periodicity of the Debris Screen check indicates it was more important, but would he think otherwise given the DECU was safety critical and a known problem? Either way:

- According to MoD, the DECU checks took up half of Sergeant Hardie's time.
- If the DECUs took priority, Debris Screen checks were missed.
- If strict orders were followed and the Debris Screens given priority, then connector checks were missed or delayed.

Nobody asked if, when the checks coincided, Hardie carried out both or Forbes helped out. An acute safety issue was glossed over, because exploring it would reveal the illegal Servicing Instruction and a possible, and plausible, cause of the accident.

More fundamentally, the volume of work to be carried out exceeded the available time. The most important and time-consuming task would not have been necessary had the airworthiness regulations been implemented. Unfamiliarity with the new Mk2, and especially the issues with FADEC, might mean crew routines had not quite settled down. Add the management of 25 passengers, some of whom might be experiencing a Chinook for the first time, and one must again question the wisdom of selecting a Chinook (quite apart from it not being permitted to fly at all).

*

Ask any apprentice how to prevent connectors coming loose and he/she will say *wire lock them*. But we also know that termination pins in connectors within engine looms were not crimped properly during assembly, pointing again to poor Quality Control. (See Annex). A wrong or worn crimping tool is the most common cause of poor solderless electrical connections. That would cause intermittent failures (the main cause of No Fault Founds), especially if strain relief cables within the looms had not been fitted correctly. All compounded if accompanied by Electro-Magnetic Interference.

What of other users? In October 1995, the US Army equivalent of the Release to Service for their MH-47E helicopter stated:

'A pre-flight inspection to check the DECU connectors for correct positioning of alignment stripes is required. These stripes shall also be checked while conducting the 30-minute ramp area check'.[80]

So, despite MoD claiming the memorandum of February 1994 as the final word on the subject, here is further evidence that the defect had not been fixed in late 1995.

The RAF Instruction remained extant in 2014.

---

80 AMSAT-R-ECC Airworthiness Release for MH-47E production helicopters, 31 October 1995.

9. Communications System

One of the enduring difficulties independent investigators have when looking at military accidents is the dearth of information in official reports. This militates against analytical depth. This is especially true of avionics, and Boards of Inquiry never list what was fitted to the aircraft, its modification state, or if the build standard was reflected in the aircraft publications and Safety Case. Like aircrew, they rely entirely on the build standard being maintained. They assume all is well, when (both) would be better advised to assume nothing is.

*

The Simultaneous Operations (SIMOPS) statement is the basis of all comms system design, where basic questions are answered and rules laid down. What comms services, including secure modes, are required at the same time? Is VHF and/or UHF Homing needed, and must it be secure? Are special role radios required, such as (at the time) Keystone and Cougarnet for Northern Ireland? All the while considering the rear crew and passengers (e.g. Troop Leaders and medics). And so on.

So, when Minister of State Baroness Symons of Vernham Dean told the House of Lords on 1 November 1999 *'They made routine calls and therefore we know that their radio was working at the time'*, this was misleading. Communications were made or attempted on separate HF and VHF radios. That is not evidence the UHF emergency radio, or the UHF functions of the Intercom, were functioning. Rather naïvely, she added:

'The noble Lord (Chalfont) *knows that we are briefed honestly as Ministers, and we give honest answers to the questions that we are asked'.*

She would not know that civilian staff in the Directorate of Helicopter Projects had recently been actively prevented from briefing the truth to Chief of Defence Procurement, Sir Robert Walmsley, on the occasion he was asked about Chinook airworthiness by the Public Accounts Committee. The Committee's other main concern? Comms Systems.[81]

Ultra High Frequency (UHF) radio

Regulations state:

'For flight safety reasons, frequency 300.800MHz has been allocated for use in the UK Low Flying System. Whenever possible, aircrew are to listen out on this

---

81 Select Committee on Public Accounts, 3 March 1999.

frequency as well as monitoring Guard'.[82]

The Board refers to a 'UHF Radio', but without mentioning or explaining the functions of the Control Unit, what model of each was fitted (especially important for the Control Unit), or what the associated Intercom and Audio Control Panel settings were. It notes that the radio was found tuned to 300.800MHz, but omits that both a manual and pre-set frequency can be selected, and that in the event of power loss it is the manual one (300.800) that will display when powered up again.

The Air Accidents Investigation Branch (AAIB) report refers to the 'UHF AM Control Unit' but not the radio, listing the positions of the various controls. Also, the settings on the associated cockpit Intercom Station Boxes (one per pilot) and the Intercom Switch Panel; but not the rear cabin equivalents. It does not say what Control Unit was fitted, but notes that the pre-set frequency selected was 284.100MHz. It is not the AAIB's role to speculate on what these selections mean, and it does not.

It is only upon studying the Release to Service that fuller detail emerges. It states *'ARI 23301/5 Plessey PTR1751WWH UHF/AM'* was fitted. Let us break this down:

- 'ARI 23301' is the MoD Airborne Radio Installation number and relates to a UHF-only installation, whereas (e.g.) ARI 23300 is a combined V/UHF system using variants of the same series of radios. A 5-digit number beginning with '2' indicates that the Intellectual Property Rights reside outwith MoD.

- '/5' is the ARI variant number. These are not simply sequential, but grouped according to functionality - in this case originally in groups of 20. So, there may be variants 1-9, 21, 41-54, and so on.

- PTR1751 is the model of radio. It operates in the 225-399.975MHz band, offering 7,000 channels with 25kHz spacing. The pilots actually see the Control Unit, which provides for selection of frequencies, pre-set channels, and functions. The radio contains a separate UHF Guard receiver constantly monitoring the 243MHz International Distress Frequency. If Guard traffic is detected, other traffic is automatically muted. It is normal for an aircraft to have at least two radios capable of monitoring UHF Guard, hitherto facilitated by the Ultra D403M Standby UHF radio. According to the RAF, Chinook had only one. (The PTR1751's main receiver and Guard receiver are not, in this sense, two 'radios', as they share common circuitry).

---

82 UK Low Flying Handbook, paragraph 15.

- Plessey were the original manufacturer, and PTR1751 is their designation (Plessey Transmitter-Receiver). The 'WWH' suffix indicates a particular set of features, for example with HaveQuick Transmission Security (frequency hopping). UHF/AM is Ultra High Frequency/Amplitude Modulation.

The combination of '/5' and 'WWH' offers the first clue something is amiss. PTR1751 originally had 50kHz channel spacing, and '/5' indicates this. But a mid-80s modification changed this to 25kHz spacing, undertaken via Air Staff Requirement 889. This, and the addition of HaveQuick, should have already changed the /number in the Mk1.

The Mk1 had PTR1751W; changed to PTR1751WWH on 27 March 1991 under Special Trials Fit/Chinook/126. The Control Unit would also change. The PTR1751WWH was retained in Mk2, but it wasn't until 14 November 1994 that /5 was changed to /565. This confirms the excessive haste with which the Mk2 was introduced, before basic configuration control could be established. Once again, the Director of Flight Safety's warnings had come to pass.

Mutual interference

Comparing the Mk1 Release to Service as of 2 June 1994, the INTERIM Mk2 Controller Aircraft Release of 9 November 1993, and the Mk2 Release to Service of 22 November 1993, reveals more anomalies.

The Mk1 Release states the radio is cleared for use, but warns:

'Interference may be expected from AD120/3 VHF(AM) and ARC340 VHF(FM) radios'.

These radios remained in the Mk2, but the warning was removed. Viewed in isolation, it might be thought the problem had been resolved. In fact, matters had regressed, the Mk2 Release now saying the equipment:

'...may be used, but no guarantee of performance can be given. This (PTR1751) *radio is likely to be unreliable when using battery power'.*

This referred to Boscombe's finding that the PTR1751 did not work throughout its specified voltage range, specifically below 24V, and in the event of power supply problems causing a voltage drop it would be useless. Not least, because the radio must be functional on battery power prior to starting the Auxiliary Power Unit. This was compounded by the 11Ah aircraft battery being unsuitable, and a poor installation design that allowed the battery to discharge rapidly when the aircraft was not in use. These are issues that the Radio Installation Memorandum must spell out.

The Release document must be annotated with sidebars to draw attention to changes. There are none. If aircrew scanning it noticed the change they would be thoroughly perplexed. More so, because these new limitations were not reflected in any amendment to the Mk1 Release; implying, yet again, the problems were new to the Mk2. So serious were these deficiencies, they influenced Boscombe's decision to declare the aircraft unairworthy.

*

Contradicting the Mk2 Release to Service, the Board confirmed:

'The VHF/AM radio also suffered from interference from the SuperTANS and IFF (Identification, Friend or Foe) *systems'.*

This had been advised in evidence by Flight Lieutenant Duncan Trapp and Air Loadmaster John Coles, who had flown in ZD576 the previous day. Coles added that interference levels varied between aircraft, both in Mk1 and Mk2. Despite the obligation to pursue these anomalies separately, no mention was made in following issues of the Release, up to and including September 1998. It is known that Flight Lieutenant Tapper was deeply concerned over these unexplained differences. (See next chapter).

Moreover, the Mk2 Release noted that secure HF transmissions caused interference on all other radios. And later, on 10 January 1996, added:

'Hydraulic system pressure gauge indications may be affected by transmissions from the VHF and UHF radios'.

The Release does not say if the gauges on the Maintenance Panel in the rear were affected, which might mean Sergeant Hardie delaying (e.g.) his DECU checks. Again, this is a reflection of initial aircraft testing having only just commenced.

Analysis of switch positions

We now move on to the positions in which ZD576's controls were found. These were listed by the AAIB but not analysed by the Board. It is important to acknowledge that switch positions may have changed at impact, much depending on the type of switch. But it is also important to ask if the combination of switch settings discovered in the wreckage has a specific meaning. The Board avoided this entirely.

Each pilot has a Station Box providing control over which radio he requires, the Intercom levels for each, and other functions. The AAIB notes the volume levels as a percentage of full scale. Most UK military aircraft Intercoms use old, wide tolerance amplifiers, so the volume an operator will set to attain a comfortable listening level varies wildly between each audio source, and between aircraft. The main effect is poor speech intelligibility, caused by an improper amplifier gain structure. (Typically, an amplifier in the chain overdriven into distortion).

Cook's UHF was at 45%, his VHF/AM at 100%, indicating he was prepared to use either. Tapper's UHF was at 5% (the minimum), his VHF/AM at 40%, indicating he was only prepared to use VHF. His father later confirmed it was his voice on the recording of the unanswered VHF call at 1755 to Scottish Air Traffic Control Centre (Military) at Prestwick. All other volumes were at minimum. It is possible, therefore, that Cook's VHF/AM setting was prompted by Tapper receiving no reply.

This in itself is unremarkable. However, both had UHF selected on their Station Box, yet Tapper's UHF volume was at minimum. There is nothing abnormal in Cook's settings - they indicate he was monitoring/using UHF. But why would Tapper have UHF selected? This is where the meaning of other switch positions becomes important...

*

Cook's Intercom was found at FAIL. One selects this if a fault becomes apparent, which is common in Chinook due to water ingress. (At the Fatal Accident Inquiry Flight Lieutenant Iain MacFarlane characterised this as a *'frequent'* occurrence). If this was the setting at impact, he had detected, or suspected, a malfunction in his part of the system. In FAIL, his telephone (what he hears) amplifier and mixer would be bypassed. He would hear what was set on Tapper's Station Box, and he would speak through it. Also, the detailed system design can, for example, set cabin Station Boxes to fail to each other, but the Forward Crewman's Station Box (MALM Forbes) to fail to a Pilot position. Lacking such detail, one cannot fully assess the impact. Nevertheless, this changes things significantly. Tapper would be unable to use another radio if Cook was using the UHF (and vice-versa) - which might explain him not following-up on the unanswered VHF call.

Furthermore, the UHF Control Unit Function Selector was set to TEST. If assessing the possibility of the Selector being moved by impact forces, one would have to know that on the PV1754AA Control Unit, which I believe was fitted to Chinook, this is one position away from 'TR' (Transmit/Receive), two positions from 'TR+G' (Transmit/Receive + Guard), and four positions from 'TR+G+H' (adding HaveQuick mode).

No report discusses the meaning of these switch positions, or comments on what position would be expected, but all the indications are they were trying to diagnose a fault. The effect is that, internally, a test tone is generated and a test routine run, resulting in an otherwise meaningless '888.888' frequency display and '88' channel display. It is an indication that most of the radio's Receiver section is fine, but does not test the Transmitter or Antennae.

Taken together, the above indicates uncertainty over whether radio transmissions were getting through, or replies made but not presented to the crew. The unanswered call to Scottish Military, and the combination of switch positions, make it reasonable to assume they suspected, at least, a developing failure of the Comms System. That is, they suspected the VHF, Cook had diagnosed a problem in his Intercom, and they were now testing the UHF. Moreover, Tapper's conflicting UHF settings might suggest he was interrupted or distracted while in the process of adjusting his controls. The possibility of an Electrical System failure emerges.

To counter any claim that such a sequence of failures and coincidence of switch positions is unlikely, let us look at an incident the following year, on 14 December 1995, involving Chinook HC Mk2 ZA708. A transient power spike disabled SuperTANS and the Instrument Landing System. In the space of less than three minutes, the UHF failed, then the captain's Intercom, then the entire Comms System. The Magnetic Brake and Longitudinal Cyclic Trim Actuators froze, and OFF flags appeared on instruments. The cabin lights dimmed and emergency lights came on. The co-pilot's landing lights failed to motor. The Automatic Flight Control Systems were thought to have failed but the aircraft was recovered before this could be confirmed. Upon landing, the engines would not shut down and the Auxiliary Power Unit would not start. Air Traffic Control confirmed that radio and Identification Friend or Foe contact was lost.

No circuit breakers had popped and no warnings appeared on the Crew Alerting Panel, except for the parking brake caption after landing. The purpose of circuit breakers is to protect the aircraft wiring, the main dangers being toxic fumes and fire. It was found that a wrongly rated circuit breaker was fitted in a Power Distribution Panel, concealing an underlying failure in the Electrical System. A potentially catastrophic failure had developed. In his comments the aircraft captain said:

> 'The _flight safety_ implications of this incident are _extremely serious_. The _lack of warnings_, the _total loss of intercom_, coupled with the noise levels in the Chinook cockpit, made effective verbal communication impossible even with helmets off. These factors, coupled with _control degradation_, made the successful recovery from this incident difficult'.

*

On 20 October 1994 the Board asked London Air Traffic Control Centre (Military) Distress and Diversion Unit at West Drayton, Middlesex to provide details of any 243MHz transmissions between 1742 and 1800 on 2 June 1994. The regulations required retention of written records for one year, and radio/radar recordings for 30 days. West Drayton replied on 24 October, saying they had wiped their tapes. Yet, when asked on 1 December 1994, RAF Machrihanish Air Traffic Control were able to access *their* archived tapes. That they apparently revealed nothing does not mean a transmission was not attempted, nor confirm that one was possible.

Why, given the 30-day limit, did the Board wait almost five months when an aircraft had crashed killing 29? Potentially, this denied them vital evidence. And if the penny dropped on 20 October 1994 that West Drayton hadn't been asked, why wait another six weeks before asking Machrihanish? The Board concluded:

'There were no significant transmissions on Guard at the time of the flight'.

How could it say this when West Drayton had no records? Taken with the sheer number of similar claims, each diverting attention from salient facts, one is entitled to be sceptical.

*

By necessity this has been a simplistic assessment. Few switch positions were noted, and no image of any Comms System unit was included in any report. (Itself a clue that the RAF did not want this area analysed too deeply, particularly when less relevant images *were* included). Nevertheless, I consider the above *prima facie* evidence of a serious malfunction in the Comms System. That in itself would not cause the accident, but would be a distraction. However, the loss of aircraft control systems most certainly could. In the ZA708 incident, one can readily see the point at which the crew would stop diagnosing a Comms failure, to concentrate on the frozen Longitudinal Cyclic Trim Actuators. The evidence points to the ZD576 pilots having to cope with similar serious malfunctions, which the ZA708 incident shows could easily arise from a developing electrical failure.

High Frequency (HF) radio

The aircraft was fitted with a Collins 718U-4A High Frequency radio, operating in the 2-29.9999MHz band. A routine transmission was made to 81SU Strike Command Integrated Communications System Tactical Control Systems South at 1746, requesting a listening watch.

The status of the HF radio in the Mk1 Controller Aircraft Release at the time of the accident was that its use was prohibited. You will recall this is mandated upon the Assistant Chief of the Air Staff. However, on 8 July 1987 he had issued a Service Deviation permitting its use, with the following warnings:

> '*Automatic Flight Control System (AFCS) disturbances when using the HF radio. Electro-Magnetic Compatibility ground tests at Boscombe have demonstrated noticeable <u>actuator movements</u> when transmitting on frequencies between 3 and 28MHz. The <u>HF-induced AFCS disturbances</u> could result, in the worst case, in a <u>multi-channel runaway of up to full stroke, which could be oscillatory</u>. The worst effects are most likely to occur during the tuning cycle. (Around 9 seconds). Boscombe warn that different aircraft will almost certainly exhibit different characteristics with respect to HF-induced AFCS disturbances, and an <u>apparently safe frequency on one aircraft cannot be read across to other aircraft</u>'.*

A former senior RAF engineering officer confirmed this:

> '*We struggled with an issue where in a stable auto hover the aircraft entered a climb when you keyed the HF. The fix was a Coca-Cola can around the vertical actuator - painted grey of course*'.[83]

Such a device, or common kitchen foil, is an invaluable diagnostic tool, but generally not the correct engineering solution. Did ZD576 have its '*Coca-Cola*' can removed during conversion? Most aircraft have similar limitations associated with their HF radio, primarily due to its high power. What stands out here is the immaturity of the clearance process. Boscombe's concern is obvious. So too the RAF's, witness a Service Deviation overruling a mandate.

Again, the Mk2 Release to Service was markedly different. At first issue, in November 1993, the HF radio was still not permitted in the aircraft. On 14 February 1994, Service Deviation 1/94 authorised the use of a Secure HF installation, fitted under Special Trials Fit/Chinook/205. This had its own Receiver, but needed to use the Collins 718 Transmitter. The contradiction is obvious - the necessary Transmitter was not permitted in the aircraft.

A belated amendment to the Controller Aircraft Release in March 1994 allowed Collins 718 to be fitted:

> '*The equipment may be used, but pending further trials no guarantee of performance can be given. HF transmissions are not to be made when using the Instrument Landing System or when using the VHF Omni-Directional Radio as a navigation aid*'. (The VOR/ILS was found switched ON at 115.2MHz).

---

83 (Withheld)/Blakeley, 13 May 2021, 16:58.

This issue had been noted by Boscombe in a report dated 15 October 1993. But the most obvious omission is the warning about the effect on the Automatic Flight Control System. Had this been corrected? Given the other remaining anomalies, unlikely.

This emphasises, again, the disconnect between what the Aircraft Project Office was doing, and the RAF's pervasive use of Special Trials Fits to bypass the airworthiness regulations. The practical effect on aircrew was lack of information, and increasing instances of Electro-Magnetic Interference and flight control disturbances.

Summary

The Board implied any unusual switch position was due to impact forces. No study of adjacent switches was carried out, nor if the combination of positions of related switches meant anything. Here they certainly did.

The Comms System was assumed to be serviceable, and that radio traffic would have to be *'sufficiently unusual or interesting to acquire the crew's attention'*. The Board noted an attempt to change the VHF/AM frequency could have been a distraction, but did not try to reconcile this hypothesis with both Station Boxes being set to UHF. Nor did it assess the probability of a major distraction caused by multiple malfunctions within (at least) the UHF sub-system. Nor, of the indication that other avionics were affected as well (e.g. SuperTANS and GPS). Circuit breakers were not mentioned.

Given Boscombe's dire warnings of obvious potential problem areas, which the RAF Director of Flight Safety had already linked to other Chinook fatal accidents, the Board's work in this area was deficient.

Finally, and of vital import to both the gross negligence allegations and cause, it is astounding that the ZA708 incident did not lead to a review of the ZD576 findings. Much worse, two months later MoD had the opportunity to advise Sheriff Young (and the families) that its ZD576 report was now seriously tainted, as the linkages were so obvious. This omission can only have been directed, as I consider it impossible that the two Chinook pilots on the Board were unaware of the ZA708 incident. Within hours, every Chinook pilot in the RAF would know of it, and in their minds ask - *is this what happened on the Mull?*

10. Navigation System

Chinook HC Mk1 was fitted with an older Tactical Navigation System (TANS 9447 F-09); pre-dating GPS, which was coming to fruition by the late 1980s. When Gulf War 1 broke out in 1990, the installation was upgraded to RNS252 SuperTANS and Trimble TNL8000 GPS, fitted under Special Trials Fit/Chinook/124. Authority to use the new system was given on 21 March 1991, with a warning:

> *'The ALERT light is difficult to see because it is very dim. Operators are to conduct regular checks of the navigation system status'.*

This is unacceptable in an aircraft with night vision capability. The cockpit lighting assessment must ensure, for example, that the lighting balance is correct and the eye not drawn to lights of lesser importance. This is not a difficult area, and all aircraft designs facilitate 'select on test' components to clamp voltages to instruments and lighting circuits. While perhaps understandable during transition to war, such deficiencies are typical of Special Trials Fits.

SuperTANS and TNL8000 were then retained in the Mk2, whose basic sensors were: Doppler (Velocity), GPS (Latitude/Longitude and Time of Day), Compass Gyro (Magnetic Heading), Air Data Computer (True Airspeed), Vertical Gyro (Pitch and Roll), Height Encoding Altimeter (Pressure Altitude) and Radar Altimeter (terrain separation).

Reliant on satellites, GPS is termed an external sensor. The remainder are internal. All outputs are fed to SuperTANS, which calculates and displays time and distance to go, and provides steering advice. The latter is not easily read on the display, but the signal is sent to the Attitude Indicator 'Steer Meter' for a more accurate presentation. As ever, the principle with the computer is 'rubbish in, rubbish out'.

Global Positioning System (GPS)

TNL8000 was a commercial unit utilising 'Coarse Acquisition' (C/A) code only, not the more accurate 'Precise' (P) military code. The Release to Service merely refers to 'SPS' (Standard Positioning Service), meaning C/A code. Initial Operating Capability (the minimum level at which a capability or service is usefully deployable) for P code was declared in July 1995. The general problem remains one of perception - that GPS is absolutely accurate and reliable. It is not. For example, C/A code had a vertical accuracy of ±512 feet, which is unacceptable in aviation.

The Chinook HC Mk2 Release to Service warned:
- *'GPS accuracy is not guaranteed to any level'.*
- *'GPS could degrade substantially without any indications to the crew'.*
- *'The "Error" figure displayed is meaningless and so no indication of the accuracy of the GPS is available to the user'.* (But it must mean something).

The cumulative effect of this immaturity meant operators experienced gross, unexpected errors, but the nature of the system meant it could recover without trace.

But these limitations were trumped by the status of the *entire* Navigation System - *not to be relied upon in any way*.[84] Had they known this, aircrew would have concluded only one thing - the Mk2 was not fit for purpose.

*

The risk, in any GPS system, is how far the position measurement can be in error without detection. Careful analyses are required to ensure this 'error detection boundary' is defined and implemented safely. Even today, uncertified commercial grade GPS sensors assume the system is working properly, and do not attempt to detect errors in the satellite measurements. When presented with incorrect data, they will calculate and display an incorrect position. That is an unsafe condition.

In 1996 an ambiguity was uncovered in ICD-GPS-060, the Interface Control Document for the Precise Time and Time Interval Interface; providing, *inter alia*, Time of Day. The resultant Bit Timing error meant system accuracy drifted over a short period. Illustrating this, on 13 July 1995 a Chinook was tasked to overfly the memorial in Flight Lieutenant Tapper's home village. With the crew having sight of the churchyard below, the same Navigation System told them they were over two miles away. But, as above, no indication of the error was available and there was no residual evidence.

*

The Release to Service stated: ***'GPS should not be used as the sole navigation aid'.*** (RAF's **bold**). This was emphasised at the Fatal Accident Inquiry by Mr Cable:

'The basic equipment was the Doppler. The GPS was an additional system'.

Yet, when asked how the crew assured themselves they remained on track,

---

84 Boscombe Down AMS 8H/05, Letter Report AMS 107/93, 15 October 1993 (Chinook HC Mk2 - INTERIM CA Release Recommendations - Navigation Systems).

Flight Lieutenant Duncan Trapp told the court:

'The primary aid would be the GPS system'.

This difference in perception is partly explained by the wording in the Aircraft Maintenance Manual, which says the GPS system comprises:

'...an RNS252 computer and a Data Transfer Device, a GPS Receiver, and a GPS Antenna'.

GPS being part of SuperTANS may seem odd, until one considers this allowed GPS to do away with its own Control and Display Unit. However, this gives the erroneous impression that the internal sensors are peripheral, and that SuperTANS is of no use without GPS.

The Manual then describes the SuperTANS system as comprising:

'...the SuperTANS computer, True Airspeed Transducer, temperature probe and an <u>Automatic Chart Display</u>'.

The Decca 1655E Automatic Chart Display was in the Mk1, fed by TANS and providing the forward aircrewman with a pictorial view of their location. But it was not in the Mk2 Release to Service, implying it was not retained. Yet, the <u>Mk2</u> Maintenance Manual insists the aircraft's position is indicated by:

'A coloured ring at the intersection of two wires which crossed at rights angles and were positioned above the chart (i.e. a map of the route), *moving laterally and vertically in response to inputs from SuperTANS'.*

Which was correct, the Master Airworthiness Reference or the Maintenance Manual? Crews were told both were the same, and accurate. Was an intended defence in depth against losing situational awareness missing? Worse, was the <u>actual</u> build standard different still? Irregularities such as this are symptomatic of the lead anomaly.

RNS252 SuperTANS

SuperTANS is an Area Navigation System, one which allows the aircraft to be navigated without the requirement to fly directly over landmarks or waypoints. This last is important, as the RAF let it be assumed the pilots intended *overflying* Waypoint A, near the lighthouse. The only requirement was to identify it, or the coastline below.[85] The benefit is that the pilot can take a more direct flight path appropriate to the route, thereby improving operating efficiency by reducing distance, flight time

---

85 Evidence of Flight Lieutenant Iain MacFarlane at the Fatal Accident Inquiry.

and fuel consumption.

SuperTANS is not an auto-pilot or part thereof. It processes data from other equipment, and displays the product. Unlike more modern systems, it does not combine the short-term accuracy of the internal systems with the (intended) long term accuracy of the external GPS. That is, it does not blend the two. Moreover, GPS is used direct, and the other inputs have no related timestamp. So, for example, while residual data showed Waypoint A was discarded and B (Corran, near Fort William) selected, it is not known when or where this took place, nor at what altitude or speed. Yet, lacking all of these parameters, the RAF used residual SuperTANS data as its primary 'evidence' against the pilots.

*

Legacy support problems remained. Primarily, and even though it had been in the Mk1 for three years, there was a dearth of information as to how the system worked or should be used. The means by which aircrew learn about this is the Aircrew Manual. In 1994 there wasn't one. At least, not one written for the Mk2. It was a copy of the old Mk1 manual, with what was termed a *'virtual swap shop'* emerging whereby units faxed each other as and when they found solutions to problems, or finally understood some functionality. This situation was not confined to the RAF. For example, when Boeing sought information on FADEC, they were given poor photocopies with illegible images.

Operation

Briefly, the navigator sets up a route using stored waypoints, or waypoints entered manually for that flight. There are two modes - Route Steer and Tactical Steer. Route Steer is intended for when the aircraft is required to maintain the course between two waypoints. Tactical Steer is used to fly the most direct course towards the next waypoint. The main delineation is visibility - Route Steer when in Instrument Meteorological Conditions, Tactical Steer when in Visual Meteorological Conditions.

The planned route was to turn slightly left before Waypoint A and hug the coastline up past Oban to Corran. (Figure 1). In which case, Flight Lieutenant Tapper would leave SuperTANS in Tactical Steer - and he did. Had he done as the RAF claimed (changed the intended route, to overfly the Mull) he would have selected Route Steer. This retention of Tactical Steer is further evidence of his intent, and that they were in Visual Meteorological Conditions.

SuperTANS generates an ALERT one minute before reaching the next waypoint - here, around 2nm from landfall. (One cannot be precise as their speed is unknown). In Route Steer the system automatically transfers to the next leg (but does not manoeuvre the aircraft in any way). But in Tactical Steer the operator must make three button presses to select the next waypoint, meaning Flight Lieutenant Tapper made a conscious decision to select Waypoint B. (SuperTANS was by his right knee and intended primarily for his use). In doing so, he discarded the only *electronic* information telling him the high ground was to his front right - clear indication that he knew it was there, and could see at least the coastline.

I submit this is *prima facie* evidence of their intention to turn left and follow the planned route.

*

The reason for the one minute ALERT is obvious, but it is worth summarising what the crew are taught to do before changing waypoints:

- Identify the waypoint and note Safety Altitude.
- Non-Handling Pilot informs Handling Pilot of the next track and distance, and any immediate hazards or avoids on the track.
- Check Barometric Altimeter, Radar Altimeter and remaining fuel.
- Make any necessary radio call and update Navigation System.

This is not comprehensive, but gives an indication of the work cycle. That Tapper changed his waypoint confirms he was not concerned about going near the high ground; and later we will see that Cook's instrument settings indicated likewise. Tapper wished to fix the equipment with reference to the next waypoint, meaning there was no need to overfly Waypoint A. This is precisely what SuperTANS is for, and how it is used. It allows one to cut the corner safely, while remaining aware of where the next waypoint is. Here, it was merely providing confirmatory information.

Neither the Board nor Reviewing Officers mentioned this ALERT, providing traction for those who claimed the crew had lost situational awareness, did not realise their proximity to the landmass, and were startled when confronted with it. In fact, the evidence indicates they knew exactly where and how far way it was, its height, and how long it would take to reach it.

The RAF claimed the aircraft was perfectly serviceable when Waypoint B was selected, saying the act of changing the waypoint proved it was under control. This does not follow. An analogy is the use of indicators in a car. They signify an intention to turn, but do not tell other road users when, nor prove the manoeuvre can be carried out. A latent control restriction might only become apparent when the turn is attempted - something the Air Staff finally admitted in 2005.[86]

The ON/OFF switch

One of the enduring mysteries is the position in which the SuperTANS power switch was found. Senior Inspector Tony Cable noted it was switched OFF <u>at</u> impact, not <u>by</u> impact. This was evidenced by sooting patterns, the standard way of determining such things after a fire if the switch position is not recorded in a data recorder. Mr Cable was reporting evidence from the scene. His colleague, Rex Parkinson, oversaw the subsequent work by Racal, who did not mention the switch. The RAF simply asserted SuperTANS was ON at impact, implying Mr Cable was mistaken. It offered no reasoning for its dismissal of this standard investigative technique. Nor did it mention if previous investigations, where it was used and accepted, would now be re-examined.

Figure 8 shows damage to the Data Entry Port (top right), but the SuperTANS is largely intact. To operate the switch (circled) the toggle must be pulled against a strong spring, and then over a ramp. Hence, the tapered shape and general size of the toggle. The ramp was undamaged, further evidence that the switch position did not change as a result of impact.

At the Fatal Accident Inquiry, Mr Cable confirmed he was *'making a distinction between power loss and point of impact'*. That, the general sequence of events was unknown. Similarly, Racal made no claim that the two coincided, only that switch positions *'may have been changed after powerdown'*. Elsewhere, they reported that 'powerdown' occurred up to *26 seconds before impact*, meaning Mr Cable's findings could be explained by Tapper, for whatever reason, switching SuperTANS off after selecting Waypoint B.

Curiously, Mr Cable's short factual statement remained in his report. Yet, when Gerald Howarth MP asked on 23 October 2000 if a copy of Mr Parkinson's statement could be placed in the House of Commons library, John Spellar MP, Parliamentary Under Secretary for Defence, refused. This potentially key evidence remains suppressed and, given the above, one is entitled to suspect it contains evidence detrimental to the RAF's case.

---

86 Directorate of Air Staff letter D/DAS/58/1/5, 8 April 2005.

Figure 8: ZD576's RNS252 SuperTANS *(AAIB)*

Only years later, when the available reports and Air Publications could be analysed together, did it become clear that both GPS and SuperTANS had battery backups. The possibility arises that the SuperTANS may have malfunctioned at waypoint change. The Racal manual suggests rebooting the system, which <u>may</u> explain the OFF position. This would result in a loss of display to Flight Lieutenant Tapper, but the data would still be held in battery powered memory - negating the RAF's entire argument.

Tending to support such a theory, Trimble's GPS report stated:

'The facility for switching the main DC power supply for the unit by utilising a low current/voltage line from the aircraft to a Field Effect Transistor (FET) within the unit did not function, in that it was <u>not possible to switch off the power supply using this facility</u>. The FET had been damaged at some time by having a <u>high voltage applied to it from the main DC power supply input to the unit</u>. The damaged FET was replaced, a bench test performed, and this remote switching of the power supply was found to function correctly'.

That is, while the SuperTANS and GPS were meant to be controlled by the power switch on SuperTANS, the faulty FET means one cannot infer SuperTANS and GPS power OFF coincided.

*

What might have caused electrical system disturbances? These are usually broken down into high and low voltage transients, power interruptions, and voltage modulation. Ripple voltage is a particular problem on DC Buses, which can be caused by instability of voltage regulators and load variations. All of these can induce failures in electronic systems. (An everyday analogy is home computers, where the quality of the voltage regulators dictates the performance and cost of the motherboard).

Aircraft power supplies must comply with Mil-Std-704 (Aircraft Electrical Power Characteristics), and all equipment must be compatible. This brings us back to Special Trials Fits. Did the RAF ensure compatibility when selecting, for example, the Commercial-Off-The-Shelf GPS unit? The practical problem is that equipment tested for functional and environmental performance in a laboratory may not work when integrated with other systems, and powered from a 'dirty' aircraft supply (i.e. with high DC ripple). When a suspect unit is removed to a workshop for testing, using a clean programmable power supply, it may work perfectly well. Declared 'No Fault Found', it might fail again when put back in the same aircraft. However, differences between aircraft power supplies might mean it works in another, and is intermittent in yet another. Thus, while 'swapping out' units between aircraft is a common diagnostic technique, and necessary to meet the operational imperative (get you flying), it is not the engineering solution. Flight Lieutenant Tapper had, that very day, reported a problem with his SuperTANS, but no fault was found and the unit refitted. Yet the evidence proved Tapper right. The system did have faults. This is one reason why the regulations require Design Authority appraisal of Service Engineered Modifications.

Technical management

MoD must appoint a System Co-ordinating Design Authority (SCDA), who takes on responsibility for the integration and performance of the System. This applies to all systems; and indeed the whole aircraft, where the Aircraft Design Authority (ADA) takes responsibility for the installed performance. In practice, the aircraft manufacturer is usually appointed as ADA, and the manufacturer of the major component of an equipment system as SCDA. For example, a comms system by the Intercom Design

Authority. This ensures each component of a system, the system, and the whole aircraft, has a named individual in MoD (the Technical Agency), and a named MoD-appointee in Industry, responsible for the build standard, Safety Case and performance. This may sound manpower intensive, but prior to March 1992 all avionics were managed by a small section of MoD civilian specialists. It is a simple but effective management structure. If applied. After 1992 it wasn't.

Hence, the caveat used throughout the Release to Service: *'This equipment may be used but pending further trials no guarantee of equipment performance can be given'*. The RAF blamed Boscombe Down for this. The real culprit was the failure to implement mandates. In fact, a common approach was *'If it works on the bench, it'll work in the aircraft'*. Despite rendering any Safety Case worthless, this was later declared acceptable by the Chinook Director General in MoD(PE).[87] Many aircrew have died as a result.

These procedures are laid down in the mandated Defence Standard 05-125/2. Had they been implemented, the Board could have asked the Navigation SCDA to prepare a report on the whole system, with independent oversight by Boscombe. However, Boards seldom avail themselves of this facility, because they are unaware it exists. Again, a prime example is the loss of Sea Kings ASaC Mk7 XV650 and XV704 on 22 March 2003. A major question was what communications had taken place, but neither the Technical Agency (the Programme Manager) nor the Comms SCDA (GEC-Marconi Secure Systems) were consulted. As a result, the Board's report was misleading, and in places completely wrong. Crucially, it missed entirely that both aircraft had the wrong build standard Comms System, and mandatory safety modifications were missing. The accident was, in many ways, a recurrence of ZD576.

Here, the Board commissioned three reports, from Racal, Trimble and the Air Accidents Investigation Branch (AAIB), covering only a small part of the Navigation System. They are contradictory yet, illogically, it accepted all three. Notably, neither company was responsible for the installed performance of any system or sub-system. This failure contaminated the entire investigation - which remains incomplete. And given the AAIB, under RAF direction, made no assessment of the reports, why was Mr Cable the one questioned about the Navigation System at the Fatal Accident Inquiry?

*

---

87 *Inter alia*, letter XD1 (304), 15 December 2000 from DPA XD1, Mr Ian Fauset.

This grave situation led to one of the most extraordinary events surrounding the case, but one which drew little comment.

I noted earlier the meaning of INTERIM. However, even this use (for ground training and familiarisation) was prohibited until the aircraft documentation was brought up to date.[88] In May 1994 this was so lacking, Flight Lieutenant Tapper felt it necessary to undertake a series of visits to Racal Avionics. His aim was to understand better the Navigation System inaccuracies and inconsistencies - anomalies unacceptable to, especially, the Special Forces Flight, whose operations rely on accurate navigation, often during long over-water transits and in poor visibility. He did this out of personal concern, and the fact he was the Squadron's Electronic Warfare Officer and subject matter expert on navigation systems. (For his part, Flight Lieutenant Cook was so concerned over the haste with which the Mk2 was being introduced, he had increased his life insurance).

Tapper had been using SuperTANS/GPS in the Mk1 since March 1991, suggesting his unease arose from differences in performance between the two aircraft - which we now know existed, through being able to compare the Releases to Service. With Doppler performance over water variable, did he fear being left with the immature GPS as the primary sensor? This was certainly part of an insidious erosion of confidence in the aircraft. In May 1994 it was a major issue. Only 14 months later, with declaration of GPS Initial Operating Capability, it would be easily dismissed. Shortly, few would remember the old days without GPS, or its teething problems.

Did he receive a satisfactory reply? In such cases both company and visitor *must* submit a visit report as part of the continuous feedback and assessment obligation set out in airworthiness regulations. (A joint one is fine). What did it say? What action was taken? What of the person who must receive and deal with the report, the Technical Agency? He is also a signatory to the declaration that publications have been validated and verified. But they had not been. Was there even a postholder, or a contract with Racal to maintain the build standard? Pointed questions given Air Member Supply and Organisation had been actively ridding itself of the posts over the past two years, and running down the contracts with the year-on-year -28% cuts. The 1992 cut was noted by the RAF Director of Flight Safety in his Chinook Airworthiness Review Team report of August 1992, when expressing concern over this precise issue.

What of the Directorate of Helicopter Projects? It could do little. The SuperTANS/GPS installation was a Special Trials Fit and outwith its

---

88 Boscombe Down Letter Report NR 108/93, paragraph 24b, 19 October 1993.

control. In any case, funding for Design Authorities to conduct trend failure analyses had been withdrawn in 1990, further hindering the work of investigators. If such core airworthiness activities are not carried out, then one cannot say the crews and maintainers are trained properly. Repairs cannot be verified, and therefore remain incomplete.

Ask any company how often a pilot pitches up at their factory asking how a piece of kit works - especially three years after it has entered service. The Board members and Reviewing Officers should have been hearing alarm bells, as there was clearly something about the Mk2 which Tapper did not recognise from the Mk1, that was causing anxiety. And his superiors at Odiham should have been demanding to know why a front line pilot was having to leave his duties to seek information that the Assistant Chief of the Air Staff had already signed to say was available.

Disorder

In 1990, MoD's Assistant Directorate responsible for Navigation Systems was in turmoil. The critical moment came when it wrongly criticised the reliability of the Sea Harrier's Microwave Assisted Digital Guidance Equipment (MADGE) to the US Department of Defense, who were on the verge of buying it for Marine Helicopter Squadron One, which flies the US President. This would have been the biggest order the UK company had ever received. The more expensive ground/ship-based part of the system was to be located in every State (2 per), and on every ship capable of taking the aircraft. (Whereas the RN had a mere handful).

In fact, there was nothing wrong with the equipment. The project office had contracted the Automatic Test Equipment to the wrong company. It didn't work, so there was no repair capability within MoD or industry; compounded by the RAF policy of scrapping unserviceable equipment to save on repair costs - but not replacing the equipment. Swiftly, the Fleet Air Arm was down to a partial Squadron fitted; which became academic when no aircraft carrier was equipped.

So shambolic was the situation, on 10 September 1990 over 600 Navigation contracts, including MADGE, were transferred to the Fire Control & Surveillance Radar, and Electronic Intelligence, project manager in a different Assistant Directorate. (Myself). The following day, 11 September, a unique event occurred. The company's entire Board of Directors was permitted to 'interview' me:

'Does the new MADGE project manager agree with his predecessor that our equipment is unreliable?'

'No, it's not unreliable, it's unavailable'.

Whereupon, I was invited to contribute to a brief for the UK Ambassador so that the US Department of Defense could be lobbied to reconsider. It wouldn't budge. Displaying remarkable restraint, the company did not seek redress. But no doubt later had words with their MP, the Defence Procurement Minister.[89]

SuperTANS and GPS reports

For many years public knowledge was based on Annexes Y and Z to the Board of Inquiry report, covering SuperTANS and GPS respectively.

Once Trimble had extracted and explained data remnants from their TNL8000 unit, the *AAIB* prepared and issued the GPS report.

However, when Racal extracted data from SuperTANS, *they* were permitted to interpret it themselves, determine what was relevant, and write the report. Neither their method of data extraction nor analysis was independently verified. The AAIB was not asked to comment, and the Board of Inquiry accepted it as written. Only four pages of narrative, comprising Section 1 (of 4), were released from a 23-page report. A second document, 'Reference 1', listing the data extracted, was withheld in its entirety. It was only in 2002 that the 23 pages, but not Reference 1, were obtained unofficially by an MP and given to the pilots' families. Notably, in 2016 another party (not myself or John) sought the report under Freedom of Information. MoD withheld it in full.[90] In fact, it now refuses to release any part of the Board's report, on the grounds it is *'part of an Inquiry'*.[91]

<u>AAIB report on Trimble TNL8000 GPS</u>

The report is a narrative of how the unit works, plus what limited data was extracted. In addition to the power supply fault already mentioned:

'The HaveQuick output was not functioning. The reason was not explored'.

The Board did not comment further. Yet the output is required by (e.g.) the UHF radio, to synchronise clocks. In 1996 it was discovered that a typical GPS unit was only specified to provide Time of Day to two loads (e.g. a radio and crypto). More risked overloading the circuitry. It was the Sea King office in the same Directorate that uncovered this, necessitating the design and manufacture of a Buffer Unit. There is no indication in any

---

89 *Inter alia*, Loose Minute D/ARad 130/3/1, 7 January 1991 'MADGE (ARI 23252/TGRI 23253) Logistic Support'; subsuming report D/ARad F5142, 2 January 1991.
90 Freedom of Information reference MoD 2016/00463.
91 Air Historical Branch letter FOI2019/07786, 16 July 2019.

version of the Release to Service that this fix was applied to Chinook. It is possible this fault is linked to the GPS power failure, and I have already mentioned the Bit Timing error. The report offers a diagram suggesting the unit is powered from the SuperTANS. But details are scarce and one cannot infer total power loss in the event of a fault. (Clearly, it continued with limited functionality). Nevertheless, further indications of power supply problems are emerging, and later we will learn of more.

Now consider what I wrote when discussing investigative techniques:

'Accident investigations attempt to uncover safety deficiencies, so that they might be eliminated. Even if such a deficiency is subsequently found to be unconnected to cause, it must be reported and resolved'.

That these matters were not followed up is a serious failure of MoD's Safety Management System, of which the Board of Inquiry is part.

The Racal SuperTANS report

The RAF claimed the suppressed information was *'commercially sensitive and withheld at the specific request of Racal'*. In fact, it is Racal's heavily caveated analysis, which is detrimental to the RAF's case. By necessity their interpretations are subjective, and they acknowledge this.

The RAF likened SuperTANS to an Accident Data Recorder (ADR). It is not, in any way. An ADR will record a comprehensive and continuous time-stamped data stream, often over the entire flight, and is designed to be resistant to extreme impact forces. The data recovered was, primarily, a snapshot of the latest inputs held in buffers. It was claimed analysis of this unverified data proved the *entire* Navigation System was both serviceable and accurate throughout the flight. In fact, in 2000 MoD claimed SuperTANS *was* the entire Navigation System.[92]

Timeline

A timeline is the heartbeat of any investigation. It is where theories emerge from, so must be verifiable. An interactive timeline allows visualisation, and for one to dig deeper into contributory factors and underlying causes. It is a living document. In this case still very much alive, because both new and fresh evidence continue to emerge.

*

---

92 MoD response to the Mull of Kintyre Group Submission, August 2000, paragraph 5.3.7.

On 22 May 1997, Defence Minister Lord Gilbert told the House of Lords:

'I should explain that the tactical air navigation system, for navigational and system operating reasons, stores <u>masses of data</u> which are retained in its memory each time the computer powers down'.[93]

What was this 'mass' of data? Four timed events were retained in GPS and SuperTANS memories, plus one calculated time:

17:06:14 Switch-on, set by the operator. Used thereafter to calculate Estimated Time of Arrival, displayed by SuperTANS.

17:07:10 Initialisation fix on position and time from GPS.

17:59:10 Loss of power to SuperTANS. (Calculated from SuperTANS runtime).

...and the only two timed events from the flight;

17:59:36 Last fix from satellites prior to power supply to the GPS unit being removed. Held in GPS Host Processor Input & Output Buffers, not yet sent to SuperTANS.

17:59:38 Internal GPS clock time that was started using SuperTANS time when it sent its first data at switch-on. Held in SuperTANS Input Buffer.

Note: SuperTANS uses UTC (Co-ordinated Universal Time), for display purposes only. This is GPS time from satellites, adjusted by the TNL8000 to subtract a 9 second offset (as of 2 June 1994).

So, in the all-important timing sense, Lord Gilbert's *'masses'* of data comprised two snapshots during the flight, two seconds apart. Degree of accuracy depends on source. The RAF assumed GPS timings to be accurate, but the Board included Maintenance Work Orders from May 1994 recording instances of ZD576's GPS data and clock *'running slow'*. It would be unaware of the specification error mentioned earlier. As SuperTANS did not use this GPS time for its calculations, one cannot associate GPS time and SuperTANS internal timing data in any way.

The time set by the operator in the battery-maintained clock (at 17:06:14) provides time and date to the system. It is not synchronised to any other source, and is stopped when SuperTANS is switched OFF. The pilot is required to confirm its correctness at switch-on via his watch, and all aircrew conduct a time check at the beginning of each day to ensure their watches are accurate. (One method is to acquire time from the 'speaking

---

93 https://api.parliament.uk/historic-hansard/lords/1997/may/22/chinook-helicopter-accident-inquiry

clock'). A small error might be expected.

The SuperTANS runtime is recorded, allowing the end time to be calculated. (17:59:10). With no weight-on-wheels input to SuperTANS, take-off time is unknown. In itself meaningless, until one appreciates GPS powerdown was 26 seconds later (17:59:36). The RAF assumed this meant the battery-maintained clock was 26 seconds in error, but operators advise this is unusually large. If one assumes for a moment the recorded GPS time is accurate, it is possible SuperTANS lost power 26 seconds before GPS, resulting in loss of display to the crew - although the data would still be held in battery-backed memory. The reality is probably somewhere between, the two main unknowns being the time on Tapper's watch and any GPS anomalies. (No report or Inquiry mentioned the watches worn by the 29 victims. Only the destroyed watches were returned to families).

In other words, it is possible there was (for example) a 10 second discrepancy between time sources, and powerdown occurred 16 seconds before impact; or variations thereof. Thus, it is impossible to know where or when the waypoint change was made.

Supporting this, SuperTANS powerdown occurred up to 195 feet below the point of initial impact. Again, the RAF simply dismissed this as an error, when it is likely the explanation is more complex. Racal defined *'powerdown'* as the voltage dropping below an unstated limit, not total loss of power - at which point the memory module is battery powered. Also, *'normal operation'* is suspended when the power supply voltage *'begins to drop'*, but the report does not say what functions are lost or degraded.

Therefore, there is no evidence at all that, even if SuperTANS remained switched ON, any data was being presented to the crew via the SuperTANS display after selection of Waypoint B.

SuperTANS revealed the waypoint change as being 0.95nm before powerdown, but not the time or position. The RAF assumed powerdown at impact, and from that an average groundspeed in the range 170-190 knots. It claimed this 'proved' it took 18-20 seconds from waypoint change to impact, from which it assumed they were flying too fast during the approach. In turn, this was based on an assumption they were in Instrument Meteorological Conditions.

In reality, the distance between waypoint change and impact is this 0.95nm, plus any distance travelled in the 0-26 second 'error'. But the data is just too inconsistent and fragmented, and all one can say is that the waypoint was changed at some point along an estimated track line.

Conclusions

Racal's report generates more questions than answers. It was written by someone intimately familiar with the system, for a similar audience with access to all the data. Few would understand it. That is not a criticism, merely a logical deduction based on Flight Lieutenant Tapper seeking help - 39 months after he had been assured the necessary information and training was available for Mk1, and seven months after receiving the same assurance for Mk2. As the full report remains unreleased, I faced the same difficulty. I cannot say I am 100% right. But I *do* say, without doubt, that the SuperTANS/GPS system was carrying faults, and MoD seriously misled aircrew and all readers of the Board's report.

There exists a series of unknowns, and the system design and data remnants do not facilitate resolution. The point is, MoD misrepresented these as knowns, and from them imagined a time of waypoint change and the speed between that change and impact, and used this to justify gross negligence findings.

The official position remains that *'all the evidence, and not just some of it'* from SuperTANS points to a deliberate decision to overfly the Mull, and selection of an inappropriate rate of climb. That, this allowed the Board to *'derive an accurate picture of the flight path'*.[94] In fact, the RAF took fragmented and unverified data, postulated a track and timeline, and from this supposed the crew's actions. All the while claiming this as *'hard fact'*, when it wasn't even a logical hypothesis. It was an outright lie.

*

Often, a degree of precision is assumed that is unattainable in a helicopter. The SuperTANS output is simply a guide. One normally flies a wind-corrected heading to achieve the track line. Trying to keep the Steer Meter in the middle is seen as pointless as it would require virtually constant heading adjustment, which is impossible at low level. Instead, one tends to fly for a while, check position, and alter heading to converge with track. One can wander left and right as the terrain and weather dictate. They were flying clear of cloud and in sight of the surface. As they approached the Mull, the advice that a left turn was needed was simply confirmation of what they already knew.

---

94 Lord Gilbert to the House of Lords, 22 May 1997.

PART 4 - AIRMANSHIP

'From everything I have seen and learnt since becoming a service pilot, I know that if anyone could have saved my father that night it would have been Jon Tapper and Rick Cook. They deserve better, and this is a stain on the conscience of the RAF and gross dereliction of duty of care by senior figures in the Military and Government. It also colours my judgment every time I climb into an aircraft, as I know the exact same cold eye would try and hang me and my crew should our own equipment ever fail us'.

Niven Phoenix, former RAF pilot, son of Detective Superintendent Ian Phoenix, RUC (late Parachute Regiment).

This section discusses various hypotheses that the pilots erred in some way. I offer counter-arguments, and note that even if error could be proven it would not necessarily be negligence.

11. Navigation

One must differentiate between human error and equipment error. If the equipment can be shown to have significant faults or defects, it is unsafe to criticise aircrew. The prevention of recurrence, and natural justice, is better served by asking why they were given unsatisfactory equipment.

*

A number of hypotheses were debated, mainly on internet forums:

- The crew mistook a signal station (little more than a shed) and a nearby small cottage for the lighthouse compound. The coastline below each runs roughly east/west, while at the lighthouse is north/south. Given the relative sizes, the crew's familiarity with the route and landmarks, and Flight Lieutenant Tapper having landed at the distinctive compound before, an error of recognition is vanishingly unlikely.

- The co-ordinates programmed into SuperTANS for Waypoint A (N55°18.50 W05°48.00) could have been set wrongly. If the '48' minutes longitude was meant to be '49', then the Waypoint would have been to the west of the lighthouse, over the sea. That is true, and waypoints may be abstract, having no obvious relationship to any physical feature. In this case, however, Waypoint A was intended to be associated with the lighthouse area, evidenced by the route planning map and Flight Lieutenant Tapper noting it was his entry point into Low Flying Area 14. (Broadly, the area north of the Highland Boundary Fault, better known historically and colloquially as The Highland Line).

- The fault line is coincident with a regional magnetic feature, dividing a string of negative anomalies in the north from positive ones in the south. The magnetic variation printed on maps was 7.5°, but the actual variation at the crash site was 12.5° and perhaps caused them to be on the wrong heading. However, this phenomenon is well understood in MoD, it being one reason why sonar and navigation trials are conducted at MoD ranges located north of the Line.

- They changed their minds as to route due to (a) the late allocation of a Mk2, with its severe restrictions, (b) the weather forecast, and (c) the perceived need to select a track over flatter ground. That, they may have intended to fly further to the east, near Southend, follow the B842 road up Conie Glen, then turn towards Machrihanish and pick up the coastline again. But why complicate matters when all one had to do was hug the western coastline, as planned? Please refer to Figure 4, showing orographic cloud extending inland on the leeward side of the hill. That would blanket Conie Glen, and the crew would know this.

- Finally, it was said they may have confused the headlights of the deputy lighthouse keeper's vehicle for the lighthouse light, as he drove down the hill. In 1994 the lighthouse had a 1,575,000 candlepower light using a 3.5 kilowatt filament lamp, flashing every 20 seconds. Quite different from a Land Rover. In any case, it was known the light was only switched on as night fell, and not used in fog or mist.

The above hypotheses overlook that they were flying under Visual Flight Rules, in Visual Meteorological Conditions. They would not have been using SuperTANS to determine where to turn, only for speed and time management. The act of changing waypoint removed the only reference they had to the danger to their right (other than their eyesight), indicating their intention to turn away from it.

Implausible implications arise, reflected in the RAF's claims. Each of the crew committed the same errors and made the wrong decisions, simultaneously. And none of the (three) forward crew were looking where they were going, and had ignored the one minute ALERT.

Even if unfamiliar with the route, it would be patently obvious that the Mull was to the front with the high ground to the right, and a slight left turn was required to skirt round it - as planned. It was clearly visible from the point at which they left the Northern Ireland coast, and they headed slightly left; confirmed by priests attending a conference at Garron Tower (St Killian's College), just north of Carnlough. (More eye-witnesses whom the Board did not interview).

Radar Altimeter procedures

The Board criticised the pilots' Radar Altimeter procedures, in particular the settings of their Low Height Warning bugs, saying this was a contributory factor. It did not examine the subject in any detail so, before proceeding, I should explain that procedures vary slightly depending on aircraft role and the use to which it is being put. I acknowledge some pilots may have marginally different views, but the essential issues remain the same.

*

The Radar Altimeter system measures the range (not height) of the aircraft from the nearest terrain within the beam pattern of the antennae. In Chinook, this is forward 36°, aft 4° and laterally 39°, relative to the aircraft's axes; meaning it cannot provide adequate warning of rising ground ahead. It is not a Ground Proximity Warning System *per se*, but still an important tool to help minimise the risk of Controlled Flight Into Terrain.

In Chinook, each pilot has a 0-5,000 feet Indicator on which he sets his bug height. The Handling Pilot will set his at, or slightly above, his low-level clearance. In this case that was 50 feet, and Flight Lieutenant Cook's bug was set at 69 feet. The Non-Handling Pilot will normally set his 20% below the clearance, so one might expect Flight Lieutenant Tapper's to be at 40 feet. However, it was at 850 feet - the basis of the Board's criticism.

VISUAL and AUDIO warnings are provided - a lamp in each Indicator and a tone in their helmets. Upon take-off, the warnings remain ON until the bug height is exceeded, although the AUDIO can be muted at any time by a switch on the Collective lever handgrip. Once above the bug setting, the warning will activate when the aircraft descends through it. It is only re-armed when it ascends through it again.

The warning sequence is intended to be VISUAL first, then AUDIO/VISUAL. The AUDIO selector switch is normally set to the Non-Handling Pilot's system, meaning if the bugs were set conventionally (~69/40), as they descended through 69 feet Cook would receive a VISUAL warning. If they continued to descend and went below 40 feet, Tapper would also receive a VISUAL, and both an AUDIO. The position of ZD576's AUDIO selector switch could not be established due to impact damage.

However, it can be seen that if everything were serviceable, the AUDIO selector set to Tapper, and if ZD576 had ascended through 850 feet, Tapper would receive a VISUAL and both an AUDIO warning as they descended through 850 feet. As they reached 69 feet, Cook would receive VISUAL only. Plainly this is not the intended sequencing, the AAIB reporting that the evidence at the scene was *'inconsistent with correct operation of the system'*.

But the limited evidence (primarily, eye-witnesses in Northern Ireland and Mr Holbrook) says they did not exceed 850 feet. Moreover, the setting is irrelevant to an overflight of the Mull, it being too low. In this sense it is meaningless.

The question, then, is why Tapper's bug was at an apparently 'wrong' setting. The clues are in the AAIB report. Both his Indicator warning lamp filaments were blown, <u>before</u> impact. The voltage to the lamps was correct when tested. But doing so on a test bench does not prove the aircraft Electrical System or the wiring looms were serviceable, only that a particular part of the circuit was intact. Nor does it prove the AUDIO warning would have worked. The Board characterised this as a *'minor fault'*. In isolation, perhaps. But not when taken with the strong evidence of other over-voltage problems.

The combination of Tapper's unserviceable Indicator, their bug settings, and incorrectly set up Transmitter/Receiver (all knowns, and reported by the AAIB), and Cook's Intercom status (suspected, with strong physical evidence), means it is likely the only warning would be a 69 feet VISUAL to Cook. But this setting makes it crystal clear he did not intend going near rising ground (as he would not receive adequate warning), and was flying visually. (In the same way Tapper's retention of Tactical Steer on the SuperTANS indicates likewise).

This is a good example of the need to assess interdependencies, systems integration, functional safety, and behaviour in the aircraft environment. Inexplicably, the Board did not.

*

Revealing a further possible scenario, Boscombe had warned:

'The Radar Altimeter may be affected by external Radio Frequency electromagnetic fields. Crews should be aware of the possibility of spurious indications when onboard radio transmitters are used'.

Such a transmission was made around five minutes before impact. There was no reply. It is normal to try three times but no more calls were recorded. If there is no reply, how do crew know if their aircraft actually radiated the transmission? They don't. The only indication they have that a small part of the Intercom is working is sidetone. Simply put, the sound of one's own voice fed to the helmet earpieces. (One experiences this in everyday use when using a telephone). If he had no sidetone, Cook <u>may</u> have selected FAIL to narrow the problem down. The evidence of cascading electrical failure grows stronger...

*

The real issue here is that equipment and information deficiencies meant the Radar Altimeter *Transmitter/Receiver*, not the Low Level bugs, had been set up incorrectly. The Air Accidents Investigation Branch reported that the Sensitivity Range Control adjustment in the Receiver module's Intermediate Frequency Amplifier was wrong, by some considerable margin. The likely effect would be erroneous range measurements and indications, as the Receiver would erratically lose/regain/lose lock.

This does not mean an error was made by maintainers at RAF Odiham. The Air Publications didn't offer a procedure or setting to use. By trial and error, a figure of 79±1dB had been arrived at when adjusting variable resistor R51 - and certainly that is what I taught diagnosticians in 1983-4. The systemic and organisational problem was that this was a local instruction, with no guarantee others were using the same figure.

It is worth pointing out here that my work was on Fleet Air Arm Radar Altimeters. The RN had taken over their own repairs from the RAF after an incorrectly repaired Transmitter/Receiver was found to be the cause of a fatal accident the previous year during the Falklands War. The RAF had missed important configuration control considerations, whereby the RN system had a Special Range Board in its Range Computer which factored range by x10, meaning the accident aircraft's Indicators were showing 10 times actual height. (This factoring, and use of different Indicators, provided greater accuracy when in the low level hover while dipping the sonar. It was also beneficial during Search and Rescue operations). The RN's actions were immediate and decisive, although not widely broadcast to avoid embarrassment. Unless one knew this background a Board of Inquiry would not know to ask the question of the RAF. Once again, the solution is to engage with the Technical Agency.

Also, there was an assembly defect whereby a component was fitted the wrong way around, and Odiham did not have the necessary information or test equipment to measure the power output. That is, they could not ensure the quality of the transmitted pulse. Lacking this assurance the device cannot be declared serviceable. Again, the Board dismissed these as *'minor faults'*. I disagree. Individually and collectively they are critical to the correct operation and accuracy of the system.

The worst aspect is that none of this came as a surprise. Odiham and Third Line workshops were denied the required test equipment, despite the impact of not being able to verify repairs being formally reported after the 1982 accident, and again in 1984. Crucially, again, the Board did not note the modification state of any part of the Radar Altimeter system, which is important here due to the number of modifications required to avoid erroneous height indications.[95]

I conclude that the above renders the Board's criticism unsafe, and note the adverse effects the lead anomaly had on the system.

---

95 Explained in 'Their Greatest Disgrace' (David Hill, 2016).

12. Incapacitation and fatigue

Flight Lieutenant Tapper had obtained permission from the 230 Squadron Duty Flight Commander to exceed, by one hour, the Northern Ireland limit of seven hours flying time within a crew duty period. In the normal course of his duties at 7 Squadron he was permitted to extend this himself, but in Northern Ireland he was part of a Chinook detachment attached to the Puma squadron, operating under different rules. Upon arrival at Fort George he would have had to seek permission from the Aldergrove Station Commander to fly back that evening. In his remarks, Group Captain Roger Wedge said:

'At the time of the accident, the crew was operating within Crew Duty Time extension which had been properly sought and granted, and fatigue was unlikely to have contributed to the cause of the accident'.

How this administrative matter would have been managed became a major discussion point, especially during the Fatal Accident Inquiry. In his written determination, Sheriff Young noted any *'minor'* question mark had:

'No bearing on Tapper's competence as a pilot and should be kept firmly in perspective against the background of the universal plaudits of those witnesses who had actually flown with him'.[96]

This was a polite way of delineating the two groups of MoD witnesses. Those intent on concealing organisational failings, whose evidence, the Sheriff noted, displayed major discrepancies. And those who spoke for the pilots, whose evidence he found compelling. He also found it *'incredible'* that the other crew members *'would have been prepared to run this risk'*.[97] Above all else, he noted that the pilots were not present to defend themselves against any allegations made against them.[98]

For fatigue to be a factor, one would have to accept all four crew were affected at the same time, in the final minute or so during the approach to the Mull. I consider this implausible.

*

It is worth digressing a little to mention an example of incapacitation due to fumes in the cockpit, and take the opportunity to discuss the Chinook

---

[96] Determination of Sheriff Sir Stephen Young, page 32.
[97] Determination of Sheriff Sir Stephen Young, page 33.
[98] Determination of Sheriff Sir Stephen Young, page 15.

Airworthiness Review Team (CHART) report of 1992. This reveals linkages.

Toxic fumes incidents had occurred in RN Lynx helicopters in 1990, caused by overheated Bakelite terminal blocks associated with the aircraft power supply to the radar. On each occasion the crews recognised the problem and landed as soon as possible, and were hospitalised for observation. RAF suppliers refused to release RN funding to make the aircraft safe. The RN could ground its Lynx fleet and come a-begging next year. As Fire Control and Surveillance Radar team leader, I suspended a low priority contract (on Hoffman Lightweight TACAN, but everything in my remit was lower priority) and used the money to fund rectification.

Had something similar occurred in ZD576 the crew would have had to land as soon as practicable. As they were under Visual Flight Rules they could land anywhere suitable, whereas under Instrument Flight Rules one needs an airfield.

*

In August 1992 the head of this supply branch, Director General Support Management Air Vice Marshal Christopher Baker, was a recipient of the CHART report from Air Commodore Martin Abbott, the RAF Director of Flight Safety, repeating warnings of systemic airworthiness failings within his command. While Baker's approach to financial probity and safety management certainly reflected RAF policy, it provides a telling backdrop to many subsequent accidents.[99] Four months later, he threatened to dismiss his civilian specialists (including myself) who had been voicing the same concerns since 1988. It was widely held by those involved that he would not make such threats without 'top cover'. The ensuing investigation by Director Internal Audit, and his report vindicating us, is the direct precursor to the Nimrod Review, in which Mr Haddon-Cave confirmed the *savings at the expense of safety* policy we were under.[100]

CHART was commissioned by the RAF Chief Engineer, Air Marshal Sir Michael Alcock. Promoted to Air Chief Marshal in 1993, in April 1994 he assumed a dual role by becoming the head of this support organisation, now renamed Air Member Logistics. In the process, he became the first non-aircrew officer to sit on the Air Force Board.

The other addressee was the Assistant Chief of the Air Staff, Air Vice Marshal (later Air Chief Marshal Sir) Anthony Bagnall who, in November

---

99 Full evidence was provided in the main submission to the Mull of Kintyre Review.
100 Report D/DIA/5/295/10, 29 June 1996 'Requirement Scrutiny'.

1993, signed the Mk2 Release to Service despite the aircraft still suffering from the failures noted in CHART. It is inconceivable he did not discuss this with the Chief of the Air Staff, Air Chief Marshal Sir Peter Harding, and Harding's successor Air Chief Marshal Sir Michael Graydon.

Here is a passage from the Air Commodore Abbott's covering letter:

'I have taken a particular interest in the operational aspects of (CHART). I am surprised to find that there is no <u>Statement of Operating Intent and Usage</u> for the helicopter fleet. And disturbed, in view of the implications for the Support area, that the Statements of Unit Policy for Chinook are outdated. Chinook tasking and fleet management appears to be not only bedevilled by a <u>lack of resources</u> but supported by a rather cumbersome management structure and faced with a less than patient customer - the Army. This is especially pertinent in Northern Ireland, where we are rather too dependent on the pragmatism of our local commanders in preventing <u>unhealthy pressure at the coal face</u>. Moreover, as the inevitable operational pressures are applied, I am keen to ensure that those aircrew that decide to carry faults always <u>involve engineers</u> in the airworthiness decision-making loop. Also, I feel that we need to look more closely at our <u>Special Trials Fit procedures</u> and the associated <u>Service Deviations</u>.

Although a certain amount of alienation might be expected in a programme involving both the Army and the Navy, it is the perceptions that organisations within the RAF have of each other that bothers me most. The Support Authority has a low opinion of engineering standards on stations, who in turn have pointed to downfalls in the Support Authority. Command and Group <u>seem to look on from outside the airworthiness loop and wait for the next crisis</u>.

I need no further convincing that the current organisational structure, and the lack of resources, are not a healthy recipe for the future sound airworthiness of the Chinook'.[101]

This is utterly pejorative. A veritable broadside. The report itself is a further 372 pages of the same level of concern, compiled by one of the RAF's most highly qualified engineers, Wing Commander Dudley Denham. I have underlined just a few of the issues discussed elsewhere, but the most basic failure is noted at the beginning. Lacking a Statement of Operating Intent and Usage, there can be no valid Safety Case.

However, the most damaging and pointed criticism is reserved to last. If we look at the Command and Group incumbents in the year or so before CHART, and the senior officer responsible for airworthiness, three familiar names emerge - Michael Graydon, Richard Johns and Michael

---

101 Loose Minute D/IFS(RAF)/125/30/2/1, 14 August 1992. (Covering CHART report).

Alcock - the officers pushed forward *in lieu* of William Wratten and John Day as soon as the serious airworthiness failings were made public in 2010.

During the Mull of Kintyre Review, Alcock briefed the media that CHART did not refer to Chinook HC Mk2. It mentioned it 284 times. His words were repeated in Ministerial briefings by the Air Staff, resulting in Defence Secretary Dr Liam Fox misleading Parliament on 13 July 2011; who was forced to retract when told the truth by several MPs.[102] However, as this was in a letter to an MP, the official record in Hansard will always show what Alcock claimed.

No action was taken against those who lied to Dr Fox, no apology was offered to Parliament, and no remorse shown to the relatives. To do so would be to admit the Houses of Commons and Lords had been serially lied to for over 17 years, and that very senior RAF officers and MoD officials had committed serious offences. Little wonder the Board of Inquiry did not mention 'airworthiness'.

The Board dismissed the general issues of fatigue and incapacitation, confirming the crew were fit and well rested. Pathology confirmed no trace of drugs, alcohol or toxic/noxious agents in the blood. I agree with the Board, but nevertheless this short chapter raises a number of pertinent issues which it did not explore, and MoD actively concealed.

---

102 *Inter alia*, Letter D/S of S/LF MC03876/2011, 5 September 2011.

13. Flying too fast and too low

This allegation was the cornerstone of the RAF's official position, but few agreed. Group Captain Crawford, RAF Odiham Station Commander:

'The implication in the Board's findings is that the transit speed approaching the Mull of Kintyre was unusually high. I doubt this. An assessment based on a time/distance calculation shows that the average Groundspeed was in the range 135-155kts. I believe the crew adopted a cruise Indicated Airspeed of 135 knots'.

Chinook VNE (Never Exceed Speed) was 160 knots Indicated Airspeed. The mooted speeds were therefore well within the capabilities of the aircraft, but an Indicated Airspeed below 140 knots was normally selected to reduce the effects of vibration. The RAF claimed this had improved in the Mk2, the Board hypothesising that Flight Lieutenant Tapper had been *'deceived by the high airspeed of the aircraft, permitted by the low vibration levels of the Chinook HC2'.*[103]

But Boscombe had already stated categorically that it had not improved:

'The vibration characteristics were similar to the Mk1 and were unsatisfactory. At speeds over 140 knots Indicated Airspeed the vibration of the aircraft increased to Vibration Assessment Rating (VAR) Scale 7 (severe), which was uncomfortable and distracting for instrument flight'[104]

VAR 7 is defined as:

'Vibration is immediately apparent to experienced aircrew even when fully occupied. Performance of primary task is affected or tasks can only be done with difficulty'.

There is more to this. Upon delivery to the UK by sea, pilots from Odiham and Boscombe collected the converted aircraft. First impressions were indeed that the vibration characteristics had improved. However, once serviced to RAF standards (different oils/fluids, rotor-tuned, etc.) it returned.

Groundspeed and Airspeed

It is important not to confuse Groundspeed and Airspeed. Airspeed is the vector difference between the Groundspeed and the wind speed. On a still day, Airspeed is equal to Groundspeed. But if the wind is blowing in the same direction that the aircraft is moving, Airspeed will be less than

---

103 Board of Inquiry report, paragraph 67c.
104 Boscombe Down Letter Report P/Chinook/41, paragraphs 21 and 23, 22 October 1993.

Groundspeed. Here, there was a 30 knot tail wind from 170°. If the Groundspeed was, for example, 150 knots, Indicated Airspeed would be just over 120 knots. Under Visual Flight Rules, if clear of cloud and in sight of the surface, 140 knots Indicated Airspeed is legal. Consistently, the RAF used Groundspeed, giving an impression of excessive speed.

Take-off was around 1742, impact around 1800, so one can calculate approximate average speed. But there is no evidence of instantaneous speed, and precious little indicating <u>when</u> any event occurred.

The best indication of Groundspeed <u>at impact</u> was from the Drift Angle Groundspeed Indicator, showing 147 knots - around 120 knots Airspeed. But as it is derived from the Doppler, the instrument does not provide a steady reading. It is continually cycling/moving, so 147 knots is an approximation. It could be up to 10 knots either side of a mean figure, depending on terrain, and varies with different aircraft.[105]

Weight, Altitude and Icing

The Chinook HC Mk2 was limited to an All Up Mass of 18,000kg, instead of the contracted 24,500kg; which was finally achieved on 30 September 1998. The original passenger manifest of 32 would have meant exceeding 18,000kg. It is likely the reduction in passenger numbers was, in part, related to the late decision to use a Mk2.

*

To assess any claim the aircraft was too low requires knowledge of its Icing Limit and Minimum Safe Altitude (MSA). One must climb to MSA when flight under Visual Flight Rules cannot be maintained. The altitude you climb to is initially the MSA for that leg - essentially the height of the highest point on the leg within a corridor either side of the route, plus a safety margin of at least 1,000 feet. Pilots view this as a 'bubble' of air space, and plan their flight based on weather forecast, terrain and the aircraft's capabilities.

The RAF claimed that between waypoint change and Waypoint A MSA was 2,800 feet, and beyond that 5,000 feet.[106] 2,800 relates to MSA on the leg from Aldergrove to the Mull. At Waypoint A and beyond it was actually 5,900 feet. Plainly, one cannot transition from 2,800 to 5,900 feet instantaneously, so the climb to MSA must be commenced earlier so that one is at MSA when it takes effect. If the intention was to overfly the Mull,

---

105 Evidence of Flight Lieutenant Iain MacFarlane to the Fatal Accident Inquiry.
106 Lord Gilbert, House of Lords 22 May 1997.

then the climb would have had to commence some miles before landfall. But there was no such intent.

*

If an aircraft does not have an Icing clearance permitting a climb to MSA, that is an unsafe condition. This aspect generated much debate, but it was never mentioned that the Icing section had been <u>removed</u> from the Release to Service in March 1994. Hitherto, the limit had been +4°C, compared to the Mk1's -6°C. (In other words, the Mk1 could operate safely in colder conditions). It was only reinserted after the accident, in July 1994. Accordingly, any reference to +4°C, and any calculation based upon it, is misleading. It was what the pilots *thought* the clearance was. (Bearing in mind there was no copy of the Release at Aldergrove).

In his statement to the Board of Inquiry, Squadron Leader Michael Stangroom, the Duty Flight Commander, confirmed both he and Flight Lieutenant Tapper *'knew the Chinook HC Mk2 had no Icing clearance'*. Most took this to mean it was inadequate for that particular flight. In fact, it had none at all. This was probably an administrative error, but is symptomatic of ongoing organisational failures which could have had serious consequences had the intention been to change the limit. Regardless, a Fleet level constraint existed whereby, when operating together, a Mk1 would have to default to the more restrictive limitation placed on the Mk2.

It was also overlooked that when (illegally) released by the Air Staff in November 1993, the aircraft only had a 5,000 feet clearance in *any* conditions, subject to *(inter alia)* FADEC being replaced with one having a manual Reversionary Mode, and its software being re-written. In March 1994 this was raised to 10,000, still far below the Mk1's 15,000 feet. When asked MoD could not demonstrate the provenance of this change. As there was no manual Reversionary Mode, and the software was not rewritten, it can be seen that this notional 10,000 feet clearance needs explaining, as it contradicts the mandate the Assistant Chief of the Air Staff was under. Is this why the RAF claimed MSA was 5,000 feet? Certainly, it is further proof of relevant evidence being concealed.

*

The RAF based its case on what the weather turned out to be, not what was forecast. It used the conditions at RAF Machrihanish, some miles north and more sheltered than the North Channel. Self-evidently, the crew only had the forecast and, showing good planning skills, predicted they <u>might</u> encounter Instrument Meteorological Conditions, necessitating a climb to 5,900 feet - breaching both their Icing and Altitude clearances (as they understood them). At the Fatal Accident Inquiry, Aircrewman John Coles, who had flown in ZD576 the previous day:

> 'Flight Lieutenant Tapper had sought advice from superiors at Odiham (Squadron Leader Milburn, 7 Squadron) as to whether *in an emergency* they could do that, and had been categorically told that if they broke any of the Controller Aircraft Release limitations then they would be personally liable for any law suit which followed'.

This was a reference to the repeal of Section 10 of the Crown Proceedings Act 1947 in May 1987. Hitherto, the Act had provided Crown Immunity to individuals who transgressed. Now they could be held liable. Faced with this refusal, the crew agreed low level flight under Visual Flight Rules was their only option. (Notably, staff with airworthiness delegation were encouraged to retain a copy of anything they signed, creating a conflict with the Official Secrets Act).

That Flight Lieutenant Tapper asked the question proves he was keenly aware that he had been tasked to operate an aircraft whose Icing Limit was below his Safety Altitude. And the reason for this Icing Limit points to possible cause - the unquantifiable risk of a FADEC software problem causing an engine malfunction had prompted the reduced maximum weight (18,000kg). But, subject to conditions that were not met.

To deliberately climb to MSA would be negligence. That is, the pilots were found guilty of gross negligence for not committing negligence.

Visual illusion

Various surface features and atmospheric conditions can create illusions of incorrect height and distance. Examples are:

- Featureless terrain such as over water, darkened areas, and snow-covered ground can give an impression of greater height.
- Rain on the windscreen and haze give an impression of greater distance.
- Bright ground lighting, especially when not illuminating surrounding terrain, can create an illusion of less distance.

The Board opined that the lack of surface texture over the sea, and the absence of an external horizon, may have produced a 'goldfish bowl' effect (whereby the sea and the horizon seem to merge). But it went no further, and did not offer an opinion as to *when* they entered any cloud. Nor did it mention the SuperTANS one minute ALERT which, coupled with familiarity with the route, provided the crew with a high degree of certainty over distance to go.

Nor did the Board say why it thought there was a lack of surface texture. There was a 30 knot tail wind from 170°. The Beaufort Scale describes the effect of a 28-33 knot wind (Force 6) as:

'Wave height 13-19 feet. Sea heaps up. Foam from breaking waves is blown into streaks along the wind direction. Moderate airborne spray'.

Mr Holbrook later described conditions as an *'uncomfortable Force 6'* and the water *'turbulent'*. The RAF dismissed his evidence, refusing to interview those who could confirm it.

It is important to note that several pilots I have spoken to harboured suspicions for many years that spatial disorientation, and specifically visual illusion, may have been a contributory factor. But when presented with the evidence that has since emerged, most have reconsidered.

Lacking voice recordings, misjudgment by spatial disorientation can only be speculation, and cannot be considered without first acknowledging the general status of the aircraft, and in particular the Navigation System. By any interpretation, this placed the crew and passengers in danger by removing a key defensive barrier. The possibility exists that this prior negligence contributed to the crew being overwhelmed.

Summary

Many have opined that, in the face of death, such niceties can be ignored. I agree. No regulations can foresee every situation. But *this* situation, for the most part, *was* foreseen. Defences in depth, intended to minimise the effect of human error, had been built, and then systematically torn down. Dire warnings were issued, yet a wilful decision made to force avoidable severe risks upon the crew (and passengers). Their subconscious would be clouded by being expressly forbidden to take intuitive action. However, survival instinct would take over, and this is why I believe something went catastrophically wrong.

A basic philosophy of helicopter airmanship is, when encountering bad weather 'go down, slow down, turn round, land on'. Low-level flying in marginal weather is routine. The flight was cleared down to 50 feet, which is normally neither onerous nor unusual. However, the Release to Service repeated a warning carried over from the Mk1:

'Prolonged cruising flight should not take place at heights below 300 feet Above Ground Level unless it is operationally essential to do so'.

I'll leave that there for the reader to contemplate, and revisit it later when discussing the reason for the limitation.

14. Air Commodore Carl Scott

I will end this section with one of the finest pieces written on behalf of the crew - the submission to Lord Philip by Air Commodore Carl Scott AFC. Personal details and references have been removed. He gave evidence in person on 23 March 2011, and was asked to capture that in writing, submitting this on 28 March 2011. The Review made no mention of it.

The majority of my career has been spent as a Chinook pilot, beginning October 1984. At the time of the accident I was a Flight Lieutenant serving as deputy commander on the Special Forces Flight of 7 Squadron. I was the tactics instructors on the unit, responsible for teaching crews to operate the aircraft under operational conditions. I was also a Unit Test Pilot. I flew with all the members of the crew who died on the Mull, and knew them and their training profiles very well.

The atmosphere on the Chinook Force
The transition between Mk1 and Mk2 was fraught, with reduced flying hours and a plethora of complex engine malfunctions as a result of the FADEC system. The conversion course was short, with some pilots (including Jonathan Tapper) reverting to flying the Mk1 for some time after conversion training and prior to his first operational flight on a Mk2. The engines at the time were prone to undemanded surges in power, inexplicable shutdown, and surging or overheating to the point of self-destruction. At the time, squadron aircrew were briefed by the Squadron Commander, Wing Commander Mike Barter, that the test pilots at Boscombe Down had ceased flying as they were unable to account for these malfunctions and believed the aircraft was, as a consequence, unsafe to fly. We were directed to keep flying as we had an operational task to fulfil.

The decision to continue flying was expressed as a 'balance of risk' and the luxury of withdrawing the aircraft from front line service was not available. Test pilots, it was suggested, did not enjoy the same high moral fibre as front line crews. It was understood that this was a question of loyalty, to the task and the command chain. It later transpired this loyalty was unidirectional.

The mood of the crew of the Mull of Kintyre aircraft
Flight Lieutenant Tapper rang me at RAF Odiham the evening before the delivery of (ZD576) to Northern Ireland. (30 May 1994). He expressed his concern that a considerable period had passed since his conversion course, and he felt unprepared to fly the aircraft. He had to (fly) a considerable number of key personnel in a single

lift, which was troubling him. He had spoken to the tasking authority (JATOC) to attempt to persuade them to spread the load between more than one aircraft, and had been refused. He had hoped Flight Lieutenant Cook, on his recent arrival in country, would have accumulated more Mk2 experience than he had, and was disappointed to find out that this was not the case. He asked if the delivery of the Mk2 could be delayed so he could execute his mission using a Mk1. I spoke to the Duty Squadron Executive, Squadron Leader Trevor Milburn, to pass on his request to delay the arrival of Mk 2. This was denied, but as the pilot delivering the aircraft (Squadron Leader David Prowse) was a flying instructor, he would offer the crews a chance to refresh their understanding of procedures for the Mk2.

I believe Flight Lieutenant Tapper was managing risk to the best of his ability, in the manner in which he had been trained. We cannot remove risk entirely from military aviation, but we can manage and mitigate it. He had appealed to his command chain in Northern Ireland and not received the support he needed. He had then turned to his home base and to those most familiar with the aircraft and its inherent problems. Having received the response he did, it is most likely that he would proceed to fly the mission as directed. A refusal to do so would have been theoretically possible, but exceedingly unusual. This was not the behaviour of a negligent pilot, but conscientious attempts of a very loyal and dedicated officer to mitigate risks he was being directed to manage by commanders.

Immediately prior to taking his pre-deployment leave, I flew the Mk2 with Flight Lieutenant Cook. During the exercise in Scotland (20 May 1994) we had flown in poor weather at low level in mountainous terrain. The abort (a rapid climb to a safe altitude) we conducted was immediate, decisive and took us well clear of the imminent threat of flying in terrain masked by cloud. I have no doubt that he understood the correct procedures for the conditions which may have prevailed on the Mull of Kintyre and, if he were to find himself in poor weather conditions with the ability to execute that manoeuvre, he would have done so.

Too little has been said of the role of the crewmen in Special Forces crews. MACR Graham Forbes and Sergeant Kevin Hardie were very experienced, mature personnel with a keen understanding of the aircraft and mission. In 7 Squadron crews in particular, they were empowered to take an active interest in the conduct of the mission, including a right of veto. Had either been unhappy with the manner in which the sortie was being conducted, they would have called for it to be terminated and the aircraft returned to base. That request would not be refused by a pilot who had achieved Special Forces mission status. To ignore such a request would have been entirely alien to the procedures and training on a unit, and would have resulted in a pilot being considered for removal from these duties.

The loss of ZD576 and those on board

I flew ZD576 on six occasions, totalling 6 hours and 50 minutes, during May 1994, after its conversion to Mk2, and immediately prior to delivery to Northern Ireland. I had a number of serious problems causing engines to be replaced twice in a very short period, alarming problems with the flying controls, and other issues including malfunctioning warning systems. It was not uncharacteristic of the Mk2 aircraft at that time.

Nonetheless, I cannot explain why the aircraft flew into the Mull of Kintyre. Nor do I believe anyone can. Too little remained of the aircraft (the absence of evidence of mechanical failure is not the same as no mechanical failure) and nothing but conjecture has ever been possible as to the actions of the crew. The ruling, that the absence of evidence of mechanical failure equates to negligence on the part of the pilots, seems to me entirely insupportable. We cannot know what was taking place in the cockpit immediately prior to its loss. It is my suspicion that the crew were placed in an untenable position by the task they had been set, the weather in which they were operating, by the unpredictable and complex technical problems of the aircraft they were flying and on which they had minimal training, and by the decisions made by their chain of command. The same chain of command, ultimately, that then condemned their failure to resolve the subsequent crisis.

Was I comfortable flying the Chinook at the time?

Not entirely, but believed greatly in my own ability, the cause in which I was engaged, and the people with whom I served. I understood there to be an operational imperative, and that risk was to be balanced and managed.

Perhaps a more pertinent question is would I, as a senior officer, ask the same of those who serve under me now? No. Categorically not. Such a position would be legally and morally untenable.

The Initial Inquiry

The Board of Inquiry conducted by Wing Commander Andrew Pulford was thorough and highly professional. However, I regret to say that I believe the subsequent decision by two senior officers to accuse the deceased of negligence was procedurally unnecessary, legally dubious, and morally bankrupt. As I have become more experienced in the conduct of operations and the management of people over the long years since this accident, I have become more, not less, convinced of this.

It was of interest that the subsequent Air Officer Commanding 1 Group, Air Vice Marshal Jock Stirrup, having recently assumed command and inspecting the Chinook detachment in the Balkans, where I was commanding at the time, called me to one side and advised me that he did not agree with the handling of the affair by his predecessor. He was under no obligation to comment, but chose to.

I may have been outspoken in suggesting 'vested interests', conscious or otherwise, in condemning the deceased. The manner in which institutions and individuals respond, collectively and individually, to protect interest is complex. The culture in the RAF at the time was most certainly a 'blame' culture; it would have been easier to keep the aircraft in service, delivering operational effect, if an individual, rather than a machine, a process or an organisation were to be found at fault. Such a judgment would not be reached today.

<u>The reputation of the 7 Squadron Special Forces Flight</u>

You referred to the reputation of the Special Forces Flight and comments that they were believed to be 'reckless'. The safety record of the Special Forces unit is second to none. The best personnel are selected and then undertake additional specialist training, which can take up to a year, before achieving mission status. The need for discreet, reliable delivery of effect is central to the operational mission. These aircraft and crews have operated throughout the world in the most extreme operational and environmental conditions since 1985, with very few incidents. A reckless pilot would be an unacceptable risk in an environment where the loss of an aircraft, or compromise of a discreet mission, would have significantly greater impact than in a conventional mission. It is testament to their professionalism that so little is known of what they do.

<u>Summary</u>

I knew the aircraft, crews and procedures involved in events surrounding the loss of ZD576 intimately, probably more so than any other surviving officer.

What took place on the Mull of Kintyre was a tragic loss and a terrible waste of talented lives. The circumstances were complex, and those who died had very limited control over the long chain of events and decisions that led to that fatal hillside. What took place afterwards, however, was a fundamental injustice which has been a weeping sore ever since. You are uniquely placed to heal this sore. I would beseech you to do so, for those who died, for those who serve, and for those who continue to grieve.

Carl Scott

*

In 1996, the then Flight Lieutenant Scott had stated in his precognition to the Fatal Accident Inquiry:

'Boeing have a vested interest in deterring any report which leaves them liable.

The company has shown a determination in the past to influence the outcome of inquiries. When Wing Commander Malcolm Pledger took command of 78 Squadron in the Falkland Islands in February 1988, I asked him to brief the Chinook Flight on the findings of the Board of Inquiry (ZA721, 7 killed), as this had not then been published. As chairman of the Board he briefed two findings: the first his own most probable cause (failure of a hydraulic jack due to poor quality control at Boeing), and then that which would actually be published due to the failure of MoD to face pressure brought to bear by Boeing (cause unknown)'.

Given the aircraft being unairworthy was concealed, this was the most incriminatory evidence heard. It can be seen he was entirely consistent. Neither MoD nor Boeing offered any challenge. Of note, Wing Commander Pledger, as Air Chief Marshal Sir, was unfairly criticised in the Nimrod Review of 2009 - something that no doubt came as a relief to those truly responsible.

Some perspective is needed here. MoD's relationship with Boeing must be considered. It would be fair to characterise this as supine appeasement. Boeing knew from long experience that MoD would do little or nothing about poor quality control. And MoD admits that, to preserve UK/US relations, it will not release or use vital information that would help prevent recurrence.

Partly as a consequence, in August 1992 the RAF Director of Flight Safety questioned Boeing's ability to act as an *'offshore Design Authority'*.[107] There can be no greater condemnation of a company purporting to be an Aircraft Design Authority, or of the organisation that made the appointment allowing it to remain. No action was taken. It is unclear if Boeing knew of this criticism.

Notwithstanding, the basic rule of risk management, 'avoid the avoidable, manage the unavoidable', went unheeded. With funding taking year on year cuts, but the workload increasing, within a few short years this became the norm. More posts disappeared. Remaining staff in MoD found themselves at the mercy of companies, given the run around, and unable to concentrate on what they were meant to be doing.

*

The intervening years tell us Air Commodore Scott was mistaken about one thing. He thought such protection of vested interests would not happen in 2011. Eight months later, on 8 November 2011, Flight Lieutenant Sean Cunningham was killed when he inadvertently ejected from Hawk

---

107 D/IFS(RAF)/125/30/2/1, 7 August 1992 - CHART report, paragraph 10.

XX177 while on the ground, and his parachute did not open. MoD and the Health and Safety Executive blamed Martin-Baker, the ejection seat manufacturer, saying the company had not provided sufficient information to service the seat correctly. Despite first-hand witnesses, Air Publications, 12 RAF-produced training videos, and even the Judge, Mrs Justice Carr DBE, naming the correct MoD recipient of the information, the company was fined £1.1M.[108]

There were other similarities. MoD concealed that the accident was a recurrence. It grossly misled legal authorities and the courts. There was no valid Safety Case. Aircraft documentation was falsely certified. The police and Crown Prosecution Service knew this, and took no action.

Knowing all this, the Health and Safety Executive proceeded with a malicious prosecution, lying to the Judge and the Cunningham family.

The lead anomaly? Precisely the same as ZD576.

---

108 'Red 5' (David Hill, 2019).

PART 5 - RAIN UNRAVELLED TALES

'It is a capital mistake to theorise before one has data. Insensibly one begins to twist facts to suit theories, instead of theories to suit facts'.
Sir Arthur Conan Doyle, 'Sherlock Holmes'

15. A second aircraft [109]

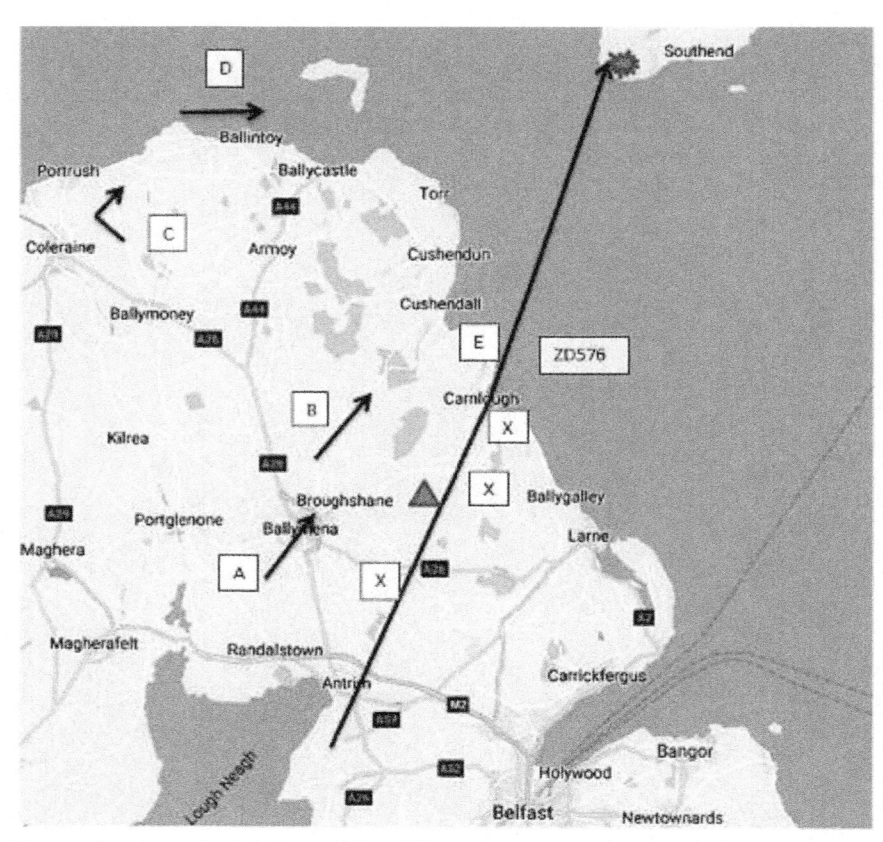

Figure 9: Aircraft sightings 1730-1755, 2 June 1994 *(Author, using MoD, RUC and witness data)*

The main track is that of ZD576, confirmed by eight interviewed witnesses (x) along the route from Antrim to Carnlough. While of course they could not say it was ZD576, the timings are consistent with take-off from Aldergrove at around 1742. The triangle is Slemish Mountain - witnesses confirmed the aircraft passed to the east.

Sighting A was by former soldier Alexander Bradley and timed at approximately 1730. The arrowhead is his position. He stated, to the Royal

---

[109] Adapted and updated from 'Their Greatest Disgrace' (David Hill, 2016).

Ulster Constabulary, that a Chinook flew directly overhead. This was not ZD576. Sighting B was by dentist Hugh McCann at Glenravel, the timing consistent with it being the same aircraft as A.

Sighting C was by school teacher Nevin Taggart and his parents at around 1730. Sighting(s) D are mentioned in Mr Taggart's evidence, the timing consistent with C - but his sources remain unconfirmed. He described the paint scheme as triple-tone, grey, light brown and dark brown.[110] ZD576 was of essentially uniform colour. It cannot be said A/B and C/D are the same aircraft, but allowing for a small margin of error by witnesses it is entirely possible.

The Board of Inquiry referred to sightings A/B, but not C/D. Until the House of Lords Select Committee sat in 2001, Mr Taggart assumed the aircraft he saw was ZD576. When it became clear the timings released by MoD precluded this, he wrote to MPs William Ross and James Arbuthnot, the latter at the time chair of the Mull of Kintyre campaign group.

On 15 February 2001, Mr Ross questioned John Spellar MP, Minister for the Armed Forces:

'How many Chinook helicopters were flown into and out of Northern Ireland on 2 June 1994; and what their flight times and routes were?'

'No Chinook helicopters flew into Northern Ireland on 2 June 1994. One flew out, that being Chinook ZD576 which left RAF Aldergrove at 1742'.

Spellar, and the Joint Air Tasking Operations Centre who tasked the flight, were only asked about Chinooks, and would only include RAF aircraft in their reply. Specifying *'into'* and *'out of'* Northern Ireland, and excluding a firm question about other operators, permitted the answer to ignore other tandemrotor aircraft, such as (US Navy) CH-46 Sea Knights, and aircraft flying solely within Northern Ireland airspace.

In a House of Lords adjournment debate on 1 November 1999, Lord Rathcavan (Hugh O'Neill) spoke of other witnesses who had not been interviewed:

'It appeared to be flying at a height of 100 feet, at which it makes a huge noise and vibrations on the ground. In Carnlough the milkman, Ambrose McSparren, remembers how it rattled windows and shook buildings. He could even see the faces of the passengers looking out of the port windows, a woman in the front window.

The Chinook gained height a little as it followed the coast beyond Carnlough

---

110 Taggart/Hill, 4 October 2016, 10:27.

harbour towards the cliff-top Catholic college of Garron Tower where priests at a conference ran out to see it fly just below them and turn out to sea, aiming slightly to the left, as they thought, of the Mull. (Sighting E).

Why did the earlier investigations not take evidence from those who saw the Chinook flying so close that they could see the faces of its unfortunate passengers? If the board of inquiry is to be reopened, it should look seriously at what appears to have been evidence previously ignored or overlooked, which raises further doubts about the previous conclusions'.

Casual observers inferred that everyone was discussing ZD576. Clearly, they were not. No Inquiry sought to resolve these contradictions. A picture tells a thousand words. Can the investigation be said to be complete lacking thorough assessment of this evidence? Mr Taggart became yet another eye-witness, along with the fishermen and yachtsman Ian MacLeod, whom the RAF refused to interview in preference to 'witnesses' who saw nothing.

Given Mr Taggart's astute observation that the track of C/D would converge with ZD576 at the Mull of Kintyre (as would A/B), one must then look further to see if there is evidence of other aircraft at the Mull, at or around the time of the accident...

*

Flight Lieutenant Hamish Millar, an Air Traffic Control Officer, gave evidence of a much slower target moving up the west coast of the Mull, between the lighthouse and Machrihanish, <u>after</u> the accident. The data he talked of was from the Beinn Haoidhinis radar station on Tiree, 90 miles north north west of the lighthouse. It could 'see' approaches from the south or south west, but with blind spots due to terrain masking. He described this track as having come from the south west (so not ZD576). Annex AJ to the Board's report ('Scottish ATCC (Military) Radar Replay Photographs') shows it then heading generally northwards after passing the lighthouse, on an erratic track. Flight Lieutenant Millar estimated its speed at 30-50 knots. Its height is not known.

The radar recorded 13 'hits' between 1802:31 and 1806:52, the target travelling around 2.2nm and moving approximately 1.1nm north. The last two hits coincide, yet are nine seconds apart. That is, the target was stationary (in a Force 6 wind), or had moved and returned to that point. The average speed is consistent with the lower end of Flight Lieutenant Millar's estimation.

Ignoring Flight Lieutenant Millar, the radar evidence and prevailing wind, the RAF's preferred hypothesis was that the radar detected airborne debris from the crash. It did not discuss the radar's capability. For example, could it detect small fragments, and would they produce a single hit at each scan after being blown in the wind for seven minutes? As the Board did not think a radar contact in the immediate vicinity, immediately after the crash, of any relevance, one can only speculate. But as the time of each hit is known, it can be deduced two of the fastest legs were directly across the wind, yet the slowest was wind assisted; suggesting controlled movement.

Taken in isolation the Tiree radar data is meaningless, in the sense it discusses a period after the crash. But it is the clue something is wrong and much is missing. Also, depending on target height, Tiree had direct line of sight to sightings C/D. It is unimaginable this was not asked, so why is there no mention? The reader should not have to infer - there should be a positive statement.

One would think such an obvious and unexplained anomaly would warrant more, but Flight Lieutenant Millar was not interviewed by the Board. With so many loose ends, probity is in doubt.

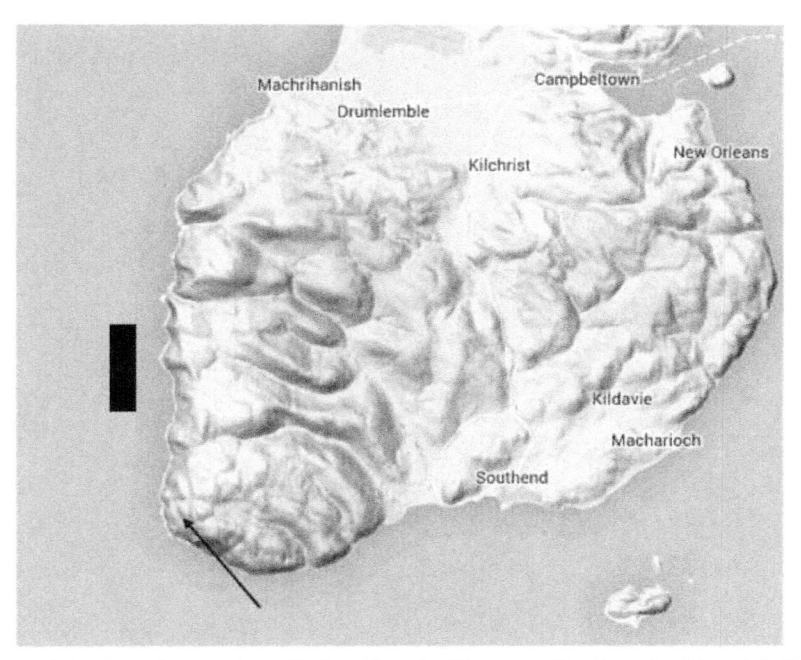

Figure 10: Southern tip of the South Kintyre Peninsula (the Mull of Kintyre) showing area of Tiree radar trace and impact site

There is another possibility - the erratic track of the radar target might suggest a collision. Or a near miss, forcing avoiding action. On 29 September 1994, Belfast Telegraph journalist Eric Waugh reported:

'Two RAF officers at a Lincolnshire base, one a senior communications officer, have confirmed that Americans (US Navy) were at the scene of the crash first. When the British servicemen asked them to explain themselves, they were told: "We are looking for something that belongs to us"'.

Did they think one of their own aircraft had crashed? And why were *they* not interviewed?

16. If there is no evidence, there is no logic

Murder / suicide by aircrew

While the very notion is distasteful, it is not unknown and the Board of Inquiry had to consider it (and dismissed it).[111]

The Board's report included, at Annex V, the report of Principal Psychologist Dr John W. Chappelow, a recognised expert in accident causation. In many ways his approach was the reverse of Group Captain Crawford; who, you will recall, wrote at length why no blame could be apportioned, then inexplicably criticised Flight Lieutenant Tapper.

Here, Dr Chappelow spent almost his entire report repeating the official line, then suddenly destroyed it at the end:

'The lack of a Cockpit Voice Recorder on the Chinook has two major consequences: the competence and skill of the crew are unavoidably but invidiously called into question in a speculative manner. And, if they did fail, the lessons that could have been learned from their tragic error are denied to their colleagues. Firm conclusions are not possible and a major distraction of unknown cause cannot be discounted'.

The Lords put this to the Board President on 27 September 2001:

'I am a little puzzled by your fairly cavalier dismissal of technical failures, and ready acceptance of a psychologist's report which does not seem to be as supportive as you suggest. (It) does not seem to be an assessment, it seems to be speculation'.

The President replied:

'The psychologist came up with their character traits and suggested what might have been'.

Annex V makes no mention of character traits, nor does it make any original suggestions.

Breakfast

The Board was required to consider whether the crew were fed and well-rested. Due to a lack of witnesses it was *'unable to ascertain whether breakfast was taken by Flight Lieutenant Tapper'*. An innocuous passage, of no consequence, and the Board dismissed the matter.

Unfortunately, this was seized upon by a retired RAF pilot who postulated,

---

111 For example, Germanwings Flight 9525, deliberately crashed by the pilot on 24 March 2015, killing 150.

on a military internet forum, self-induced fatigue, with Flight Lieutenant Tapper's alleged negligence made worse by not eating since the previous evening. Such jumps, from *unable to ascertain* to *definitely happened*, were a constant feature of the RAF's case. He avoided the fact that the Board confirmed Flight Lieutenant Cook, the handling pilot, had been served breakfast. And, given the flight took off in the early evening, it might anyway have been more appropriate to confirm the crew had eaten lunch.

Many asked who was pressing his buttons. In time, misguided allegiances became clear. He had served on the staff of Air Vice Marshal Day.

Tampering with FADEC software

This was suggested by Dublin magazine, Phoenix. (Unconnected to Dr Susan Phoenix). It assumes the software in the Digital Electronic Control Units was written with the facility to remotely increase, decrease or cease fuel flow to the engines. By no means technically impossible, but...

The feature would have to be incorporated during development, in such a way as to avoid detection during independent verification. Later, the necessary remote-control device would have to find its way into the hands of an (unidentified) operator, who would be hoping a Mk2 was selected for the flight to Fort George. Always assuming he/she was aware of the highly classified details surrounding the transport arrangements. And so on...

There are aspects of the case where embarrassing information was relatively easy to conceal, as it remained under the control of those who had most reason to hide it. Here, however, the sheer number of people involved, from disparate organisations, and over a long period, meant control of information would be impossible. Nevertheless, it served as a reminder that poor, unverified software could cause unplanned and catastrophic changes in fuel flow.

IRA / Bomb / Projectile

The possibility of a terrorist attack was quickly mooted in the media. The indecent haste with which the Government implied pilot error in poor weather provided ammunition. Also, Mr Holbrook was asked if had seen mortar tubes or rocket launch equipment on the Scottish fishing vessels he had passed. But, surely, the perpetrator(s) would have publicised such a triumph? And see above - the same obstacles exist.

If there was one person in 1994 who would recognise bomb damage, it was Tony Cable. He had been the Senior Air Accidents Investigation Branch

Inspector when Pan Am Flight 103 exploded over Lockerbie on 21 December 1988. I know Mr Cable well, and always find him open and honest, as well as supremely competent. Yes, often that honesty results in an answer of *'I don't know'*, but that is the nature of accident investigation. It breeds a cautious attitude. To make a positive statement requires proof, and Inspectors know they will be required to substantiate their statements in court. (Whereas, MoD is not). They are always aware that the unscrupulous will twist their words.

Mr Cable concluded there was no evidence of bombs or explosive projectiles. That should be good enough, but was corroborated by Dr Henry Drysdale, a consultant in forensic pathology employed by the RAF Institute of Pathology and Tropical medicine:

'In the event no such (shrapnel) wounds were discovered and no fragments were recovered from within the bodies, burned or unburned. They had suffered internal rather than penetrant forces'.[112]

I accept this evidence without hesitation.

---

112 Board of Inquiry report, Annex G.

17. State sponsored murder

This chapter discusses four intertwined hypotheses. I am not entirely sure the first three named are real identities, and so similar is their work it is possible they are one and the same person, or a collective. None have replied to my approaches. However, it is necessary to mention them as they all cite the hypothesis of the fourth contributor, Walter Kennedy, that an unknown person lured the aircraft onto Beinn na Lice by means of a covert homing device.

'Finian Cunningham', 'Peter Eyre' and 'Trowbridge H. Ford'

Mr Cunningham's primary article was published in November 2011, following the overturn of the findings, and has now been deleted. He believes the accident was an *'inside job'* by the British authorities, to bring about an end to the conflict in Northern Ireland.

> *'Nearly three months after the Chinook deaths, the IRA announced what many analysts had believed would be unthinkable - its historic ceasefire on 31 August 1994, calling for a "complete cessation of armed struggle". That move paved the way for the Good Friday Agreement in 1998. The men onboard that Chinook would take to their graves many dark secrets about Britain's "dirty war" operations, including how British forces colluded with Protestant loyalist death squads. From the British Government point of view, they would have been viewed as an obstacle to the peace process'.*

Mr Kennedy often supported this view[113], and Mr Cunningham goes on to summarise and agree with his hypothesis, quoting him thus:

> *'From the very beginning, this has smacked of a cover-up. The official account is demonstrably not true in light of the flight and instrument data. Given the strong political motives, there is powerful reason for why it could have been sabotage. And now there is evidence of the technical means by which this sabotage could have been carried out'.*

*

Mr Eyre insists all 29 occupants were shot in the head. He agrees 29 bodies were recovered, so one is left to infer that the assassin (or assassins, he doesn't say) parachuted to safety somewhere close to the coastline beneath the lighthouse. He claims, variously, the perpetrators belonged to MI5,

---

113 https://www.pprune.org/military-aviation/39182-chinook-still-hitting-back-3-merged-124.html, Walter Kennedy, 2 August 2006.

MI6 and the Department of Trade and Industry.[114]

Mr Eyre also agrees with Mr Kennedy's hypothesis, implying two assassination teams, one onboard and one on the hill.

At the time, the police were required to follow any evidence deemed credible by virtue of being submitted by a credible witness. Mr Eyre reports that the (Derbyshire) police ignored him.

Why do I repeat such a hypothesis? Mr Eyre formally submitted it to the Mull of Kintyre Review, which was required to consider it, however briefly. In doing so, he implied that various campaigners, including myself, John and the late Captain Ralph Kohn, agreed with him. A formal denial had to be issued.[115]

*

In December 2011 Mr Ford published a piece 'MI5 killers sabotaged Chinook helicopter that crashed at Mull of Kintyre in 1994 finally exposed?', claiming it was a combined MI5/British Army Force Research Unit operation. The tone and political leaning is similar to that of Mr Cunningham but, again, suddenly veers off (this time uncredited) into Mr Kennedy's hypothesis. However, Mr Ford's premise is that the crew intended landing near the crash site, to pick up IRA informer Martin McGartland and take him to Fort George.[116]

Mr Walter Kennedy

Mr Kennedy has stated he does not wish to be associated with Messrs Eyre, Cunningham or Trowbridge - who simply agree with him without analysing his hypothesis or acknowledging contradictions.[117]

Rather, he believes the RAF was seeking to conduct an *ad hoc* demonstration of the Covert Personnel Locator System (CPLS), to Security Forces and Army personnel who would soon use it. But, there was *'malpractice by someone on the ground'* who misled the pilots regarding range and bearing to the intended landing zone, luring them on to higher ground by means of a PRC-112 radio, which the CPLS homed on to.[118]

---

114 https://eyreinternational.wordpress.com/2011/05/25/
115 Kohn/Passa (Mull of Kintyre Review Secretary), 4 November 2010, 15:12.
116 https://flyingcuttlefish.wordpress.com/2011/12/04/sabotaged- Chinook/
117 E-mail Kennedy/Hill, 30 November 2020 16:22.
118 https://www.pprune.org/military-aviation/39182-chinook-still-hitting-back-3-merged-179.html Walter Kennedy, 4 August 2008.

'I believe that the person with the PRC-112 was wilfully out of position, that this crash was contrived'.[119]

I agree it is possible a UK/US collaborative trial was being planned, and ZD576 fitted with CPLS in anticipation. The RAF will not say if it *was* fitted, but an aircrewman on the delivery flight to Aldergrove advises that it was. While I cannot confirm this, he was specific enough to say where - on an avionic pallet previously fitted to Mk1, which is consistent with the later Service Deviation permitting use of CPLS in Mk2.[120] [121] This is a good example of the difficulties families and campaigners faced - a barrage of disinformation from RAF pilots on the internet claimed the equipment simply did not exist. Despite the Service Deviation, to this day (and much to Mr Kennedy's frustration), they continue to insist there is no such thing.

In my opinion no such trial would be approved or attempted during this sortie. While that does not preclude an unofficial trial (which are common), I do not believe any pilot would trust such a beacon when approaching mist-covered ground.

While drafting this chapter I prepared a lengthy analysis of Mr Kennedy's hypothesis. (It is more than that - it is part theory because CPLS exists and was fitted to Chinook). But upon reflection, to give it more space than others would be to lend it credence, when in fact it ignores most of the known facts I have outlined. In particular, it does not address a fundamental question: *Why would they discard the relevant waypoint if intending to land at or close to it?*

Ironically, while I disagree with Mr Kennedy's conclusion, his work relies entirely on the lead anomaly, revealing a more plausible cause...

Classified equipment

Classified equipment *must* be listed in a Classified Supplement to the Release to Service. The Table of Contents *must* note if there is a Supplement, but it is only issued on a 'need to know' basis. If there is no Supplement, it must say 'NONE'. No version of the Release gives any indication, either way. However, the Board of Inquiry revealed that classified equipment was fitted to ZD576. Squadron Leader Stephen

---

119 https://www.pprune.org/military-aviation/39182-chinook-still-hitting-back-3-merged-381.html Walter Kennedy, 22 March 2011.

120 Witness/Hill, 2 April 2009.

121 Service Deviation 30/95 (Category 1) - Homer for Covert Personnel Locator System (CPLS), 9 November 1995.

Brough, an engineer with 7 Squadron at RAF Odiham, provided the detail in his statement, but MoD redacted it in the version supplied to families:

'The only classified item in the Chinook HC2 standard Northern Ireland role fit is the ▮▮▮▮▮▮▮▮▮▮▮▮▮▮▮▮▮▮▮▮▮▮▮▮.'

Mr Kennedy maintained for many years that this conceals *'Covert Personnel Locator System'*, and indeed this is a close fit. But on 24 August 2020 the Air Historical Branch (RAF) confirmed the redaction referred to *'a power control unit that has no locational, navigational, or communication function'*.[122] That only leaves the *'ALQ-157 IRJ Control Power Supply Unit'*, which is a precise fit. (IRJ - Infra-Red Jammer). This was the only approved and classified role equipment in Mk2. Mr Kennedy has, reasonably, pointed out to me that only by using the acronym does this fit. All I can say is that, having managed this equipment for the Fleet Air Arm from 1985-87, 'IRJ' was always used; and I believe Squadron Leader Brough would do likewise. In any case, current pilots have confirmed the content to me.

There is no valid security reason for the redaction. It is the detailed function of the Control Power Supply Unit (CPSU) that is SECRET. Its existence and basic function are not. The Air Accidents Investigation Branch did not mention the system, so its status cannot be known. None of the images released show any part of it. Almost certainly, the RAF sought to conceal the presence of a high powered (>2kW) equipment known to cause serious Electro-Magnetic Interference in the aircraft. It knew it <u>could</u> have contributed to cause, but wasn't wise enough to realise that the admission it was on board revealed a serious breach of the airworthiness regulations.

ALQ-157 system description

ALQ-157 is an omni-directional Countermeasures System. Its purpose is to protect the aircraft from heat-seeking missiles, and indeed the Board noted the *'realistic'* threat of Surface to Air Missiles.[123] Their guidance system is jammed by radiating controlled, pulsed, high intensity infra-red energy. There are five pre-set jamming patterns, and more can be programmed. It is the detail of these patterns that is classified.

The Transmitters are located aft, one under each engine, each providing 180° coverage. The Control Indicator is a simple press-to-test device with a lamp for each Transmitter. The 'brain' of the system is the CPSU, located

---

122 Letter D/AHB(RAF)928/2020, 24 August 2020.
123 Board of Inquiry report, Part 2, paragraph 33.

in the cabin (on the pallet also hosting CPLS).

The system was approved for Chinook HC Mk1 in 1988. The Release to Service carried various warnings, including an adverse effect on the Gyro Magnetic Compass. Incorrectly, it was included in Section L (Radio) of the Release. This may seem minor, but if aircrew were seeking to remind themselves about Electronic Warfare or Role Equipment limitations, they would tend not to look in the Radio section.

Figure 11: AN/ALQ-157 Infra-Red Countermeasures System (l-r Transmitter (1), Control Power Supply Unit, EMI Filter, Transmitter (2) and (front) Control Indicator). *(Loral Electro-Optical Systems)*

It was not included in any Boscombe Down assessment at the point of Mk2 Release to Service (November 1993). In March 1994 it was inserted for the first time, in Section T (Role Equipment). The extensive Mk1 warnings and limitations were replaced with a simple statement:

'This equipment may be used but pending further trials no guarantee of equipment performance can be given'.[124]

This speaks volumes about immaturity of the Mk2 trials and release process. Aircrew would query why the 'new' Mk2 had regressed, after an expensive upgrade. Just as it had regressed in other areas.

Concurrently, the Transmitters were repositioned under Special Trials Fit/Chinook/204. No reason was given, but this might imply poor performance in the original Mk1 positions, partial mitigation of known Electro-Magnetic Compatibility problems, or a need to create distance

---

124 Release to Service, Section T (Role Equipment), paragraph 6.

from susceptible equipment or wiring. As ever, this must be qualified by the aircraft's overall status - *not to be relied upon in any way*.

The above implies the system was removed before or during conversion to Mk2. It is known Boeing were, rightly, concerned over the undocumented standard of the first aircraft delivered for conversion, removing and setting aside everything they had not appraised or had not been contracted to incorporate into the design. This is why, in late-October 1993, Boscombe still did not have a representative Mk2 to trial.

When equipment is fitted under Service Engineered Modifications or Special Trials Fits (ostensibly to save time and money, but often at the expense of performance and safety) the airworthiness audit trail is almost always broken. Primarily, there is seldom supporting documentation, and no Safety Case update. MoD leaves itself no choice but to allow Aircraft Design Authorities to ignore such changes, as no company can be expected to underwrite the safety of a modification it has no say in.

Once fitted, if MoD decides to integrate it with existing aircraft systems (by no means a given) it is especially important that the installation design is appraised by the Aircraft Design Authority. As mentioned before, the oversight committee whose role it was to police this was disbanded in June 1991, without replacement.

In other words, Boeing would/could only underwrite a build standard that corresponded with the Master Record Index. The significant undocumented gaps between the Boeing and RAF build standards are indicative of total breakdown of configuration control. This is what the Director of Flight Safety had warned the RAF Chief Engineer and the Assistant Chief of the Air Staff about in August 1992.

But here, matters are potentially far more serious. By the RAF's own admission, ALQ-157 caused Electro-Magnetic Interference. If it proved to be a root cause of the accident, then Boeing would have every right to walk away. Doubly so if the affected equipment had also been installed without Boeing's involvement, or had been declared *'positively dangerous'*. MoD pays Design Authorities vast sums to accept responsibility for product safety and underwrite installed performance. But then proceeds to waive any right to make a claim by breaching its own airworthiness regulations. The company engineers shake their heads in wonderment and despair. Their accountants and lawyers rub their hands in glee.

*

The proper mitigation is to agree, before contract award, the 'Induction Build Standard', and to ensure the contract includes, at least, Cover

Modification action. Preferably Superseding Cover Modification action, whereby the design responsibility transfers to the company. Bypassing this process guarantees subsequent problems. As it did in 2011, when the upgrade to Chinook Mk4 under 'Project Julius' had no agreed Induction Build Standard, significantly delaying armament safety certification.

This lack of effective configuration control had been identified by the resident RAF team in Philadelphia in 1983. The RAF had lost three Chinooks during the Falklands War the previous year, and ordered another eight to supplement the first buy of 33. During final assembly of the first aircraft, RAF engineers identified a host of faults. Checking the minutes of original acceptance meeting for the first batch, when there were numerous requests for changes and all incorporated in the 33, these changes were now absent from the new batch. Boeing sought to persuade the senior RAF officer that the aircraft should be released to the UK, and a working party would make the necessary changes at Odiham. He correctly declined, and after much argument the changes were made on the production line in Philadelphia. That is, either a deliberate decision was made by Boeing to omit them, or the drawings were not up-to-date.

Yet nothing was done to correct the root failure. In 1992/93, Air Technical Publications staff from Glasgow encountered the same problem when visiting Philadelphia to try to understand why the Mk1 (and hence Mk2) publications were so poor. In fact, the civilian head of the Department (a former RAF engineer) developed a 'get well' programme for Boeing, who republished it in their own name. But it is clear from the evidence of Chief of Defence Procurement Sir Robert Walmsley, to the Public Accounts Committee on 3 March 1999, that it wasn't implemented and sustained.

*

In 2011 the Chinook Project Team underwent a Military Aviation Authority (MAA) audit, following the formation of the MAA post-Nimrod Review. It received a 'Very Good' pass. One can only assume this airworthiness audit overlooked the basic components of airworthiness.

In 2012 integration of ALQ-157 into a Defensive Aids Suite upgrade was being planned. As the CPSU had a history of catching fire (!), an audit was undertaken to ensure there was a stable airworthiness and contractual baseline. As with the FADEC software, there was no Certificate of Design and Performance, a pre-requisite to equipment being permitted in the aircraft. There was no recorded build standard or Radio Installation Memorandum, and the system was still not under configuration control. There was no safety statement, so it had not been included in the Chinook

Whole Aircraft Safety Case - 19 years after the Assistant Chief of the Air Staff had signed to say he was satisfied all this had been carried out.

Conclusions

Mr Kennedy's work served to highlight that classified equipment got on board, despite there being no clearance. It doesn't matter if it was Covert Personnel Locator System or the Control Power Supply Unit. By the RAF's own admission it was there, when it shouldn't have been, and there was potential for it to cause flight safety critical problems.

But wilder hypotheses provide only a welcome diversion for MoD, and anguish for the families. There is nothing to support the suggestion of State sponsored murder. The fundamental obstacle is that the would-be perpetrators would have to dictate and control every event. It is usually wiser to look at things from another direction.

Therefore, I reject the notion, while mindful of the possibility of a high-power system causing Electro-Magnetic Inference, and in turn a FADEC-related Undemanded Flight Control Movement. As ever, the best clues can be found in what MoD is prepared to conceal and lie about...

PART 6 - UNDEMANDED FLIGHT CONTROL MOVEMENTS (UFCM)

MoD defines Undemanded Flight Control Movement as:

'An unexplained change of aircraft in-flight attitude without a legitimate flying control input, or any movement of flying control input controls when there should be none, or any movement of flying control surfaces or systems without a corresponding legitimate input'.

Flight Lieutenant Iain MacFarlane to the Fatal Accident Inquiry:

'It would not make sense to practise for these emergencies, because there is no course of action which is going to get you out of the problem. To that extent they are feared. At least if an engine stops or catches fire you can do something about it. I don't believe the Board have taken full account of the possibility of pre-impact control malfunction, i.e. intermittent jams'.

18. UFCM history 1994-2001

In June 2000 MoD advised Martin Bell MP of six UFCMs involving Chinooks in 1994, five in 1995, six in 1996, five in 1997, seven in 1998 and six in 1999 - 35 incidents since the accident, in six of which the cause was never found. The following year, Robert Key MP asked how many had occurred since 1 January 1999. MoD revealed there had been 24 in the 28 month period to July 2001. In all but one the cause was a faulty Automatic Flight Control System and/or faulty Directional Gyro.

Due to the conversion programme there were fewer Chinooks available in 1994/5, but it can be seen the rate of arisings is fairly constant (and high, in a small fleet), despite understanding improving. MoD did not expand on causes, or if any were found to be defects (whereby the basic quality of the design is to blame). Nor did it say what, if anything, was being done. Did the RAF simply decide to accept the risk of this rate of UFCMs continuing unchecked? Were UFCMs even acknowledged as a risk in the first place? We have already seen that a notification from February 1994 had still not been promulgated to aircrew after the accident, despite recurrences.

Mr Key further asked the Secretary of State to list:

'Each occasion on which pilots have temporarily lost control of RAF Chinook helicopters during an uncommanded flying control movement'.

Minister for the Armed Forces Adam Ingram MP replied:

'No such instances have occurred. Aircrew have retained full control whenever an uncommanded flying control movement has taken place'.

This was an outright lie, the most obvious example being the loss of ZA721 in February 1987, killing seven. (Discussed later). MoD's position, confirmed by Mr Ingram, was that these historical failures were irrelevant if it could not be proven they occurred on ZD576 on 2 June 1994.[125]

Why would MoD say something so obviously irrational, defying good engineering practice and its own safety regulations? Because it was stuck firmly between a rock and a hard place. Having ceased trend failure analysis some years earlier (particularly on avionics), it could hardly admit it was a vital tool in maintaining airworthiness.

---

125 Letter from Adam Ingram MP, /Min(AF)/AI 4573/05/C/LN, 10 November 2005. (Trend failures, as applied to ZD576).

Automatic Flight Control System (AFCS)

The main functions of the dual AFCS provide:

- Stability about all axes
- Bank angle, heading, airspeed and pitch attitude hold
- Positive stick gradient
- Heading select
- Longitudinal Cyclic Trim

With both systems ON, each provides half of the required control input. With one ON, the single system provides the total required input. That is simplistic - there are many interrelated and interdependent components.

Squadron Leader Robert Burke's evidence now assumes greater import. He characterised these AFCS faults, resulting in violent porpoising, as a *'constant occurrence'*. The Board would understand that test pilots solve problems by exposing themselves to often unquantifiable risk, and develop solutions which are then used in pilot training. So poor was the information available on Chinook, Burke's vast experience made him uniquely qualified to help understand the accident. Yet he was ordered not to assist the investigation, and not called as a witness by the Board. Why?

Aircrew perspective

The reaction time to major emergencies can be long. First response will usually take a few seconds. However an insidious failure, or a set of circumstances not covered by the Flight Reference Cards, or not practised in the simulator (if a suitable one exists), can lead to significantly longer reaction times. First the crew must recognise something is wrong - difficult when faced with false warnings and little helpful information. They must then diagnose the problem and work out what to do. The first rule is 'fly the aircraft', but that might not be possible with a UFCM.

Various types of UFCM were a known occurrence. Squadron Leader Burke was able to recover on the occasions it happened to him, as he had sufficient height. A loss of around 1500 feet during certain events could be expected. ZD576 was cleared down to 50 feet. To approve such a clearance, one must be very confident that the risk of UFCMs occurring is negligible. And that is what the Assistant Chief of the Air Staff did say, when issuing his Release to Service. What evidence did he use, given the ongoing investigations into serious UFCMs that were puzzling other users?

*

ZD576 was flying below cloud and in sight of the surface, towards a headland whose upper slopes were shrouded in low level localised mist, on a regular route requiring a slight left turn to handrail the coast, where visibility remained good. The obvious question is: *Why did it not make that turn?* The Board of Inquiry postulated a 'cruise climb' was attempted, but an inappropriate rate of climb selected - 1,000 feet per minute, at 150 knots Indicated Airspeed. (~180 knots Groundspeed). The Commanding Officer at RAF Odiham, Group Captain Crawford, rejected the notion as an *'unrecognisable'* Chinook technique.[126]

Let us pause and consider this extraordinary put-down. Crawford was provided with an advance draft of the Board's report, and he asked some of his senior pilots to read it and comment.[127] It is inconceivable he did not discuss his (and the pilots') concerns with the President. There would be a conversation among gentlemen. Crawford would tell the Board members what he intended saying, who would realise they would endure a degree of ridicule - which they subsequently did.

The only conclusion I can draw is that a higher authority was dictating the report's content. I have already noted that Air Vice Marshal Day's remarks were seemingly written before Crawford's were finalised. It is also known that the engineering member's sections were returned for re-write - something of great professional concern to him.

The Board maintained that the aircraft impacted at 150 knots Indicated Airspeed, ignoring the evidence that it was around 120 knots. This was not a confusion over Groundspeed and Airspeed, as the passage finishes *'coupled with the strong tailwind component, would have produced a high Groundspeed and closure rate'*.[128] By assuming the aircraft flew in a straight line between these points, while initiating a climb, it arrived at a figure of 18-20 seconds between waypoint change and impact. This 'straight-line theory', as it became known, ignored UFCM-induced porpoising mentioned earlier, and yaw kicks whereby the aircraft would suddenly begin to turn sideways. Such events would alter the speed and altitude.

The Board based its hypothesis on the alleged position and time at SuperTANS powerdown - which, ignoring the physical evidence, it assumed was at impact. From that, it imagined the time, latitude, longitude and altitude when Waypoint B was selected - and from that the supposed speed. It presented these parameters as fact, when they weren't even

---

126 Board of Inquiry report, Part 3, paragraph 1.
127 Evidence of Flight Lieutenant Iain MacFarlane at Fatal Accident Inquiry.
128 Board of Inquiry report, Part 2, paragraph 59.

educated guesses. By fixating on pilot error, contrary evidence was discarded and all other lines of inquiry closed off.

*

At the time there was no Freedom of Information Act, and none of the reports were available. The internet was in its infancy, dissemination was difficult, and very few people were involved or even interested. Most commentators took the RAF's claims as gospel. But, gradually, understanding grew as to how tenuous they were, and it became clear there were far more plausible explanations for most of the RAF's 'facts'.

But, and I make no apology for repeating this, at the most basic level the very act of selecting Waypoint B shows Flight Lieutenant Tapper made a command decision to stick to his planned route. Flight Lieutenant Iain MacFarlane, to the House of Lords on 16 October 2001:

'I would expect that they were visual with the landmass when they made that waypoint change, for a number of reasons. If they were not visual they would have kept the waypoint in the navigation equipment to give them greater situational awareness of where the landmass was.

If they were planning to continue to Corran, I would expect them to change to Waypoint B, which is what the crew elected to do, and if they were planning to change from Visual Flight Rules (VFR) to Instrument Flight Rules I would have expected them to change the waypoint to an aviation facility, probably Glasgow, Prestwick or Aldergrove, because once they had committed themselves to instrument flight they would have to get back down again at some point.

Icing limitations would not allow that descent in the Inverness area because they could not get over the Grampians with the icing clearance the aircraft had, so they would have had to get back down to VFR somewhere in the south of Scotland or Northern Ireland. I would suggest if they could not, then that would be a sortie termination with a recovery to Aldergrove'.

Twisting this, the RAF claimed the failure to turn left meant a decision had been made not to. This was illogical and not evidence-based. It did not take into account previous occurrences explaining an inability to turn, or that the waypoint change and retention of Tactical Steer mode was incompatible with a transition to Instrument Flight Rules. Why would it omit this? Again, because to mention it would swiftly reveal the aircraft was unairworthy, and that those blaming the pilots knew this. Rate of climb was a red herring. They had no intention of going over the Mull. They planned to go around it.

*

The RAF claimed ZD576 was under full control. Evidenced in part, it said, by the position the yaw ('rudder') pedals were recovered in - the left was found depressed 77%. It omitted that the pedals are connected by a fixed link, meaning a 77% displacement of one will result in a 77% displacement of the other in the opposite direction. The impact forces were principally to the starboard side of the cockpit; pushing the right pedal up and depressing the left, with feedback from distortion or severing of the control runs a predominant factor.

The initial impact damaged the cockpit and cabin, tearing off the ramp. The aircraft inverted, and the second impact completely destroyed it. The Air Accidents Investigation Branch reported:

'A number of items from the periphery of the <u>right</u> side of the cockpit were spread along the centre of the (debris) trail. These consisted of parts of the right-hand pilot's <u>rudder</u> pedal mechanism and broken-up pedal mounting box, together with the cockpit right door and door frame'.

Moreover, above 40 knots the pedals are only used to maintain balanced flight, the aircraft turned by banking using the Cyclic stick. That is, using a yaw pedal pivots the aircraft left or right about the cockpit. Turning is a secondary effect.

Ignoring this, it was claimed the position of the left pedal proved Flight Lieutenant Cook had attempted a last second flare manoeuvre by trying to climb and turn left. It also ignored the possibility that the slight nose up attitude at impact may have been an attempt to recover from a nose low attitude, or a natural upswing while 'porpoising'.

When the above is taken into account, nothing meaningful can be deduced from the pedal positions. But MoD cited Boeing's analysis, which was based on severely damaged actuators. This is what Squadron Leader Burke was investigating when told to stop assisting Mr Cable. *('There was a very strange DASH extension on the aircraft and nobody could work it out')*. But with Burke ordered to stand down, conjecture quickly became accepted 'fact' - and remains so among those who have yet to read the evidence. When Boeing took a step back after their reassessment of June 2002, MoD refused to budge.

The evidence strongly suggests Flight Lieutenant Cook either could not command the left turn, or the aircraft failed to respond correctly. If he experienced the same UFCM(s) as others, he would not retain full control. Why did the RAF discount this? Because it would reveal that aircrew had not been informed of the UFCMs Burke spoke of, nor fully trained in what to do. (It was not a scenario in the simulator, which was little more than a procedural trainer and did not 'fly' like a Chinook). The airworthiness status would be revealed. One <u>always</u> comes back to this lead anomaly.

*

The Board knew of these possibilities (in fact, probabilities). The now Group Captain Pulford told the House of Lords:

> 'Indeed, on one occasion I recall discussing the possibility of a DASH (Differential Airspeed Hold) *runaway with Squadron Leader Burke during lunch in the Officers' Mess'.*

Without elaborating, he also confirmed he was aware of FADEC failures, undemanded engine shutdowns, engine run-ups, spurious engine failure captions, and misleading and confusing cockpit engine indications. Why did he not explore this? Why did he not call Burke as a witness? It is unthinkable that Burke did not take the conversation one step further, reminding Pulford that one reason Boscombe refused to sign-off on airworthiness was because an 'essential' modification to the DASH was still outstanding from the 1987 fatal accident in the Falklands. An accident he was intimately familiar with, losing two of his engineering test team, so had made it his business to establish cause when the Board was instructed to leave well alone. Pulford would also know that Burke had prepared numerous papers and recommendations on how to manage such failures.[129] Also, the Chinook/Puma Maintenance School had submitted proposals, demonstrating wider concern about the design and likely links to the accident.[130]

Had the Board reported this evidence, it would be clear their preferred scenario was in reality a remote possibility.

Prior warnings

Before moving on to the known causes of UFCMs, I wish to discuss prior warnings by RAF Director of Flight Safety Air Commodore Martin Abbott. In August 1992 he submitted his Chinook Airworthiness Review Team (CHART) report to the RAF Chief Engineer and Assistant Chief of the Air Staff. The section 'Chinook Major Components/Systems' begins:

> *'The airworthiness of major Chinook components has been of concern for some*

---

[129] For example, ODI/79/FS/44, 6 September 1989 'Chinook Flying Control Operation in the Roll Axis', and ODI/79/FS/44, 1 August 1994 'Proposed modification to Chinook Mk2 DASH Logic'. (Both Squadron Leader Robert Burke).

[130] For example, 'Chinook HC2 Full Differential Airspeed Hold Runaway Protection', July 1994. (Sergeant R J Setter, Chinook/Puma Maintenance School).

time'.

And at Annex N, discussing their visit to RNAY Fleetlands:

> 'Of concern was the <u>large number of cracks</u> found, and partial <u>wear on flying control bearings</u> which could induce <u>Uncommanded Flight Control inputs</u>. Typical faults are <u>non-standard</u> temporary repairs (and) <u>cracked</u> Auxiliary Power Unit support brackets'.

The report dwells on transmissions, which were a general concern among both military and civilian Chinook users at the time. But at paragraph 110a, it mentions UFCMs again:

> *'In September 1991 ZA760 experienced a UFCM, characterised by a progressive roll. Although there had been many previous incidents (25 reported from 1985 to present), it was not until November 1991 that UFCM fault finding procedures were published in AP101C-0501-2(R)1 Leaflet 002. Since the introduction of the procedure there have been four UFCM incidents'.*

What the report (prepared between May and early-July 1992) omits is that these procedures were embryonic at best. And the increasing <u>rate</u> of UFCMs - from 25 in seven years, to four in seven months. The problems increased in Mk2, with (as mentioned already) 24 in the 28 months to July 2001. The section concludes:

> *'The Chinook has suffered for a long time from inadequate <u>Configuration Control</u>, mechanical design <u>faults</u> and poor <u>Air Publications</u>...exacerbated by a <u>lack of resources</u>'.*

This one sentence lists four (underlined) core components of maintaining airworthiness (specifically, the build standard); which, after all, was the whole point of the exercise. Yet the RAF later claimed CHART did not call into question the airworthiness of the aircraft. The report noted that year's 25% cut in support funding, the second of three consecutive such cuts. But the authors were kept unaware of directives <u>not</u> to maintain Configuration Control or Air Publications, and to cease fault investigations. By the RAF department which, in June 1994, was headed by the same RAF Chief Engineer who later actively campaigned against the pilots.[131]

*

On 3 March 1999, Chief of Defence Procurement Sir Robert Walmsley confirmed to the Public Accounts Committee that these failings remained:

> *'We simply have not been having access to convenient enough systems to record*

---

131 See main submission to the Mull of Kintyre Review for full details.
https://sites.google.com/site/militaryairworthiness/their-greatest-disgrace-2016

modification states... I hope these new computer systems will be friendly enough to the airmen, to the soldiers, to the sailors who have to put the data in so that it can be the right data because the computer systems will have that capability to record it and we will then be able to attach it under resource accounting and budgeting to the increased value of the aircraft with the investment we have made in it via the modification'.[132]

Walmsley was given notice of what he would be questioned on, and staff (myself included) were tasked with preparing briefings. We did so, but the truth was considered so unacceptable we were frozen out by intermediate managers. Persons outwith not only the Directorate, but MoD(PE) entirely, were told what to write, on subjects they knew nothing about.[133]

He was implying that maintaining correct records (i.e. the airworthiness audit trail) was impossible without a 'new' computer system. This ignored that the process to digitise these records had commenced in 1995, in the Directorate of Helicopter Projects. A young student on work experience was tasked with developing the database, working at home due to London Underground strikes that summer. No-one thought to ask how this work had been managed previously. (Properly trained staff, adequate resources, adherence to mandated regulations, and a sharp pencil).

If MoD was prepared to admit to such a gross failing, what was it hiding? The short answer is maladministration and fraud, leading to *savings at the expense of safety* and systemic airworthiness failings. A longer answer is in the 2009 Nimrod Review report. The comprehensive and definitive answer is in the main submission to the Mull of Kintyre Review.

The Committee didn't grasp the implications, or that this should have been sufficient to overturn the negligence findings.

Twelve years after these assurances were made, a check of the Chinook fleet showed a less than 15% match between recorded and actual modification configurations. The Local Technical Committee, chaired by the Technical Agency and the primary control mechanism for maintaining airworthiness, had not been held since 2004.[134]

*

I return now to Special Flying Instruction/Chinook/12 of 28 February 1994, which warned:

'*Chinook HC Mk2. Undemanded Flight Control Movement. There have been a*

---
132 Select Committee on Public Accounts, 3 March 1999. (Paragraph 78).
133 *Inter alia*, e-mail DHP H/SK2 (the author)/DHSA HS11, 19 February 1999 09:34.
134 (Withheld)/Hill, 18 September 2011, 21:02.

number of incidents of yaw kicks on Chinook HC Mk2 ZA718 during recent flight trials at Boscombe Down. The characteristic is manifested by <u>very sharp uncommanded inputs to the yaw axis which result in a rapid 3-4 degree change in aircraft heading, in both the hover and when in forward flight when the aircraft is subject to high levels of vibration</u>. Any aircraft exhibiting these characteristics is to be treated as having an Undemanded Flight Control Movement (UFCM). The heading hold is to be disengaged and the aircraft is to be landed as soon as practicable. Engineering modification action is in hand to cure the cause of the problem and this SFI will be cancelled once the modifications have been carried out'.

Some obvious issues arise. *'Very sharp uncommanded inputs'* would explain a failure to make a controlled turn. Little input was required during a straight transit across the North Channel, and pilots had previously experienced UFCMs only upon demanding a turn.

'Modification action is in hand' and *'modifications'* (plural) implies a maturity of knowledge and process. But these modifications were not in ZD576. Where would this maturity of knowledge come from? The experiences of the likes of Squadron Leader Burke. Yet MoD dismissed his evidence as lies when he spoke of identical and, on occasion, catastrophic events. In 2010, he confirmed he had never seen this Instruction:

'No. I did not know of this SFI. I suspect very few people did, either aircrew or groundcrew, as when another pilot - by coincidence Witness A to the House of Lords (Flight Lieutenant Iain MacFarlane) - *had this problem quite severely in Northern Ireland, and I was called over there to fly the aircraft sometime <u>after</u> the Mull accident, we were not aware that this was a known problem. Often, SFIs took a long time to reach the actual front line operators, getting bogged down in the various layers of admin and command'.*[135]

Concealing this Instruction prevented any further challenge. It was later removed (not redacted) from every version of the Release to Service provided under Freedom of Information. Did the Board know of this notification that perfectly explained the accident?

Two other Special Flying Instructions were never mentioned:
- SFI(RAF) Chinook 13 - Use of FADEC in Reversionary Mode (25 March 1994). *'Following a recent incident in which an engine flamed out upon selecting Reversionary Control, the following restrictions are to be observed until further notice... If either engine fails from primary FADEC control...it is to be landed as soon as practicable'.*

---

135 E-mail Burke/Hill, 13 September 2010, 1510.

- SFI(RAF) Chinook 14 - Tripping circuit breakers to simulate emergencies (28 July 1994). *'The tripping of circuit breakers on the Chinook Mk2 can induce failure modes in the FADEC system... This SFI will be reviewed once full software verification has been completed'.*

The significance of the first is that the incident was one of two which prompted Boscombe to halt trials and ground their Chinook. (Boscombe's aircraft was part of the MoD(PE) Fleet, not an RAF aircraft, and flown under different rules allowing the operating envelope to be explored by test pilots). It is difficult to reconcile this grounding with ZD576's low level clearance of 50 feet.

The significance of the second is in the final sentence, a clear admission that FADEC's safety critical software remained unverified two months after the accident, and nine months after Air Vice Marshal Bagnall had assured aircrew it was. Unverified? Not permitted in RAF aircraft.

*

UFCMs were treated as random events, but there are factors that render them more likely. For example, when the components of the flight control system have recently been changed or disturbed - such as occurred to ZD576 shortly before the accident when a balance spring was detached in the control closet. (Discussed later). Hence, the concept of 'disturbed systems testing'. I note the deaths of two Red Arrows pilots caused by the failure to conduct such testing - Flight Lieutenant Simon Burgess on 13 February 1996, and Flight Lieutenant Sean Cunningham on 8 November 2011.[136]

UFCMs are unpredictable in nature. Altitude plays a significant part. Recovery is possible, although not always a conscious act. Diagnosis always proves difficult, with a high incidence of No Fault Found. Foreknowledge is indicated by SFI(RAF)/Chinook/12, but this did not form part of the pilots' Mk2 conversion course. What of the maintainers' training? And who was developing the modifications? Boeing? The RAF? We don't know, because the issue was glossed over.

On 27 June 2000, in reply to Martin Bell MP, Defence Minister Dr Lewis Moonie stated UFCM problems *'could easily have been dealt with'*. The list of dead from other Chinook UFCM accidents suggests otherwise.

---

136 'Red 5' (David Hill, 2019)

19. Known causes of UFCMs in Chinook

Control jam

I mentioned earlier the Thrust/Yaw and Roll/Pitch Control Pallets. A detached pallet, or component thereof, can jam the controls before the pilot's commands are fed into the control hydraulics. Squadron Leader (later Air Marshal Sir) Barry North at the Fatal Accident Inquiry:

'On 10 May 1994, (in ZD576) when I pulled the (Collective) there was a noise and a ratchety feel, and I asked Sergeant Hardie to pull aside the soundproofing. We saw a spring hanging down with what appeared to be a piece of bulkhead hanging on to it. The bonding had not been completed correctly. I was going on was a two-ship sortie. My immediate concern was for my fellow pilot on the other aircraft (Flight Lieutenant Cook), and I sent Sergeant Hardie across with an engineer to make sure the other aircraft was serviceable for full flight'.

The balance spring is about 6" long and 1.5" diameter, and is retained only by its own tension. A spring and/or bracket detachment would render the probability of a control jam high. Squadron Leader Stephen Brough, at RAF Odiham, reported that upon completing a visual inspection a pallet was robbed from another aircraft, as there were no spares. He finished:

'The main flight safety concern is the danger of a loose article within the flying control closet. Detachment of the bracket during flight could present a serious safety hazard, with a detached bracket fouling adjacent flying controls. A means of restraining the bracket/spring assembly (is recommended) should it become loose, pending confidence of the existing design being assured. However, the following points may be of interest:

1. The AFCS (Automatic Flight Control System) section of the control closet (broom cupboard) of the Mk2 Chinook was completely different to that of the Mk1. I stress that this was a complete redesign which hardly even resembled that of the Mk1 physically, let alone in its internal workings.

2. The ability of the simulator to reproduce a number of the AFCS faults that I had experienced in those early Mk2 days was very limited; not only due to the limited abilities of the equipment, but also to the inexperience of the operators, who, just like the aircrew, were new to the Mk2. The aircrew, as well as the groundcrew and the simulator instructors, were in no way helped in those early days by the appalling lack of proper, up-to-date, paperwork. For the pilots this was made even worse by the flying restrictions placed on the circumstances in which they could practice AFCS failures in the air. Basically these were that the AFCS could only be taken out in Visual Meteorological Conditions with the aircraft straight and level. When one got a real AFCS malfunction, of which I suffered a fairly large number, they invariably showed themselves during manoeuvre. These could be quite random and of dramatically different intensities.[137]

The refusal of the RAF to consider the likelihood of an AFCS malfunction served one purpose. To admit the possibility would completely destroy its repeated assertion that the pilots were in full control of the aircraft as it flew in to high ground - an allegation fundamental to its case that the pilots were grossly negligent.

*

Servicing Instruction/Chinook/060 was issued requiring *'detailed examination of the flying control pallets for component security'*. A Fleet inspection was carried out. Forty-seven threaded bonded inserts had to be checked in each aircraft. The Instruction was then cancelled. Almost immediately there were three more occurrences on aircraft that had passed their checks only a few days earlier - ZD574, ZD674, and ZA677.

When inspected upon arrival at Aldergrove on 31 May, a pallet in ZD576 was <u>again</u> found to be detached, raised 1.5" off the floor. Aircrew were invited to inspect the fault before a repair was attempted. The aircraft was confined to a hangar overnight to allow the bonding adhesive/epoxy to cure, as the outside temperature was too low. Was the hangar warm enough? A slight temperature change can have an exponential impact on curing time. Was the temperature difference between the epoxy and the materials being bonded (pallet, insert, superstructure) too great? And the temperature of the materials is even more important than that of the epoxy. Was the working time of the epoxy exceeded, meaning it could not be moulded without structural damage? And were the damaged fixing points still viable?

Post-accident, Tony Cable immediately reported detached inserts in ZD576, his report repeating Squadron Leader Brough's concerns and strongly criticising the method of securing components of the flight control system. He stated that these visual checks were insufficient to detect a weakness of the bracket and imminence of failure.

A further more detailed Servicing Instruction (Chinook/071) was issued on 21 June 1994. Maintainers were instructed to, *'as far as possible'*, conduct a visual and manual examination. This correctly implied the pallets are not easily accessible, meaning loose inserts might not be identified. Once

---

137 Serious Fault Signal HJH/H8O/OGH/KQA/H8G from 7 Squadron (Brough), 11 May 1994.

again, the root cause was one of design.

In March 2006, QinetiQ issued a Nimrod Fuel Leak Study Report. It noted the habitual use of an unheated hangar, resulting in *'poor adhesion of sealant'*, and *'variable cure times'*, leading to *'increased possibility of failure of the repair'*. They recommended the installation of a thermohydrograph for continuous monitoring of temperature and humidity. Yet again, MoD had compartmentalised what were systemic failings.

*

But the most noteworthy part of the Servicing Instruction was:

'The Boeing Field Representative at RAF Odiham has passed a US Army repair scheme for the mounting pallet inserts, but Boeing wish to review the situation and develop their own scheme to re-secure loose inserts'.

The US Army task was dated 1990. This is a prime example of what the Director of Flight Safety warned of in August 1992. A breakdown of build standard control between Boeing and the US Army; and the RAF out on a limb because it was no longer policy to maintain the build standard.

Why did Boeing have no scheme of their own? Did the US Army advise Boeing of what it had conceived? In the UK, while the Services have authority to develop their own repair schemes (something I did in 1984, on Chinook transmissions), the Design Authority must appraise them if there are possible safety implications. This procedure is managed by the MoD Technical Agency. And what would RAF engineers' attitude be toward the rest of the Mk2 technical data? We know part of the answer - they preferred using captured Argentinian publications. For example, the UK manuals did not include information on the rotor heads.

At the Fatal Accident Inquiry this was only discussed during Tony Cable's evidence. The questioning of him was belligerent, as if he were somehow at fault. He made it clear that material evidence had been denied him. That MoD and Boeing should be answering the questions.

Mr Cable also reported that a tie bolt retaining the Thrust/Roll output bellcrank (located in the same area, below the balance springs) had fractured - at the point where an additional hole (for a split pin) had been drilled in the threaded part of the bolt.[138] I have already mentioned the loss of ZA721 in the Falklands, in 1987, killing seven. There, Mr Cable reported a hole had not been drilled in an actuator, allowing it to unwind. In both cases, loss of control would be inevitable.

---

138 Air Accidents Investigation Branch report, paragraph 7.4.2.

The RAF claimed the Board of Inquiry conducted a thorough engineering investigation. Yet, it failed to mention this recurrence of Quality Control failures, or that the aircraft was neither airworthy nor serviceable. That is like writing a book about the Bible and not mentioning Jesus.

*

In October 2001 the Senior Reviewing Officers gave evidence to the House of Lords Select Committee, who were caustic:

'Sir John Day discounted the possibility of a control jam, saying the crew flew "a serviceable aircraft" into the hill. Nevertheless, he later said that he could not exclude the possibility of a control jam having played a part in the accident; and his acceptance that evidence of emergency power having been pulled could have been destroyed necessarily weakens his argument against such a jam having taken place. Likewise, Sir William Wratten conceded the possibility of a control jam or engine malfunction'.

In 2005 the Air Staff finally agreed a control jam may have occurred during the leg to the Mull, only manifesting itself when the planned turn was attempted. Director of Air Staff, Air Commodore (later Air Marshal Sir) Richard Garwood:

'If at any point the Chinook had a latent control jam preventing the helicopter from turning, but the helicopter was continuing on a straight course, the aircrew may not have had any indication that there was a problem. <u>The problem would only become apparent when they tried to instigate a change of course away from dead ahead'.</u>[139]

He did not mention that a warning had been <u>actively</u> concealed, removed from copies of the Release to Service whenever sought by Inquiries, families or the public. Nor that he was repeating, exactly, the evidence of Squadron Leader Burke - who his predecessors had accused of lying, with other parts of MoD still rejecting his evidence. Nevertheless, together with Lord Bach's withdrawal of the claim that cloud extended out from the Mull, this admission completely destroyed the arguments of the Senior Reviewing Officers. But their findings were not reviewed.

Hydraulic oil contamination

I discussed earlier the instruction to check the Transmission Debris Screens every five minutes. On 22 October 2001 Captain Ralph Kohn offered written evidence along similar lines to the House of Lords Select

---

[139] Directorate of Air Staff letter D/DAS/58/1/5, 8 April 2005.

Committee:

'We must remember Undemanded Flight Control Movements caused by hydraulic contamination. Metal particles found in a hydraulic system were similar to contamination found on a CH-47D US Army Chinook after it rolled of its own accord onto its back, then completed the roll through 360° to a wheels down attitude at 250 feet, narrowly avoiding a crash in 1997'.

The US report Captain Kohn referred to said this:

'CH-47D helicopters are experiencing uncommanded oscillations, flight control movements, and flight attitude changes that may be related to the performance of the Upper Boost Actuators. Three primary upper boost critical areas are metal contamination in the control head, dead band travel distances, and side loading discovered in the end caps. <u>The anomaly occurs, then returns to normal</u> operations on a test stand or in the aircraft.

A critical area is the Integrated Lower Control Actuators (ILCA). The metal contamination and moisture found in the pitch, roll, and yaw ILCAs are considered CRITICAL TO FLIGHT SAFETY. The amount of contamination found in the pitch and roll ILCAs were considered sufficient to cause a <u>disturbance in the normal operation of these components at any time</u>. If the primary valve jams, in this situation, the capability to direct hydraulic fluid flow ceases.

These two areas are CRITICAL TO FLIGHT SAFETY, PERSONNEL SAFETY, AND EQUIPMENT SAFETY.

During Aft Swivelling Boost removal, maintenance personnel discovered that the plain press bushing was <u>not installed</u>. Installation procedures show the requirement for two washers and not the required bushing. Without this bushing, uneven loading is placed on the bolt and clevis. Uneven loading and <u>missing bushings have proven to be directly related to fatigue failure</u>'.[140]

In his evidence to the House of Lords, Tony Cable substantiated the above conclusions. Did the US Army realise its concerns <u>repeated</u> those of the Mr Cable following the loss of ZA721 in the Falklands in 1987?

Up to a point, MoD's system worked. In 1992, the Director of Flight Safety expressed grave concern over Boeing's Quality Control System. Perhaps if he had been heeded...

Power Supply failure and interrupts

During engine start up, when switching over from the Auxiliary Power

---

140 Extract from US Army 'Flightfax' October 2000, and Analytical Investigation Branch, Corpus Christi Army Depot (Ruben Burgos).

Unit generator to the main generators there is a power interrupt which affects sensitive equipment. After a time, it was realised which equipment had to be kept switched off until the main generators were on line. This is not uncommon, and equipment must pass power interrupt tests during repair, using Power Interrupt Units, to ensure it either continues working during the interrupt, or recovers correctly within a given time.

MoD Third Line workshops were left to devise a best-guess in-house test procedure for these Units. This is part of a dangerous chain of organisational failures. The effect is cumulative. The Air Accidents Investigation Branch noted RAF Odiham lacked the correct equipment to test torquemeters and triple tachometers, and crucial Radar Altimeter settings could not be ensured. Previously, when investigating the loss of ZA721 in 1987, it noted Odiham could not test actuators. This illustrates how an entire safety-related process can be compromised by a decision to task repairs to a workshop, but not provide the wherewithal. Not unlike Boeing and Boscombe, who did not have access to FADEC documentation. And the pilots, who were tasked to fly an unairworthy aircraft.

*

Geoffrey Clifton-Brown MP in the House of Commons on 26 June 2000:

'Mr Brian Trubshaw, the Concorde pilot, wrote to me on 12 October 1999. The letter, a copy of which I sent to MoD, refers to a Chinook crash in the United States in 1996. It states: "Subsequent investigation found <u>electrical failure</u> and the pilots were cleared of blame. Boeing settled for $4 million". The Minister for the Armed Forces also makes no reference to Boeing's admittance that all Chinooks flying between 1992 and 1996 were subject to <u>power problems</u> due to salt water seepage. It is clear that technical doubts exist'.

On 7 March 1996 a US Army Chinook crashed during a snowstorm, killing five. Unable to recover from a turn to align with the runway, the aircraft had plunged from 3,300 feet. Post-accident, the US Army raised two 'product quality deficiency reports' relating to circuit breaker failures. And another, a result of an on-board fire over the Atlantic Ocean the same year. A report dated 16 June 1996 noted *'this is the third incident...of water causing smoke or fire in the Power Distribution Panel'*. It was recommended that the aircraft's electrical system be configured *'so that a single fault cannot cause a complete failure'*. In 1999 MoD admitted it still awaited advice from Boeing.

And on 18 February 2007 a US Army Chinook crashed in Afghanistan, killing 8 and injuring 14. The investigation concluded an engine suddenly flamed out, a fuel computer shutting down due to an electrical anomaly.

Differential Airspeed Hold (DASH) runaway

DASH comprises electrically controlled actuators connected in series with the fore and aft function of the Cyclic stick. It has two parts, one for each Automatic Flight Control System (AFCS). If one fails, the other is designed to compensate. DASH corrects an awkward characteristic of the Chinook - in flight above 40 knots it has a negative stick gradient, meaning the Cyclic counter-intuitively moves backwards. DASH cancels this, working primarily to push it forward; but also has a pitch-damping role.

A double DASH runaway is an emergency that has a severe effect on the pilot's ability to control the aircraft. It is difficult to diagnose quickly and accurately, partly because the symptoms are similar to other UFCMs. At first, it appears to be a failure of the main Attitude Indicator. It then becomes apparent there is a control malfunction. The pilot may be unable to prevent major oscillations in pitch (porpoising) before regaining control. The correct emergency action involves test of the AFCS - each is turned off in turn to find out if one is faulty. This is difficult to achieve if tackling a major loss of control. Until sure it is an AFCS problem, one is reluctant to switch both systems off as they are what are providing a vestige of control. The subsequent loss of yaw control makes the decision doubly difficult, especially at low level. For obvious reasons, it is an unrehearsed emergency in cloud.

Squadron Leader Robert Burke wrote to his superiors seven weeks after the accident:

'PROPOSED MODIFICATION TO CHINOOK Mk2 DASH LOGIC

Reference: ODI/720/4/Eng dated 21 Jul 94

Both the Chinook Mk1 and Mk2 can suffer from DASH runaways. The consequences can vary dramatically depending on the nature and the flight conditions. I have experienced a variety of single DASH failures from full single runaways to the DASH cycling from full retract to full extend and back again. A single DASH failure in Visual Meteorological Conditions above about 300 feet is no real problem. Any DASH failure in cloud can cause control problems which can so disorientate the pilot as to lead to loss of control. A double DASH runaway, either in cloud or close to the ground, will cause major problems with the high probability of a crash. <u>*This state of affairs has long been recognised and Boscombe have cleared neither Mk1 nor Mk2 for prolonged transit flights under 300 feet Above Ground Level.*</u>

One of the major control modifications sought by the Air Staff, at the request of the aircrew, was some DASH runaway protection. Aircrew were briefed this feature had been incorporated in the Mk2. A number of us doubted this, and indeed we now know that with the exception of occasions when power to the AFCS is switched off or interrupted there is no runaway protection.

(The proposed modification) has a fundamental flaw, in that if rapid large fore and aft Cyclic stick displacements were to be applied resulting in rapid changes in fuselage attitude or airspeed, the DASH low rate circuitry would be activated resulting in quite unpredictable control problems for the pilot. Such control inputs are only likely to be used in fairly demanding flight regimes - typically in a low level quick stop manoeuvre very close to the ground. The proposed modification, as drafted, would cause far more problems than it would solve.

The problem of DASH runaways has been ignored for far too long. If Boeing cannot come up with an acceptable runaway protection system, I believe the fitment of the DASH position indicator, as suggested some years ago, could provide a reasonable compromise'.

*

Let us discuss the 300 feet limitation, as it is revealing of the thought processes that lead to airworthiness certification. (Or in this case, non-certification). The Release to Service actually says:

'Prolonged cruising flight should not take place at heights below 300 feet Above Ground Level unless it is operationally essential to do so'.

'Prolonged' is not defined, but ultimately limited by the range of the aircraft. Yet another distraction nagging away in the pilot's mind. *How long am I allowed to stay below 300 feet?* Boscombe's concern arose from these repeated DASH runaways but, as Squadron Leader Burke pointed out, 300 feet only refers to a single DASH failure. If there is a double DASH runaway, at any height, an accident becomes more likely.

Boscombe must evaluate the effect of such problems, and the Aircraft Project Office is required to conduct an investigation (via Boeing) or give reasons why it thinks this unnecessary. Among many references are two Boscombe reports:

- Letter Report PE/Chinook/41, APF/247/Annex, 22 October 1993 'Chinook HC Mk2 - INTERIM CA Release Recommendations':

    'The Differential Airspeed Hold (DASH) Low Rate caption was not consistent with the DASH feedback signal, and was not an indication of any rate of actuator movement. The title of the caption is inaccurate'.

- Annex A to Letter Report TM2210, 26 October 1993 'Chinook HC Mk2 - Document in the form of an INTERIM CA Release':

    'There remains a requirement for a DASH actuator runaway warning device. This requirement, often stated by Boscombe Down and most recently justified

at Reference C (letter APF/246/13 dated 11 April 1990), was considered Essential for CA Release for the Chinook HC Mk1, and remains so for the HC Mk2. This matter will be covered in detail in the definitive CA Release recommendations, but it is considered relevant to restate the Establishment's position once again at this stage'.

The Release *must* list 'Essential Modifications'. The Mk2 Release states 'NONE', meaning a modification considered essential to safety following the 1987 Falklands crash had not been developed. ('Essential' also serves to inform the Chairman of the HQ Modifications Committee as to what classification he should apply to the modification). Boscombe cited this as one reason why the Mk2 was not airworthy.

By definition, then, the Mk1 Release to Service was also unsound, because the Safety Case was incomplete and there was no audit trail. This is crucial, because that Mk1 build standard (including the Safety Case) formed the contractual baseline for the upgrade programme. As this was contaminated, one must ask what chance the Mid-Life Upgrade had of ever succeeding. (Despite the RAF accepting the Mk2 into service, by no stretch of the imagination can a programme be considered a success if the output is not considered airworthy).

Once again the RAF rolled the dice, choosing to interpret *'operationally essential'* as *'all flying is operationally essentially, so the limitation can be ignored'*. The reason is simple. Lacking a low level clearance, Chinook is useless as a Support Helicopter.

Why would Boscombe insert the 300 feet limitation, but not refer to the concern over double DASH failures? The answer lies in this report merely being an early assessment of the trials task - due to commence in April 1994 but delayed pending verification of the FADEC software. Boscombe are reserving their final position in the hope the RAF finally comes to its senses and schemes the modification in time for embodiment into the trials aircraft. Their frustration is clear at having to quote a 4-year old letter which they have received no reply to.

What were Boeing's thoughts on this, having accepted a contract to modify an aircraft knowing that the contracted baseline contained this fundamental flaw? And what of the Design Review and Acceptance process that allowed this situation to remain?

At this stage (October 1993), the Boscombe trials manager would not be anticipating the RAF actually flying the aircraft. But no progress was made between then and June 1994. In fact, matters got worse, with his aircraft grounded twice for airworthiness reasons.

Flight below 300 feet was an unquantifiable risk, yet ZD576 was cleared for low level flight down to 50 feet. I cannot speak for those involved, and there exists the operational imperative, but to operators the underlying issues would be largely invisible. Few would know that the concerns had been festering for seven years. That, this was not a simple binary decision. It was a complex problem and risks were being compounded. It is plain the Authorising Officer for the final flight, Flight Lieutenant Tapper, did not truly understand what he was signing for. That was an organisational fault, not a personal failing.

Where was the acceptance of this risk recorded, and by whom? Given risks must be assessed regularly, and the top 10 every month by a 2-Star, many Air Officers must have just waved through extensions over a period of years. Did the Air Staff not ask why this restriction had been carried over from the Mk1, when the upgrade programme was the ideal opportunity to clear it? This should have been one of the primary aims, and the programme not approved until it was included.

Here is an overwhelming reason why the RAF would not want Squadron Leader Burke or Boscombe Down speaking to any Inquiry.

20. Four examples of UFCMs

1. Chinook HC Mk1 ZA721, Falkland Islands, 1987

On 27 February 1987, during an air test, the aircraft pitched nose down until almost vertical and dived into the ground, killing all seven on board. Officially, cause was unknown. The evidence said otherwise. Flight Lieutenant (later Air Commodore) Carl Scott's statement to the ZD576 Fatal Accident Inquiry in January 1996 bears repeating:

'When Wing Commander Malcolm Pledger took command of 78 Squadron in the Falkland Islands in February 1988, I asked him to brief the Chinook Flight on the findings of the Board of Inquiry (ZA721, 7 killed), as this had not then been published. As chairman of the Board he briefed two findings: the first his own most probable cause (failure of a hydraulic jack due to poor quality control at Boeing), and then that which would actually be published due to the failure of MoD to face pressure brought to bear by Boeing (cause unknown)'.

Wing Commander Pledger issued the most condemning set of conclusions and recommendations imaginable:

'The Board uncovered several areas of potential disaster within the flying controls and their associated hydraulics'.

*

With a civil accident, the Air Accidents Investigation Branch (AAIB) will look into airworthiness certification, previous incidents and accidents, maintenance standards and practices. The Engineering, Operations and Flight Recorder Inspectors will then analyse all the evidence and try to reach conclusions about events and factors that possibly or probably contributed to the cause.

With military accidents, the AAIB's brief is to provide the Board with a factual statement on the evidence found at the scene. Its report forms an Annex to the Board's. Airworthiness and organisational aspects are covered by the Board. On this occasion, both were robust in their criticism of Boeing. The Board was *'disappointed'*, saying some information was *'parochial, contradictory, misleading and unacceptable'*.

This reflected the experiences of the AAIB:

'Evidence of a number of pre-impact defects (in actuators) was found. Co-operation from Boeing was generally good, but <u>little in-depth knowledge</u> of the actuators was apparent in the responsible Design Groups.

<u>Forward-Swivelling Upper Boost Actuator</u>

No upper roll pin or locking wire was present. The clevis attaching rod had <u>not been drilled</u> to accept the pin. These were clearly <u>assembly omissions</u>. Relatively deep witness marks were found on the rod, indicative of it having been <u>carelessly clamped</u> in a vice or grips prior to final assembly.

Aft-Pivoting Upper Boost Actuator

Seals in the head housing assembly had been <u>incorrectly installed</u>. One back-up ring on System 1 and two on System 2 were found with bevelled ends <u>crossed over</u>. <u>Incorrect back-up rings had been fitted</u> in the 1.5" diameter seal between the piston bearing sleeve and the outer cylinder in both Systems 1 and 2. Continuous back-rings should have been used, but scarf cut rings were fitted. (This same defect was discovered in the Aft-Swivelling Upper Boost Actuator). The outer seal in System 2 between the core of the head housing assembly and the piston assembly was <u>incorrectly assembled</u> and had suffered a <u>gross failure</u>. The inner back-up ring was <u>missing</u>, and the evidence clearly indicated it had <u>not been installed</u> at assembly. A 0.5" circumferential length of the O-Ring and the outer back-up ring was <u>missing</u>, providing a large overboard <u>leakage path</u> for System 2 fluid'.

The Board concluded the most likely cause was a jammed Forward-Swivelling Upper Boost Actuator, with an Aft Longitudinal Cyclic Trim Actuator (LCTA) malfunction a likely contributory factor.

You do not have to be an engineer to grasp something is very wrong here. Vital parts were missing or wrongly installed. Not drilling a hole for the roll pin is scandalous, and *'made possible the potentially catastrophic jam or runaway of the Forward-Swivelling Upper Boost Actuator'.*

Let me be clear. Legal action should have been taken. Too strong? Ask the families of those killed.

*

Independently of the Board, experienced Chinook pilots submitted a short paper to superiors. They concluded three interrelated factors forced the aircraft into its nose-down attitude:

- Differential Airspeed Hold (DASH) actuator motor stall.
- Aft LCTA clutch slippage (compounded by the Aft-Pivoting Upper Boost Actuator problem).
- Forward and Aft Rotor Head lift imbalance.

The first two were logical deductions based on physical evidence, and had been experienced before. The last was only alluded to by the Board, and relates to incorrect adjustment of the Pitch Links. Consequently, the apportionment of lift between the forward and aft rotors is wrong. One effect would be to reduce the authority of the DASH actuator, ultimately preventing any further reduction of, for example, aft pitch - with the aft rotor wanting to overtake the forward, causing a nose down attitude. In each scenario normal control is lost, recovery dependent upon height.

Separately, the Flight Safety Cell at HQ Strike Command was so unhappy with the official version, Squadron Leader Robert Burke was sent an original copy of the Board's report and allocated simulator time at Mannheim with the US Army. He wrote a test schedule, and the Flight Commander on the Operational Conversion Unit was able to repeatedly replicate the crash. The only way to avoid the accident was to take off all power by lowering the Collective (thrust) lever completely, thus slowing the aircraft down. This is counter intuitive. Given the directive to find 'cause unknown', the RAF would not wish this to be made public; at the time, or later during ZD576 investigations.

Burke also developed the necessary training to aid recovery from DASH and LCTA failures. Neither pilot in ZA721 had received this and would have been taken by surprise. With their height reducing, the crash swiftly became inevitable. Additionally, he had developed an air test schedule, approved and issued by the RAF Handling Squadron at Boscombe Down. This included, at about 85 knots, a check on the action of the LCTAs against the cockpit indicators, to be done before transitioning to fast forward flight. If there is an LCTA problem it will show up here, as will unusual fore and aft stick positioning. The Board's timeline reveals this check was not carried out, probably due to ZA721 being asked by Air Traffic Control to expedite clearing the approach path because of a TriStar returning to the dispersal area. Thus, the aircraft accelerated with, certainly, a faulty aft LCTA and a handling pilot who was unaware of the correct recovery procedures. Not dissimilar to...

2. Australian Defence Force Chinook, 2011 [141]

On 30 May 2011 a CH-47D Chinook of Australian Army Rotary Wing Group 6, callsign Brahman 12, encountered turbulence and experienced a large and uncommanded nose-up pitch of 15 to 20 degrees. As per their training neither the co-pilot, who was flying, nor the aircraft commander, took any action to damp the excursion, which developed into oscillations that rapidly:

'Became divergent to a point reaching or exceeding the aircraft's flight limits of

---

141 https://www.flightsafetyaustralia.com/2015/07/saturation-confusion-impact-the-wild-ride-of-brahman-12/

30 degrees in the pitch axis in the third oscillation, and ending with the fourth oscillation involving a nose-down attitude in excess of 90 degrees'.

Late in the fourth oscillation the aircraft commander ignored what he had been taught and took the controls. He was able to recover level flight but could not stop the helicopter from hitting the ground. The aircraft rolled after impact and caught fire. One passenger became weightless above the aircraft loading ramp due to g forces, fell out, and was killed.

Like all tandemrotor helicopters, Chinook is fundamentally unstable in pitch. It will not automatically return to its trimmed state after a disturbance such as a wind gust - static instability. And once disturbed it will engage in increasingly large oscillations from its flight path - dynamic instability. These instabilities are a consequence of aerodynamic interference from the forward rotor to the aft rotor. The Automatic Flight Control System (AFCS) manages this, making its own control inputs; however, it can be overwhelmed causing DASH runaway (saturation), which the pilot must correct.

Pilot-induced oscillation can occur in any fixed or rotary wing aircraft. The correct response is to make no control input - the opposite of the action required to correct an externally caused upset (above). But the pilots had been taught to make no input in both scenarios. No-one had challenged or questioned this, instead becoming accepted practice.

The Defence Force Commission heard that AFCS saturation *'was not taught or understood by the vast majority of the wider Chinook community'*, including the UK and US. But Squadron Leader Burke understood it and tried to disseminate his experiences, but was ignored.

Porpoising had been experienced in Afghanistan, but only reported informally:

'...such reporting may remain within the confines of a particular unit and not receive wider dissemination within the Australian Defence Force aviation community, which dissemination could provide greater appreciation of potential problems and greater resources to address, and possibly solve, such potential problems'.

This mirrors similar failures within the RAF. For example, aircrew not having seen the UFCM Special Flying Instruction in 1994, exacerbated by the denial of funding for investigations from 1991-on, which naturally developed into ambivalence and a perception that there was no point reporting problems.

After the accident, Boeing issued Service Note 145-092 to address Chinooks being flown by pilots with an *'inattentive flying technique'*; which sounds like a dig at the pilots to divert attention from the lack of proper manuals.

When Brahman 12 hit the ground it was the final act in a sequence that had begun much earlier and very quietly, with unquestioned assumptions, lack of information flow, and their inevitable consequence - the wrong response.

3. US Army barrel roll, 1998 [142]

A US Army Chinook, while in cruise at around 1,100 feet at 130-135 knots Indicated Airspeed, barrel rolled. The nose began a slight pitch down. The pilot applied aft cyclic to correct, but the nose began a slow left yaw he could not control with full right pedal. The aircraft then began a slow left roll to about 90 degrees, and then continued with a snap roll through the remaining 270 degrees. With both pilots now fighting the controls, the aircraft returned to its correct attitude at about 250 feet, and the pilots touched down. The droop stops were damaged, and during shut down a rotor disc clipped the fuselage. This was a perfect example of a fully developed UFCM.

A six-month investigation concluded the probable cause was a sticking Upper Boost Actuator, caused by particle contamination of the hydraulic fluid. The investigators had an intact aircraft to deal with, but still had major difficulty identifying the problem. It is rather obvious that, with an aircraft that has thoroughly crashed and been consumed by fire, evidence of a pre-impact malfunction might not be there to be found, irrespective of the quality of the investigation. Nevertheless, the same contamination was found in ZD576.

One lesson this incident emphasised, and contrary to the RAF's assertion, was that it does not require a simultaneous jam in all control channels to make the aircraft unflyable. The aircraft needed over 1,000 feet to recover. Even then, it was not entirely conscious. ZD576 was at around 200-400 feet when over the sea. Perhaps Flight Lieutenant Cook simply did not have enough height. But that is not the same as flying 'too low'.

4. Chinook HC Mk2 ZD981, 1999 [143]

ZD981 was the lead aircraft of two transiting from RAF Shawbury to

---

142 US Army report SIOCC-QP-AIUSASC 97-305.
143 Adapted from Air Incident Report ODI/381/99 (Crew Report).

Odiham at 2,000 feet. Approximately 10 minutes after departing a jolt was felt throughout the airframe and the captain, in the right-hand seat, noticed that some of his flight instrument power flags briefly showed, and the Master Caution Panel lights flashed on and then off.

Two minutes later this occurred again. The jolts were similar to that felt when the AFCS extendible links centre after a power interrupt, and the crew concentrated on that possibility. Approximately one minute later further jolts and power interrupts were experienced. The captain switched the AFCS off.

Almost immediately, the Master Cautions and all the captions illuminated dimly. All power was lost to the primary flight instruments, including the main Attitude Indicator and Horizontal Situation Indicator, and to the engine instruments. The only services remaining were those powered by the essential battery busbar. A loud hum was also heard through the Intercom, pulsing in phase with the warning captions.

All circuit breakers were checked and confirmed to be okay. The forward Longitudinal Cyclic Trim Actuator (LCTA) was seen to be in the fully retracted position, so speed was reduced to approximately 80 knots as a precaution. (See above, Burke's air test schedule). The captain ordered all non-essential equipment to be switched off and the formation was turned back towards Shawbury. An emergency was declared.

The Flight Reference Cards were unhelpful, but the captain had recently discussed electrical problems with the simulator staff and recalled a similar scenario, where isolating the AC and DC cross-ties enabled one of the two electrical systems to be brought back on line. No.1 Power Distribution Panel DC and AC cross-ties were tripped, but to no effect.

The captain then tripped No.2 cross-ties. Tripping the AC cross-tie restored his flight instruments and the No.2 Electrical Control Unit indications, but all the services powered by No.1 Power Distribution Panel were still inoperative. The warning captions partially cleared with the following remaining: Low Fuel Pressure, Rectifier 1, Automatic Flight Control Systems 1&2, and Transmission oil pressure & Transmission Auxiliary oil pressure.

With partial power restored and the aircraft in a relatively stable configuration, the Flight Reference Cards were checked again. Warning caption indications were now similar to a single Transformer Rectifier Unit failure with no cross-tie, so the captain decided not to re-set his cross-tie circuit breaker. The cross-feed was selected OPEN to start balancing fuel, without success. The crewman then operated the cross-feed valves manually, which cleared the Low Fuel Pressure caption.

An unsuccessful attempt was then made to program the forward and aft LCTAs in manual. On short finals to land, the LCTAs were selected to retract for 30 seconds. At this point No.2 aircraft of the formation informed the lead aircraft that his aft wheels had swivelled through approximately 45 degrees. The captain took control and made a vertical landing, followed by a gentle taxi forward to straighten the wheels.

The fault was later rectified by replacing No.1 AC Generator Control Unit and the Generator Contactor. The incident lasted 20 minutes. Indications were complex and confusing, and the Flight Reference Cards of limited use. The event was considered a major safety hazard, and had the crew been less experienced on Mk2, alone, or at a lower level, the outcome might have been considerably different. The crew of ZD576 were disadvantaged in all these respects.

PART 7 - THE END OF THE BEGINNING

'To exercise power without having it is an abuse of power, and that is what has happened in this case'.
Lord Desmond Ackner, Lord of Appeal, 5 March 2001

21. Concealed evidence

The ghost of electricity

Even the most technologically advanced domains suffer from Electro-Magnetic Interference (EMI). In 2009 the Formula 1 car driven by Rubens Barrichello suffered a gearbox failure caused by interference from the subway system beneath the Marina Bay circuit in Singapore. The point being, no-one else did, including his team-mate in an identical car. Rubens pitted safely. In aviation, matters are not so straight forward.

*

A designer must always ask: *If a device is malfunctioning how does this manifest itself, is it evident to the operator, and will he know what to do?* If this cannot be answered the design is likely to be immature, and possibly defective. Importantly, if an unforeseen malfunction occurs, it must be investigated, understood and corrected. However, one must accept that all electronic devices may be prone to malfunctions caused by EMI, especially in the confined space of a helicopter where sufficient physical separation is often impossible. A functional safety and performance assessment is necessary; of individual equipments, then as integrated systems, and then as a whole aircraft system of systems, in order to articulate any Limitations in the Release to Service and train aircrew to cope with them.

Here, terminology is important. Limitations are something that can be 'worked around', and are acceptable so long as they are understood. Constraints, in this sense on operational capability and safety, cannot be worked around. They are unacceptable, and their existence is what drives the prioritisation of expenditure. Clearing engineering Limitations is the role of the HQ Provisioning Authority, mentioned earlier. Clearing Constraints is the role of the Service Operational Requirements Branches, today called the Directorates of Equipment Capability. But the *savings at the expense of safety* forced ever more Constraints upon Front Line.

*

One of Boscombe Down's most important tasks is to put the trials aircraft through the Radio Frequency Environment Generator (REG). In addition to being bombarded with RF signals of varying field strength and frequency, the aircraft's own emitters are used as an illuminating source, the aim being to reveal susceptibilities. So important is this, the REG is a UK strategic asset.

This is but one step in establishing the installed performance of every item of electronic equipment; crucial, because during *any* upgrade or modification programme the contractor is contracted to 'not degrade the installed performance'. It is Boscombe's job to verify this. Therefore, MoD must be able to state what that performance is, and the contractor agree to it. Otherwise, MoD has little option but to agree a 'test and declare' status; meaning the contractor can say *'We've done the work, we've tested it, we declare it doesn't work and/or isn't safe, please pay us in full'*.

This became increasingly common as unappraised Service Engineered Modifications and Special Trials Fits proliferated, and unverified 'read across' was claimed from other aircraft types. It lies at the root of other fatal accidents since 1994, such as the Tornado/PATRIOT shootdown on 23 March 2003. (Two RAF aircrew killed).[144] What was to be the primary focus on Chinook Mk2? The new fuel computers, but they were uncertified so any testing would be nugatory.

Personal Electronic Devices

While there remains a plethora of concealed evidence, I concentrate here on physical evidence that was removed from the scene and never returned to the Board of Inquiry - the phones, cameras and personal computers carried by the deceased.

It was widely assumed, because MoD said so, that EMI from these devices had been eliminated as a cause. But Boscombe's brief reports, forming Annex AD to the Board's report, are simply a general analysis. One is headed 'Assessment of two portable phones', <u>but these were not devices from the wreckage</u>. To every Inquiry, MoD let it be assumed they were, the Board claiming:

'The worst effect of any interference would have been to cause the SuperTANS to revert to Doppler'.[145] (That is, degrade the GPS).

On <u>10 January 1996</u>, as a result of initial testing, an amendment was issued to the Release to Service:

'Electronic equipment such as video cameras and laptop computers are potential sources of <u>significant</u> Electro-Magnetic Interference (particularly from the monitor screens) and may interfere with the <u>Automatic Flight Control System, engine/fuel control units, Radar Altimeter, navigation and communications equipment, including the Intercom and UHF radios'.[146]

---

144 'Breaking the Military Covenant' (David Hill, 2019)
145 Board of Inquiry report, paragraph 37.
146 Chinook HC Mk2 Release to Service, Section T, paragraph 12.6. ('UHF Radios' is

The Board President then gave evidence to the Fatal Accident Inquiry on 24 January 1996. Advocate Depute, John Mitchell QC:

'I believe the conclusion was that there was <u>no possibility</u> of any equipment that was likely to be there being able to generate a sufficient field to cause any upset to the <u>Automatic Flight Control System</u>; is that right?'

'That is correct'.

Compounding this, the now Group Captain Pulford told the House of Lords in 2001:

'As far as the aircraft systems, the <u>Automatic Flight Control System, the FADEC</u>, neither personal computers nor mobile phones would have any effect at all'.[147]

Based on this claim, the Lords referred to *'scientific analysis of <u>the</u> portable electronic equipment'* carried by passengers, saying *'the Board concluded that Electro-Magnetic Interference was not a factor in the accident'*.[148]

It is an understatement to say the above statements cannot be reconciled. *'No possibility'* implies full testing of the actual devices in a representative environment. The amendment of two weeks earlier was not mentioned at the Fatal Accident Inquiry, and confining the question to the AFCS omitted the effect on other systems that were known to be vulnerable. The Sheriff, the Lords, and most importantly the families, were deceived. One might think there was a duty to reveal the whole truth. Did the President mislead by omission, or did he just answer the exam question? A fine line. A plausible cause of the accident was swiftly forgotten.

Removal and concealment

The Air Accidents Investigation Branch report revealed:

'Luggage and personal effects were removed from the site rapidly, <u>largely before AAIB detailed examination of the site</u>'. [149]

This was the only mention, buried in an Annex of the Board's report that only became partially available in late 2001, via Hansard.

On 30 September 2009 the Air Staff were asked to provide details of recovered Personal Electronic Devices by type, quantity, frequency (or band) of transmission, maximum transmission power, network provider,

---

erroneous. There was one UHF radio authorised in Chinook HC Mk2).
147 Evidence of Wing Commander Andrew Pulford to House of Lords Select Committee, 27 September 2001, paragraph 95.
148 House of Lords Select Committee Oral Evidence, September 2001, paragraph 37.
149 Air Accidents Investigation Branch report, paragraph 5.3

and whether each was found switched on or off. They refused to reply, but after intervention by the Information Commissioner did so on 11 February 2010. They still did not provide the information, but admitted:

> 'The tests carried out were generic, rather than relating to specific known items of equipment; this may be taken as an indication that the <u>AAIB and RAF investigations did not have access to or specific knowledge of any items that were recovered from the scene. It may be that, given the identities of the passengers, all such devices and equipment were removed by the police or the security services, and were excluded from the RAF investigation</u>'.

The reply does not say it *was* the *'police or security services'* (and note, it does not say *the* Security Service), but why speculate at all? The Air Staff either know, or they do not. They exclude the RAF's Mountain Rescue Teams and everyone else who was there, so are presumably satisfied *they* were not involved. Plainly, they know precisely who it was. But to reveal the truth would imply the existence of correspondence between the Board President, the Air Staff, and these other agencies. Also, it would be an admission that control of the accident scene and evidential trail was lost.

Consequently the *'generic'* testing was irrelevant, and does not offer any assurance that a transmission from within or outwith the aircraft did not interfere with its systems.

Motive, means and opportunity (the building blocks of guilt)

Who would order the removal of the devices, carry it out, and direct that they were not to be returned to investigators? And who would ensure the official reports were sufficiently ambiguous to make the families and all Inquiries believe the investigators had the actual devices to study?

- *Initial* motivation is clear. MI5, Army Intelligence and the RUC would not want any information pertaining to their roles falling into the wrong hands. Or each other's. But the purging of classified data is irrelevant to an EMI assessment, and no reason to exclude the devices from the investigation. Whoever made and agreed with *that* decision had a different motivation, and was content to undermine the investigation and perpetuate the lie of gross negligence.
- Means would require the above three Services to attend the site and/or a compliant party begin the search before they or investigators arrived. Both scenarios occurred.
- To assess opportunity a timeline must be constructed to determine who was at the scene before the AAIB and Board arrived. The reports of RAF

Mountain Rescue Teams, along with local media articles and confirmation by actual attendees, provide the best insight as to who (they thought) were there, and when. Given the Air Staff's admission, we now know where to focus...

Police

This can be Strathclyde, RAF, or the Royal Ulster Constabulary.

Campbeltown Police Office covers almost the entire South Kintyre peninsula, including the islands of Islay, Jura and Gigha, and so has quite wide-ranging resources. The accident occurred in the area covered by L Division of Strathclyde Police, one of 15, headquartered in Dumbarton, 22 miles west of Glasgow and 130 miles north of the crash site.

Local officers arrived within 40 minutes and took charge. The remainder of their colleagues were recalled to duty, arriving with other emergency services over the next few hours. The senior officer at Campbeltown, Chief Inspector James Dorward, arrived at 2200. The site was only cordoned off *after* he arrived - a significant window of opportunity.

At 2230, seven officers arrived from Glasgow via an RN Sea King from HMS Gannet (Prestwick). An RAF Boulmer Sea King later collected more, but their time of arrival was not revealed.

Detective Chief Inspector Janet Joyce from Dumbarton, and Scenes of Crime Officers from Glasgow, arrived the following day, the latter staying for three days. Their photographs and video have never been released.

That same morning, RUC Special Branch Superintendents Trevor Campbell and Paul Leighton (later Deputy Chief Constable of the PSNI) arrived at 0650, having taken the ferry from Larne to Stranraer and driven 230 miles to the scene in six hours. After the bodies were searched and removed, they combed the area for classified papers and personal effects.

The Board stated *'appropriate site control measures were evident by the time of the Board's arrival on 3 June'*. Yet, it also reported discussing the lack of RAF Police at the crash site with a Group Flight Safety Officer from the Inspectorate of Flight Safety, whose purpose was to guide them as to procedures. This implies Wing Commander Pulford, while content at the initial response, became unhappy over his crash scene being contaminated as ever more non-MoD personnel arrived.

The first police officers to arrive would almost certainly not interfere with evidence without orders, their immediate concern being any survivors. If they gathered any devices they would simply secure them. The significant players are those flown in from Glasgow, almost certainly including a Security Service contingent, and US forces stationed at Machrihanish.

Security services

'Security services' can be *the* Security Service (MI5), Army Intelligence or RUC Special Branch. More meaningfully, it can be the RAF Provost and Security Service (P&SS), at the time headquartered at RAF Rudloe Manor. The clue is in the ambiguous presentation of the Board's report, using the acronym but without spelling it out, and burying the single reference in a paragraph unrelated to the *effect* of the devices:

> *'Loss of, and damage to, classified material was incurred. This is being investigated by HQ P&SS. Their report will be forwarded under separate cover'.*

A request was made to the RAF Provost and Security Service on 22 January 2021, seeking their report to the Board. On 17 March MoD replied saying processing was delayed due to COVID-19. In isolation, that may seem reasonable. However, one must appreciate that the campaign to clear the pilots, and numerous other investigations by the public into fatal military accidents, faced the same stone-walling. In September 2021 MoD claimed not to have the report.[150] Yet more accident papers had gone missing.

As MI5 are exempt from the Freedom of Information Act, they will not discuss the matter. But it must be assumed the Home Office would afford them primacy over Strathclyde Police.

An Army Intelligence Corps Captain from G2 (Security and Intelligence) was sent from Northern Ireland. It is not known if he was accompanied.

Finally, journalist David Walmsley reported:

> *'I arrived the morning of 3 June, though the crash site was still sealed off with no access. I spoke to US Navy SEALs above the site, so can confirm their presence and their involvement in a recovery operation'.*

These US personnel also stayed on the scene until 5 June. It cannot be said they were merely helping with casualty recovery, because that was completed on 3 June.

Mountain Rescue Teams (MRTs)

The RAF Kinloss advance party arrived at 2030 and were prevented from entering the crash scene by Strathclyde Police. Reports suggest this was

---

150 Letter FOI 2012/00775, 1 September 2021.

more than a polite verbal exchange, only resolved later in the evening by the RAF Machrihanish Station Commander. One must assume the police were acting under orders, but those same orders apparently told them to allow US Forces to undertake a search. The matter is complicated by a long-running feud between MoD and Emergency Services over primacy. Initially this rests with the civilian police, as the removal of bodies must be co-ordinated (in Scotland) by the Crown Office.

Of those present, only the MRTs provided reports (at Annex S of the Board's report). The Kinloss MRT leader said this:

'It very soon became apparent that the cordoning of the site and the exclusion of people from within it would not be carried out in accordance with RAF regulations. At one time, a large inflatable tent was erected 15 metres from the aircraft wreckage while 40 Fire Brigade personnel smoked and had a meal. Fire Brigade, police and Coastguard personnel continued to arrive over the initial four hours, and entered the site for a "look" until the eventual intervention of the RAF Machrihanish Station Commander'.

The advice to Service personnel is to wait until Fire and Rescue Services operations are complete before *'attempting'* to take control. This is unhelpful when there is an obvious security risk.

In summary, it can be gleaned the site was insecure until around 2230, just as darkness fell; at which point the RAF Leuchars MRT established a long-term crash guard, but remained hindered in their task.

Investigators

The Air Accidents Investigation Branch (AAIB) Inspectors and the Board of Inquiry members arrived on the scene between 1130 and 1200 on 3 June. (The Board had arrived at RAF Machrihanish at 0630). Thereafter details are scant, but it is clear from the AAIB comment in their report that the devices had largely been collected by this time. Separately, the RAF searched for the classified equipment that only it knew the Chinook carried; which was also not offered for technical analysis.

Unfortunately, much of the AAIB's records have been lost or corrupted in a migration from Mac to PC and, a few years later, back again. (What price back-ups?!). But Senior Inspector Tony Cable recently expanded on this:

'The Fire Service and the police were on site well before me, as were RAF and Security people. I recall seeing a collection of personal devices picked up from around the site, mostly cameras and phones. I understood that the Board was arranging specialist examination of these; by whom I am uncertain, but I think it

was Security Services.[151]

That is, the devices were visible to Mr Cable, but he was not afforded sufficient access to note the types, or even count them. Yet, his job was to report on evidence from the scene. Plainly, he was obstructed.

At 1310 on Monday 7 June the Board President gave permission for the RN Mobile Aircraft Support Unit to commence removal of wreckage. But some of the most vital evidence was already gone, and out of his control.

Assessment

Of the three Strathclyde Police officers and two civilian employees who appeared at the Fatal Accident Inquiry, two were questioned about physical evidence by the Advocate Depute - Detective Chief Inspector Joyce and Leonard Warren, a Scenes of Crime Officer:

'Am I right in thinking great care was taken at the site to mark out the items of personal property which were recovered and in so far as they could they were allocated to individual deceased; is that right?'

(Joyce) *'That is correct, yes'.*

'Was it your understanding that apart from removing the bodies of the deceased that the wreckage had been left untouched and was guarded so that it was untouched until you took these photographs?'

(Warren) *'To the best of my knowledge, yes'.*

As ever, carefully selected questions were asked of carefully selected witnesses, the aim being to conceal the truth. The families could only infer that no items had been removed. But both officers had only arrived at the scene the following day. No-one who was there on the evening of the crash or the following morning was asked, the entire matter dismissed in two meaningless questions. That the court was misled is now exposed by the admission that items *were* removed, by people who got there before.

The chain of custody was broken and the devices not returned for technical examination, fatally undermining the Board's report. In a criminal case that would (or should) preclude prosecution even being considered, never mind a manslaughter conviction.

Where is the missing evidence?

While researching this book, on 15 September 2020 I asked Police

---

151 E-mail Cable/Hill, 15 October 2020, 12:14.

Scotland:

> 'The RAF Directorate of the Air Staff have confirmed that physical evidence (Personal Electronic Devices) was removed from the crash scene by "police or security service", before the arrival of the accident investigators at 1130 on 3 June 1994. Would you please list any such items removed by the then Strathclyde Police, to whom it was sent, and under what authority'.

Each police officer must submit a report to the Divisional Commander, and he to the Chief Constable. At which point a consolidated Strathclyde Police report would have to be sent to the Procurator Fiscal and Board of Inquiry. This principle would apply to all emergency services, so I also asked for this report.

Police Scotland replied that they could *'neither confirm nor deny'* they held any information, claiming public interest immunity. When asked to review their decisions they were obtuse, conflating cause of death and cause of accident.

I submitted an appeal to the Information Commissioner for Scotland. His office responded promptly in several personal phone calls. On 17 February 2021 it upheld my appeal on the grounds this was a public interest matter, instructing Police Scotland to firmly state whether or not they have, or had, the devices, and any report to the Board of Inquiry. On 26 February 2021, the police wrote:

> 'I can advise that Police Scotland no longer wish to rely on Section 18 of the Act (Neither confirm nor deny), in conjunction with Section 34 (Investigations). I can advise that we now replace this with Section 17 - Information not held'.[152]

Why not say this in the first place? Plainly there is something to hide, and it took six months to concoct *'not held'*. Given the Government undertaking that all ZD576 papers shall be retained, the implication is that no report was prepared. I consider this impossible; so it is likely the report has been deposited somewhere else, to permit plausible deniability.

*

In parallel, I asked the Crown Office (COPFS) in Glasgow:

> *1. Would you please advise if COPFS, and through it Sheriff Sir Stephen Young or the legal representatives of the victims, were advised that evidence that may have revealed cause or contributory factors, in the form of Personal Electronic Devices, was removed from the scene and not made available to MoD or the Air Accidents Investigation Branch for assessment?*

---

152 Letter from Police Scotland IM-FOI-2020-1610, 26 February 2021.

2. *Would you be able to provide a copy of the report submitted to you by Strathclyde Police; or, if not, would you confirm one was submitted and when?*

In reply, it stated that it does not retain records about deaths after 10 years.[153] An astounding position in the face of 29 unexplained and uninvestigated deaths. I again note the Government's undertaking in 2019 to retain ZD576 records.

*

On 3 October 2020 two former RUC officers, one of them present in the aftermath, were asked about the devices, initially claiming the force did not have cell phones in 1994. When challenged they declined to say more.[154] Why say such a thing in the face of RUC widows, whom they knew well, confirming their husbands had phones and they were not returned?

On 9 October 2020, I asked the Police Service of Northern Ireland (PSNI):

'Did (the RUC) remove, or assist in the removal, of said devices? If so, where are the devices now, and could you provide details of them (not their content, which I accept is classified). For example, Orange or One to One phones'.

The PSNI replied in an almost identical *'neither confirm nor deny'* letter. I appealed to the Information Commissioner in Northern Ireland who, on 5 March 2021, replied saying he had passed the matter to his counterpart in England. On 18 March 2021 the English office wrote asking that all the papers be resubmitted - seemingly they had not been forwarded from Northern Ireland. A Decision Notice was issued almost two years after the original request, on 31 August 2022. The Information Commissioner upheld the PSNI's right to *neither confirm nor deny*, on the following grounds:

'Confirmation or denial that PSNI holds relevant information could have a detrimental effect on current counterterrorism work. The Commissioner considers that information relating to the personal electronic devices described in the request may well be of value in the present day'.

Quite how the number and type of devices could be of value to terrorists in 2022 is beyond me. Equally odd is the refusal to confirm or deny their staff helped retrieve the devices, given the officers concerned have confirmed this in media interviews. I conclude that PSNI are obstructing the course of justice, in concert with MoD and the Home Office.

---

153 Crown Office & Procurator Fiscal Service letter R024249, 9 November 2020.
154 Telecon with former RUC officers (names withheld), 3 October 2020, 10:30.

Above the law

In his Mull of Kintyre Review report, Lord Philip confirmed:

'A Board of Inquiry was an internal process convened for the Armed Services to determine how a serious incident happened and why, and to make recommendations to prevent a recurrence. <u>The Board of Inquiry was not a substitute for a legal inquiry into cause and circumstances of death</u>'.[155]

This was the view taken by then Lord Advocate, Donald Mackay, Baron Mackay of Drumadoon. However, the current incumbent, James Wolffe QC, disagrees. He insists a Fatal Accident Inquiry replicates the work of the MoD Inquiry, so is unnecessary.[156] He will not say why he disagrees with Baron Mackay and Lord Philip, and indeed the law he is bound by. He overlooks that a Board may hear evidence that is not admissible in court, meaning the court and families are denied vital information and, logically, the Crown Office must separately order the police to investigate that evidence which MoD ignores or will not release. In reality it never does, and the police show no inclination.

This is a direct insult to the bereaved. The MoD Inquiry is a one-way street, with families not permitted to ask questions or be represented. A Fatal Accident Inquiry, like a Coroner's Inquest, is their only opportunity to have MoD cross-examined. The Inquiries have different aims: MoD's to determine cause of the accident, the judiciary's to determine cause of death - the overlap being to prevent recurrence. Mr Wolffe *must* realise this, so who is he protecting? He is fully aware that the families were lied to, and that untrue statements were carelessly and negligently made in court without checking their veracity. That, the obligation to be candid in matters of fact was disregarded. In Scotland that is termed 'defeating the ends of justice' - a crime against the justice system itself as it prevents courts from getting to the truth.

*

In 2020 a new Head of the Scottish Fatalities Investigation Unit in the Crown Office was appointed, former Procurator Fiscal for North Strathclyde Laura Mundell. A renewed submission was sent on 16 November 2020 advising her of the above, in particular the deception over airworthiness status and the testing of Personal Electronic Devices.

On 17 February 2021 she replied, saying the Crown Office was *'not currently*

---

155 Mull of Kintyre Review report, paragraph 3.1.2.
156 *Inter alia*, letter R020188, 5 June 2019, from Lord Advocate James Wolffe QC to Douglas Ross MP.

in receipt of any _new_ evidence supporting an allegation of potential criminality'.[157] This ignored that she already held the _fresh_ evidence set out in this book. On 22 February 2021 a full submission was made; once again enclosing not only the evidence about electronic devices, but the fresh evidence submitted to the Mull of Kintyre Review in 2010/11. Hasteners were sent in August and December 2021, and November 2022.

Finally, on 12 December 2022 Ms Mundell's successor, Katrina Parkes, replied. She stated that my submission contained no new or fresh evidence relevant to the accident or deaths. I replied:

'You say that none of the evidence submitted constitutes new or fresh evidence.

By definition, then, the Crown Office has always known that, for example:

- The aircraft was not airworthy, serviceable or fit for purpose, but a false declaration made to the crew that it was.
- The aircraft's fuel computers were "positively dangerous".
- The crew were not permitted to rely upon the aircraft "in any way whatsoever", but were not told this.
- Physical evidence crucial to establishing the accident timeline was removed from the scene by the police and/or security services prior to investigators arriving, and was not examined.
- False evidence was given to the Fatal Accident Inquiry on all the above.

Could you now say what action will be taken in respect of the offences I have outlined, in particular the failure of the Crown Office to notify this prior knowledge to the court and Mull of Kintyre Review?'

No reply.

*

Here, it is necessary to say that the Crown Office is well-known for colluding with MoD on these matters. For example, in the case of a Tornado mid-air collision over the Moray Firth in 2012 (3 killed), Richard Lockhead MSP wrote to Mr Wolffe in November 2017 enclosing a discussion document containing fresh evidence should a Fatal Accident Inquiry be held. The 11-page document was marked CONFIDENTIAL on every page, and the covering letter made it clear that it should not be passed on. At a meeting in May 2018 Ms Mundell's predecessor, David Green, asked if he could pass the document on to MoD. It was made clear that he could not, without the express permission of the Service Inquiry President, an RN Commander, who had been quoted therein. This was

---

157 Crown Office & Procurator Fiscal Service letter, R014375, 17 February 2021.

confirmed and acknowledged in follow-up e-mails. Also agreed was that any MoD comments would be made available to all parties. However, in August 2019 Mr Green was forced to admit he had immediately sent the document to Air Marshal Richard Garwood, Director General Defence Safety Authority, without consulting with or advising the President or Mr Lockhead. The Crown Office refuses to release this correspondence, or Mr Green's briefing to Mr Wolffe. Of the 30 issues raised, only three were addressed by the Lord Advocate, and these were the minor ones.

The Crown Office has claimed the circumstances of this Tornado accident and loss of life have been fully investigated. A lie. The final acts have been looked at by MoD, but the causes and circumstances of the deaths have not. There has been no cross-examination, no involvement of families, no submissions by independent experts, and there is no report covering the events of the Crown Office claim. What we have is in-house evaluation of some alleged facts by non-specialists in this very specialised field. Let the Crown Office produce the report into its alleged *'full investigation'* for public scrutiny. It cannot, in the same way it cannot on Chinook ZD576. An open judicial inquiry is required into this malpractice and malfeasance.

Summary

It is one thing to secure classified data, but quite another to conceal material evidence when it might offer an explanation for the accident. To persist, knowing that its very existence casts doubt on charges laid against the deceased, is the worst kind of misconduct in public office. Plainly, MoD and the police were willing to risk this, but remain nervous over their failure to gather evidence and investigate; and MoD concerned that radio frequency emissions may have caused malfunctions in the aircraft.

The removal of these devices should have formed a major part of the Board's report, the President declaring his investigation blighted - not least because it was his sole responsibility to determine when wreckage could be removed. It is likely he noted this to, at least, the Group Flight Safety Officer who was advising him. Both were in the unusual position of having to deal with senior officers from multiple other agencies. Indeed, not only was the Safety Officer an ever-present, he saw the report after the Reviewing Officers (Group Captains Wedge and Crawford) remarked, but before it was passed to Air Vice Marshal Day. It could be said that, without actually signing it, he was in a unique position to influence it.

The Inspectorate of Flight Safety knew the aircraft's airworthiness was in doubt. But the previous Director, Air Commodore Martin Abbott, had left post in April 1994. Was his successor, Air Commodore Rick Peacock-Edwards, briefed by the Group Safety Officers? It is known he advised the Chief of the Air Staff, Air Chief Marshal Graydon, against the gross negligence findings, saying they were unsustainable. Given his role, this advice would be solely aircraft safety-based. He was interviewed by the Mull of Kintyre Review, who no doubt found all this compelling corroboration of the main submission it had received.

It is thought provoking that MoD, Police Scotland, the Police Service of Northern Ireland and the Crown Office remain unmoved over these violations, and the cause of 29 deaths. My belief is that, above operational level, all conspired to conceal the truth, and continue to do so. And the Information Commissioner for England and Wales has colluded. The factual evidence is overwhelming.

*

The most likely scenario is that MI5, the RUC and Army Intelligence were allowed to purge classified data from the devices carried by their personnel, which were then transferred to the RAF Provost and Security Service. Similarly, it is likely the latter took possession of the classified ALQ-157 equipment.

But regardless of the precise details, the Board of Inquiry was denied crucial material evidence, and this was not revealed to families or Inquiries. The control of these items was governed by the Criminal Procedure (Scotland) Act 1975 and the Service Codes of Practice. The significant legal issue is that evidence left the Crown Office's jurisdiction, apparently without it knowing. But it does now.

Finally, and briefly, precisely the same thing occurred after the death of Corporal Jon Bayliss on 20 March 2018, when the Hawk he was a passenger in crashed at RAF Valley. His phone and GoPro were removed from the scene by the police, MoD denying in court that they contained retrievable data. This proved to be a lie.[158] They were returned only after four years, the Coroner refusing to take action against those who lied to her court.

---

158 'A Noble Anger' (David Hill, 2022).

22. Power destroys all reason

AP3207, the RAF Manual of Flight Safety, requires:

'Where a person fails, whether negligent or not, the Board should consider the possible human failings of others who placed that person in the situation'.

In this sense, the 'Board' includes all the Reviewing Officers. How was this requirement satisfied? It wasn't, despite the 1992 CHART report, and internal investigations and audits into *savings at the expense of safety*, having confirmed systemic Organisational failings.

Also, it was required to consider 'Unsatisfactory Equipment' as a causal factor. But it was left to campaigners to uncover proof of this, Lord Philip reiterating the mandate placed upon the Air Staff that the Chinook HC Mk2 was *not to be relied upon in any way*. Moreover, the Air Accidents Investigation Branch noted Technical Faults (and worse, defects) in both ZD576 and the wider Chinook fleet.

Why would the Board ignore such a significant body of evidence? To make a finding of gross negligence, the Senior Reviewing Officers had to positively eliminate other possible causes, and give reasons why. They did not even attempt to, because the Organisational failings were so great they led directly to the Unsatisfactory Equipment and Technical Faults.

For 17 years the focus was on the RAF's inability to prove guilt without any doubt whatsoever. In fact, before this question even arose its case failed the very first hurdle - the question of duty of care owed the pilots, aircrewmen, passengers and those whom the aircraft overflew. (One must never forget it was sheer luck that hill-walkers were not killed or injured). The pilots were left alone to deal with chronic management failures and refusal to respond to notifications of critical risks. The cumulative effect means Controlled Flight Into Terrain becomes less and less likely, and Uncontrolled Flight all the more likely.

Today, despite the gross negligence findings being overturned, they have not been replaced with anything. The reasons are clear.

Culpability

Air Vice Marshal Anthony Bagnall held a duty of care to ensure the Mk2 was airworthy before issuing his Release to Service. He failed in this duty, making a false declaration that he had satisfied it. An accident was a reasonably foreseeable consequence of ordering aircrew to fly an unairworthy aircraft. As a pilot he would know this. Moreover, his proximity to the pilots is demonstrated by the fact they relied entirely upon the accuracy of his Release to Service. That is, he cannot claim to be so removed from the event that his actions were irrelevant. Logically, therefore, a duty of care responsibility for the safety of the aircraft could not be delegated to the pilots.

As the officer charged with signing the Master Airworthiness Reference, it is reasonable to expect him to understand the rules he was bound by, and what he was signing for. He had been in post for 15 months, and on his first day had received the CHART report repeating previous warnings. If he didn't know what it meant, he should have made it his business to find out. (And if he did not know, what does that say about a system that permitted his appointment?). Whether or not he understood this may never be known. He has never spoken.

But while the signatory, he would not have acted alone on such a vital matter. The decision to take such a gamble lay above him, not only with the Chief of the Air Staff but in the political arena. Was the Secretary of State, Sir Malcolm Rifkind, told? He was not. In fact, he was lied to. Therefore, *he* cannot be held liable. Matters are narrowed considerably...

*

It is inconceivable Chief of the Air Staff, Air Chief Marshal Sir Michael Graydon, was unaware of CHART. He took up post in November 1992, a full year before Bagnall issued his Release to Service. In that time, his Air Staff subordinates were inundated with notifications that the Mk2 was not airworthy. It is unthinkable that he was not aware of this. His subsequent actions are revealing. For example, the claims he made to Sir John Grandy and, in the same letter, his description of Wing Commander Pulford's performance as *'barely adequate'*. But at least Pulford was alive to defend himself, if he wished to.

CHART was commissioned by Air Chief Marshal Sir Michael Alcock, the RAF Chief Engineer. It was his duty to ensure that its recommendations - in reality pre-conditions to achieving airworthiness - were implemented. They were not, evidenced by Sir Robert Walmsley's confirmation to the Public Accounts Committee in March 1999 that the main failures remained. Likewise, Alcock's subsequent actions are revealing.

Air Chief Marshals Sir William Wratten and Sir John Day were not in post on 2 June 1994. They inherited a situation not of their own making. *Their* wrongdoing relates to the findings against the pilots, delivered in the certain knowledge that the standard of proof had not been met. The Lords dismissed their evidence.

There is nothing I can say that can make the actions of these officers seem any worse. Wilfully blind to the known facts, they knowingly and maliciously blamed the wrong people and deceived Inquiries. This, and the rejection of legal obligations, is behaviour beyond how a reasonable person is expected to act. So, too, is the behaviour of those who knew the aircraft was unairworthy, but actively concealed this.

In summary, there is irrefutable evidence of:

- The existence of a duty of care.
- An indifference to a notified risk of injury or death.
- A determination to run the risk regardless, and a deliberate decision to actively deceive those required to take the risk.
- A failure to mitigate that went beyond inadvertence.

...by the Air Staff, not the pilots.

Lord Craig of Radley, former Chief of the Defence Staff and Marshal of the Royal Air Force, to the House of Lords in 1997:

'Negligence is defined as: "The doing of something which in the circumstances a reasonable person would not do or do differently". It is not reasonable to put at risk your aircraft and the lives of all on board'.[159]

But he wanted it both ways. It was fine for the Air Staff to place the aircraft and all those on board at risk. *Their* negligence was not to be considered. His former Personal Staff Officer, Air Chief Marshal Sir Peter Squire, agreed. More linkages.

Intent

Degree of intent is important, not least because of the uncertainty in legal circles over the concept of manslaughter by gross negligence. Indeed, many argue that if there is intent, then the offence is greater than mere manslaughter.

One intention was to run down airworthiness management, generating funding to compensate for conscious and gross waste. That was fraud by misrepresentation. Twenty years later, in 2009, the Nimrod Review confirmed the success of this policy. The Government and MoD accepted its findings. The main submission to the Mull of Kintyre Review was based on the same known facts.

---

159 https://api.parliament.uk/historic-hansard/lords/1997/may/22/chinook-helicopter-accident-inquiry

The policy led directly to scores of avoidable deaths. There was no intent to kill, but that was an easily foreseeable outcome so at the very least there was indifference. The risks were notified by civilian staff from (at least) January 1988-on, and were repeated by the Director of Flight Safety in August 1992. The punitive action taken against these staff, and the failure to advise aircrew of the risks, involved conduct so appalling, so inexcusable, I consider it outwith the bounds of acceptable behaviour. But, infinitely worse, a false declaration was made that all risks were As Low As Reasonably Practicable.

I believe these actions meet the criteria for gross negligence manslaughter. I accept this is generous. The impact for the bereaved is no less than that of murder.

23. Conclusions

Recap

Over a minute before impact, around the time Mr Holbrook saw the aircraft, SuperTANS produced an ALERT signifying Waypoint A was coming up. The system was indicating time and distance to go, and instruments were showing airspeed, groundspeed, altitude, height and attitude. Flight Lieutenant Tapper selected Waypoint B, signalling an intention to turn slightly left and follow their agreed low-level flight plan. His retention of Tactical Steer mode in SuperTANS, other equipment settings, and eye-witness testimony, indicates they were in Visual Meteorological Conditions and had no intention of overflying the Mull.

The Board of Inquiry rejected all this, claiming Flight Lieutenant Tapper made an error of judgment by instructing Flight Lieutenant Cook to select an inappropriate rate of climb. But, that there were no failings on the part of Flight Lieutenant Cook for failing to identify this 'error'. It speculated that <u>after</u> changing waypoints, Tapper suddenly decided to depart from the agreed plan. That, Cook's situational awareness had degraded due to the weather, and he simply followed Tapper's instruction.[160]

The Senior Reviewing Officers, Air Chief Marshal Wratten and Air Vice Marshal Day, disagreed with the Board. They found <u>both</u> pilots negligent to a gross degree, saying Cook should have recognised Tapper's *'unsound course of action'* and refused to take it. This implies they considered and rejected <u>all</u> scenarios whereby only one pilot was at fault. Also, that the aircraft remained under full control, and the crewmen were not party to the conversation in the cockpit or assisting with navigation.[161]

The unofficial third Senior Reviewing Officer, Air Chief Marshal Graydon, disagreed with everyone before him. He claimed the aircraft was *'off course by some miles'*, implying Cook aimed the aircraft at a visible landmass they had no intention of going within miles of, and Tapper recognised and allowed this.

Known facts

The lead anomaly was that the aircraft was not airworthy, serviceable or fit for purpose. Its level of clearance was 'INTERIM', meaning *not to be*

---

160 Board of Inquiry report, paragraphs 67 & 68.
161 Board of Inquiry report, Parts 4 & 5.

relied upon in any way. The primary root cause was notified to the correct people, at least six years before the accident. This was confirmed by various internal audits and, in 2009, the Nimrod Review. In 2011 the Mull of Kintyre Review reiterated the effect on Chinook.

Underpinning this are known constraints, faults, defects, unresolved issues and pending engineering investigations; among them:

- Safety Critical fuel control software was illegal, unverifiable, and its implementation *'positively dangerous'*, meaning associated risks were unquantifiable.
- ZD576's Icing Limit was below Minimum Safe Altitude.
- The GPS had a faulty power supply and Time of Day output.
- The UHF radio was in TEST mode and the Intercom in FAIL mode.
- The Radar Altimeter had an initial assembly defect and incorrectly set Sensitivity Range Control, and Flight Lieutenant Tapper's Indicator was unserviceable.
- There was a defective tie bolt securing the Thrust/Roll output bellcrank, due to superfluous hole which weakened its structure.
- Undemanded Flight Control Movements, and engine run-ups, run-downs and flameouts were prevalent.
- Essential modifications had not yet been designed.
- Electro-Magnetic Compatibility testing had barely commenced.

As MoD has conceded all this I have not sought to debate the points, merely explain them and offer context. All are contributory factors, and many point to plausible and probable cause. All were known before the accident. There can be no valid reason for accepting such an aircraft off-contract, or ordering Service regulated flying in it.

MoD's arguments do not stand up when exposed to this evidence. The suggestion of gross negligence by the pilots was based on lies, false propositions and palpably absurd assumptions. The case against the pilots was contrived, to conceal gross misconduct at the highest levels of the RAF.

The lead anomaly, the fact that the Chinook HC Mk2 was not airworthy, dominates this entire case. The decision to make a false declaration that it *was* airworthy was the decisive violation. No investigation should have proceeded until this known fact was aired and fully understood. Until then, the proximate cause (the final act) should not even have been be considered.

Cause

The combination of known faults, defects and performance degradation points inexorably towards technical failure. When the above facts are viewed as a whole, there is convincing evidence of malfunctions or disturbances affecting multiple aircraft systems. They had happened before, and happened again, in what RAF engineers and aircrew described as *flight safety critical events*.

Ironically, I gravitate towards the RAF's own words. The Special Flying Instruction of 28 February 1994, warning of Undemanded Flight Control Movements (UFCMs), is compelling. It explains perfectly what is known about the final moments, and reveals serious shortcomings in the RAF's application of MoD's Safety Management System.

Additionally, the testimony of Squadron Leader Robert Burke and Flight Lieutenant Iain MacFarlane regarding these UFCMs, and of Air Commodore Carl Scott regarding behavioural patterns and the problems during introduction to service, is persuasive. When combined with Flight Lieutenant Tapper's actions, and the known status of the aircraft, the argument for technical failure becomes overwhelming.

I conclude, therefore, that Flight Lieutenant Cook attempted the turn but something prevented it. The most likely cause was UFCM. I offer three interconnected scenarios:

1. A recurrence of an engine runaway up and rotor overspeed, caused by a malfunction of the unverified and uncertified Full Authority Digital Engine Control (FADEC); which itself was susceptible to recurring Electro-Magnetic Interference.

2. A recurrence of an Automatic Flight Control System (AFCS) fault, particularly a recurring Differential Airspeed Hold (DASH) runaway.

3. A recurrence of Control Pallet debonding and/or balance spring detachment, causing a transitory or complete control jam.

Events may have been exacerbated by the resultant violent movements causing a recurrence of a Digital Engine Control Unit (DECU) connector, or pins/wiring within the connectors, working loose; in turn causing spurious warnings and fuel control malfunction. Conversely, these extant and recurring connector/wiring defects may have caused severe UFCMs.

Finally, and perhaps critically, I note the strong evidence of progressive electrical failures that could explain (1) and (2) above.

Any of the above, or combination thereof, and the resultant partial or full loss of control, would explain the failure to avoid the high ground they had intended turning away from. <u>Only this theory is consistent with all the known facts</u>.

My conclusion is reinforced by the inescapable fact that MoD lied to families, Ministers, every Inquiry and the media, about almost every aspect of the accident: from the maladministration of the preceding years, through the Air Staff releasing an unairworthy aircraft to service, to the ongoing concealment and destruction of material evidence.

In the months and years before June 1994, the RAF gambled on there not being <u>another</u> fatal accident caused by UFCM. Given its actions, it is reasonable to assume it was nervous over this being the cause again. It knew that disclosure would be of assistance to investigators and families. That is a powerful motive to deceive.

Culpability

There exists a contract between aircrew and MoD. The former accept a range of risks on the understanding MoD will mitigate them, as far as reasonably practicable. MoD tore this contract up. It violated its own rules, and operated outwith the constraints of its Safety Management System. Hazards were allowed to develop, the pilots harbouring deep suspicions about the aircraft. And had the passengers been told the aircraft's airworthiness certification was a fabrication, it is unlikely any would have boarded. Instead, they were all sent to their deaths in an unsafe aircraft.

The lessons of failure were there, but MoD and the RAF did not have the courage to face their failings. It is easy to follow the pack. True leaders would have spoken up. Instead, they reacted with cowardly malice against those who sought to correct the failings, and those who suffered from them. ZD576 was a recurrence, and subsequent fatal accidents have been caused by the same organisational and systemic failures. And there can be little doubt that, thankfully, further catastrophes have been avoided only by some members of the public challenging MoD's illegal actions.

The official silence is shameful, and dishonours the dead.

ANNEX A

Review of the Airworthiness, Engineering and Maintenance aspects of the Board of Inquiry into Chinook HC Mk2 ZD576

by Air Commodore John Blakeley

Introduction

In 2003 JB Consultancy was asked by Michael Tapper to review the airworthiness, engineering standards and maintenance issues revealed by the RAF Board of Inquiry (the 'Board') into the accident to RAF Chinook HC Mk2 ZD576 on 2 June 1994. This work was carried out *pro bono*.

The original report was based on the incomplete information made available by MoD. This 2011 update reflects further information provided to the Mull Group under the Freedom of Information Act, or other requests for documents. It concentrates on issues that should have been before the Board, including the Reviewing Officers.

It also looks at later evidence, particularly that given to the House of Lords Select Committee, and the latest position stated by MoD. Thus, there will be many similarities with the points made by others when questioning the decision to find the pilots grossly negligent.

The key element of the original review was to make an assessment as to whether the status of the Chinook's airworthiness, or other engineering or maintenance factors, could have been a cause of, or played a part in, the accident, and thus offering a further credible alternative to the findings of gross negligence. The conclusion of the original review was that both the airworthiness and serviceability of ZD576 must be called into question, and this finding has been further reinforced by all that we have learnt since then. Of particular interest is that although the original review was made available to MoD, it has neither carried out any detailed assessment of its findings, nor commented on its contents other than to reject it under the standard 'no new evidence' response.

I was a copy addressee, and concur with, the contents of David Hill's airworthiness submission to Lord Philip. This paper is intended to complement it by adding an In-Service/Operational viewpoint.

Background

Given that even the Senior Reviewing Officer, Air Chief Marshal Wratten, prefaces his findings with the comment that in the absence of an Accident Data Recorder no-one can ever be sure of the causes of this accident, both the findings of gross negligence and the subsequent MoD support for this decision, in the face of very significant and consistent legal opinion against these findings, is both surprising and worrying. However, better qualified men and women have already covered this issue, and I will not repeat their arguments, save to say that the original and subsequent reviews of the airworthiness and engineering audit trail cast even more doubt as to the safety of this verdict.

In my professional view, the competence and impartiality of the Board in reaching their decision, ranging from the original balance of probabilities position of 'pilot error' for the main Board, to the verdict of 'gross negligence' of the Senior Reviewing Officers, does not stand up to any serious scrutiny.

Also, the conduct of the Board, their apparently superficial look at the maintenance issues and documentation, and their choice and questioning of witnesses, confirms they immediately supposed pilot error - a position they maintained even when witness evidence questioned this approach. This presumption, I suggest, coloured everything that then happened, and may even have led to a failure to carry out a proper engineering review of the findings (since there is no evidence of this having taken place). As a result, pertinent facts were not put before the Reviewing Officers.

Support for these views is given by the failure of the Board to study:

- The Release to Service limitations. (Some are selectively mentioned).
- The workmanship standards achieved during the modification programme. (Particularly with respect to wiring defects).
- The design standards used by Boeing. (See Air Accidents Investigation Branch comments below on bonding).
- The Boscombe Down position. (Even if they had not seen the correspondence, it is known the Board President spoke to Boscombe).
- Their failure to follow up the outcome of the range of defects and faults on ZD576 that were still under investigation, or, indeed, confirm that these investigations had been authorised and were taking place.
- Their failure to interview the engineering managers on the status of ZD576, and how they ensured an airworthy aircraft was selected.
- Their failure to review the Wilmington incident of 1989 to see if any of the underlying problems there could have applied to ZD576. (Whereby an RAF Chinook was severely damaged due to poor software design. The software behaved as it was designed to, but almost destroyed the aircraft. MoD withheld this from all Inquiries despite it offering a plausible explanation for the loss of ZD576).
- Their failure to investigate the systems implications of the Power Turbine Inlet Temperature gauge problems, and how they might link to the incident that caused Boscombe to cease trials for the second time.
- Their failure to check whether all essential preparations had been made

for the Chinook HC Mk2 to be supported in Northern Ireland. (ZD576 was the first Mk2 in theatre).

The only conclusion is that the Board was (a) totally lacking in competence (and any investigative initiative) in the engineering area, and/or (b) had been told which direction to take. Even then, we know the Board did not go far enough in the eyes of senior Air Officers. Evidence of this is contained in a letter from Chief of the Air Staff Air Chief Marshal Graydon to Marshal of the Royal Air Force Sir John Grandy of 4 February 1997, where Graydon, being more than economical with the truth, commented:

> *'An exhaustive Board of Inquiry took place in which the President carried out a barely adequate job, avoiding any attribution of negligence to the pilots concerned. After considerable review, Air Officer Commanding 1 Group (Air Vice Marshal John Day), himself an extremely experienced helicopter pilot, concluded from his own analysis and that of the Farnborough scientists, that aircrew error must have been the primary factor of the accident. In essence there was no evidence to indicate any unserviceability of the aircraft when it hit the ground, it was off course by some miles, and it was proceeding at virtually maximum speed in very poor weather'.*

If we analyse just this single paragraph, we find quite a few areas of major concern - not least that the Chief of the Air Staff appears happy to lie to protect the RAF's position.

The only MoD Farnborough reports to the Board were by the Navigation System Research department, and School of Aviation Medicine. The former confirmed the SuperTANS/GPS system was vulnerable to interference from mobile phones, whereby the GPS ceased to track the satellites, generating an ALERT. The latter is primarily an analysis of the crash dynamics, concentrating on the pilots' seats. Neither report speculates as to cause, never mind liability. So, who are these people that Air Vice Marshal Day used, and what was their evidence? What was Day's analysis, and where is it documented in the Board's report? If Day and his 'scientists' wanted to change the conclusions of the main Board, why are they operating outside the Board process - apparently in some separate cabal of senior Air Officers? If these officers did not believe the Board's conclusions, and had evidence of their own, it should have been re-run with better terms of reference to include this evidence.

How did Graydon know the aircraft was serviceable? Even the Board does not go that far. Why does he say the aircraft was *'off course by some miles'*? It was not. If it had been, it would not have hit the Mull.

The aircraft was operating in Visual Meteorological Conditions and at a legal speed, but Graydon ignores these facts to indulge in speculation aimed at justifying the vilification of the pilots.

Graydon criticised the performance of the President of the Board in order to justify Day's actions. On the other hand, in the Lords debate on the Select Committee report, Lord Craig said the following in order to help justify the vote against accepting the Select Committee's Report:

> 'I was surprised that the Committee criticised the appointment of Wing Commander Pulford as board president because he had not previously conducted a Board of Inquiry. But the Royal Air Force has had few major accidents in recent years. Only one affected the Chinook fleet, over five years before the Mull accident. Previous experience of inquiries into fatal accidents is thus extremely limited. Of far greater importance in an Inquiry is current knowledge of the operation of the aircraft type in question. On those grounds, Wing Commander Pulford was very highly qualified - one of the most experienced helicopter pilots of his rank in the Royal Air Force. Expert advice was constantly available to him from flight safety and technical staff throughout the Inquiry. I believe that the Committee's criticism of his selection is both unfair and unwarranted'.

As they say - one of them must be wrong! A fairly minor point perhaps, but further evidence that 'protecting' the RAF was a higher priority than justice - a position made clear in the remarks by the same Reviewing Officers in the case of the Glen Ogle Tornado crash in September 1994.

Moreover, Craig was wrong to say there had only been one previous accident - an error repeating that of Assistant Chief of the Air Staff, Air Vice Marshal Tim Jenner, to the House of Commons Defence Select Committee on 4 March 1998, even though Jenner had been forced to belatedly correct himself. The most serious accident prior to ZD576 was in the Falkland Islands on 27 February 1987, killing seven. The reason why MoD misled over this loss was because the Board President, Wing Commander Malcolm Pledger, had been instructed to find 'cause unknown', when the same Air Accidents Investigation Branch Inspector, Tony Cable, had uncovered a root cause - poor Quality Control at Boeing.

*

The Board confirm their starting position on page 1:

> 'There was sufficient evidence to eliminate as possible causes: major technical malfunction or structural failure of the aircraft prior to impact. Therefore, the Inquiry focused on the crew's handling and operation of the aircraft'.

Where this decision was made, and on what evidence, is not stated. Indeed, it is not even supported by subsequent comments of the Board itself, and I will give further examples of this major inconsistency.

If the technical evidence is never fully analysed (and it is my contention that it was not), and if known facts that do not support the aircrew error hypothesis are ignored or not pursued, then alternative explanations will never be found. This ignoring of information and facts not only applies to the Board's deliberations, but has been a constant theme in MoD's responses to the various Inquiries and Committees. Yet each has still found against the gross negligence decision.

The Air Accidents Investigation Branch (AAIB) report, which has been widely misquoted, certainly does not eliminate a technical cause for the accident. I comment later on the control problems suffered by ZD576 just days before the accident, and on the comments of one expert witness to the House of Lords, test pilot Robert Burke. The AAIB stated:

- The possibility of control system jam could not be positively dismissed.
- Most attachment inserts on both flight control system pallets had detached, including the Balance Spring Bracket that had previously detached from ZD576's thrust/yaw pallet, with little evidence available to eliminate the possibility of pre-impact detachment.
- The method of attaching components to the pallets appeared less positive and less verifiable than would normally be expected for a flight control system application.

If we now add the response received by Lord Anthony Jacobs from the Director of Air Staff when he asked when a latent control jam would manifest itself:

'If at any point the Chinook had a latent control jam preventing the helicopter from turning, but the helicopter was continuing on a straight course, the aircrew may not have had any indication that there was a problem. <u>The problem would only become apparent when they tried to instigate a change of course away from dead ahead</u>'.

This was neither rocket science nor based on new understanding. The same comment would have applied if the Board had asked itself, as it should have done, the same question. Neither an earlier incident on 10 May 1994 (discussed later), nor the AAIB report, should have been ignored. If taken into account, there is no way the possibility of a control jam being a cause of the accident could have been discounted.

The airworthiness chain

JSP318 (Regulation of Ministry of Defence Aircraft) defines airworthiness:

'The ability of an aircraft or other airborne equipment or system to operate

without significant hazard to aircrew, groundcrew, passengers or the general public over which the airborne systems are flown'.

It is interesting to note that the Board's Terms of Reference do not specifically task it to look at whether either the Chinook fleet, or ZD576 as an individual aircraft, were airworthy at the time of the accident. This despite the fleet problems at that time being well known to supervisors and commanders. The Board was, though, specifically tasked to assess the equivalent human failings. The Board, including the Reviewing Officers, does not mention the word 'airworthiness' at any point.

When this definition is taken into account, it becomes easier to see the 'advantages' of this being an aircrew accident rather than having some basic and difficult-to-answer questions raised. Such questions, by either the Board or the Review process, would quickly extend to the RAF's decision to continue to operate the aircraft at all; as well as questioning whether maintenance errors and lack of engineering supervision contributed to a major airworthiness breakdown. Of equal concern must be that throughout all of MoD's reviews, and Ministers' 'soul searching' since the findings were challenged, nobody has looked at this area from MoD's side. One must draw one's own conclusion as to why.

*

To assess whether the Board conducted a thorough and competent investigation of the possible non-aircrew causes of the accident, and the relevance of the problems being experienced with the aircraft's entry into service, it is first necessary to understand how the airworthiness of any aircraft and its systems is established. In this short paper it is not feasible to cover all the issues (MoD's Defence Standard 00-970 on airworthiness runs to thousands of pages), but it is worth mentioning the core components. As a matter of policy, those marked * were deficient across MoD Air Systems at the time of the accident. That is, they were systemic failings. Those marked # were deficient on Chinook HC Mk2.

- System definition #
- Contract requirements #
- Design and Development - hardware and software #
- Qualification testing of components and systems #
- Verification and validation of software *
- Quality Control and Assurance systems and standards *
- Flight Trials - both manufacturer's and MoD's *

- Certification *
- Recommendations from Boscombe Down
- Release to Service, including flight limitations *
- Configuration Management *
- Training of air and ground crews *
- Documentation, Publications and Orders including such vital publications as Flight Reference Cards - the first line of reference in any emergency *
- Servicing recommendations *
- Maintenance standards, Recording systems and responsibilities *
- Fault Investigation, feedback, continuous review and remedial action *

It was probably easier to say that only Boscombe Down behaved and performed as required - perhaps the best illustration of why they were excluded from the investigation and Inquiries. Their ability to conduct their business relied entirely on these core activities being delivered.

Fleet level examples include FADEC software, despite its key role in the safe operation of the aircraft, being neither designed nor documented to flight critical software standards. Subsequent unexplained failures, with the lack of an audit trail, was one of the reasons why Boscombe had stopped flight trials at the time of the accident.

Indeed, initially, MoD implied that this was the only reason why Boscombe had stopped trials. We now know differently. It was because, in their view, there were too many (15 since October 1993) engine related incidents for which there was no satisfactory explanation - the last of these being one of four causing particular concern, on ZD576, just two weeks before the accident.

We also now know that Boscombe had refused to issue Controller Aircraft Release Recommendations for the Chinook HC Mk2, and in their letter of 6 June 1994 (which was drafted before the accident) said:

'The unquantifiable risks identified at the <u>INTERIM</u> Controller Aircraft Release at this stage may not in themselves have changed, but some have become more clearly defined by events, to an extent where we now consider the consequences of the risks and the probability of an occurrence to be unacceptable'.

In other words, matters had become worse. This letter was either ignored by, or not given to, the main Board. But the office of the Senior Reviewing Officer saw it, because a reply was drafted.

There were also major concerns in areas such as the Navigation,

Communications and Electrical Systems, training, and aircrew documentation. (The Board does not seem to have considered these issues at all as far as the maintenance crews were concerned).

Also, at the time of the accident the RAF operational fleet was operating to quite restrictive flight limitations, and suffering a significant number of unexplained, and sometimes flight safety related, incidents. In my view, and supported by a number of witness statements, these incidents had become the 'norm', to the extent they not only hid 'real' defects (a frequent occurrence in my experience), but the responsible commanders and flight supervisors were so used to them occurring that they were no longer questioning the underlying airworthiness.

The high possibility of distraction is a position acknowledged by Station Commander RAF Odiham, and even accepted as a possibility by the Board. The Board must have known that the Release to Service contained a quite extraordinary (in airworthiness terms, for a helicopter operating day-to-day at low level with still uncertified FADEC software) warning:

'Pending manufacturers investigations and a remedial solution, the "Eng Fail" caption may illuminate spuriously on the Caution Advisory Panel, with a corresponding illumination of the master caution light. The pilot must immediately verify the status of the engine by a scan of engine instruments. If engine operation is normal, aircrew should expect the "Eng Fail" light to extinguish after a 12 second lapse time'.

'Eng Fail' indicates to the pilot that an engine is in the process of running down. Boscombe Down report E1109, 26 October 1993, paragraph 11h (1)(I) recommended changing the amber captions to red (i.e. warnings, not cautions) and incorporating an associated audio warning Attention Getter. It had previously stated, on 22 October, that the Caution Advisory Panel and Attention Getters *'could be dimmed to extinction, leaving the aircrew unaware of major malfunctions'*. The Board of Inquiry did not say if these changes had been incorporated.

Nor did the Board assess the potential for distraction if the scan of engine instruments confirmed a problem. (See PTIT, above). What were the odds of both engine fail captions illuminating at the same time, which would very definitely be a major distraction? The Tornado GR1 originally had a similar situation with spurious engine oil temp lights, except that to be on the safe side the 'offending' engine was shut down. I well recall the day when both lights came on simultaneously. Fortunately, the pilot did <u>not</u> follow the Flight Reference Cards and shut down both engines, but he was high level and had time to make a full analysis of what was happening, as well as an alternative means of landing.

These 'fleet' issues contributed to an overall unsatisfactory set of procedures and standards for introducing the Mk2 into service. I have no doubt they were a possible cause of, or contributor to, the accident, and raise the obvious question as to why the RAF was operating the Mk2 at all. Also, why an aircraft that was suffering from these problems, and which in June 1994, based on the witness statements to the Board, did not meet the definition of airworthiness, was chosen for such a sensitive and high-profile passenger sortie. Especially when it was not an operational one and could have been flown by any passenger aircraft, including a civilian one. The fact that the Board ignored these issues shows just how fixed their mind set was (or had been directed).

Many areas in the above list apply to ZD576 itself. This is a different, but complementary, story to that of the Mk2 'fleet' airworthiness, and I will look at these areas in the following sections.

Conduct of the Board

Although the Terms of Reference for the Board were not prescriptive - indeed they are typical of any Board of this type - anyone reading the report and the witness questioning must come to the conclusion that the Board <u>never</u> felt the accident was caused by maintenance or engineering/equipment deficiencies; and they are quick to confirm this.

Worrying, given the problems with the Mk2 (which were known to the Convening Authority and the Board), is the fact that the Board was not specifically tasked to look at the status of the overall Mid-Life Upgrade programme to see if any of these issues had a bearing on the accident.

Whether this failure, and the concentration on aircrew performance, was caused by direction from above (and from experience I can confirm this happens), or whether it was because the Board did not possess the necessary knowledge and competence, only the officers concerned can tell us. But, it must be suspected that the content of the Chinook Airworthiness Review Team report - uncovered by David Hill in 2010 - played a part, as it had notified the Air Staff of just such issues.

What is certain is that the general tenor is that of 'situating the appreciation' that this was an aircrew error accident. When the remarks of the two Station Commanders are also taken into account, then in my view it is likely that the Board was directed down certain paths.

Nevertheless, and despite their early decision to eliminate technical malfunctions as a cause, the Board did do some limited, and as a result of their decision not to follow things up, inconclusive, work in this area. The following comments are relevant examples of this:

- Paragraph 36d: 'An unforeseen technical malfunction of the type being experienced on the Chinook HC Mk2, which would not necessarily have left any physical evidence, remained a possibility, and could not be discounted'.
- Paragraph 46c: 'The HC Mk2 has experienced a number of unforeseen technical occurrences since its introduction to service, and although the technical investigation provided no evidence of any technical malfunction, the possibility of the crew being distracted by a technical fault which had left no trace could not be dismissed. The Board concluded that distraction by a technical malfunction could have been a contributory factor in the accident'.

What is not clear is why the Board decided it could only have been a 'distraction'. Witness 20, Squadron Leader David Morgan, a Qualified Helicopter Instructor on the Operational Conversion Unit, commented:

'The unforeseen malfunctions on the Chinook HC Mk2 of a <u>flight critical nature</u> have mainly been associated with the engine system FADEC. They have resulted in undemanded engine shutdown, engine run-up, spurious engine failure captions and misleading and confusing cockpit indications'.

The Board's Engineering Member was a 1 Group Staff Officer and not a current or experienced Chinook engineering officer. Whilst he had done the Manager's Course, his day-to-day experience with maintaining the aircraft was limited; perhaps non-existent. If anyone had thought that the accident might have had an engineering or maintenance cause, this would have been a surprising choice. It removed the first link in the staff review of the Board's report - the Staff Officer concerned was a member of the Board and hence was unlikely against it at the review stage. I note his next posting was to Boscombe Down as a rotary wing trials officer. Perhaps if he had been there first...

*

The Board makes no attempt to assess and confirm the training, qualifications and experience of the tradesmen involved in maintaining the aircraft at Aldergrove. Particularly on the Mk2, as this was the first time it had been deployed to Aldergrove - and ZD576 had only arrived two days before (and was in maintenance for much of that time). Obvious questions, which the Board do not seem to have addressed, are:

- Was this the first time these tradesmen had worked on the Mk2, or had they gained the required and relevant experience at Odiham before going on the detachment?
- Did engineering personnel change upon ZD576's arrival?

The Board did not consider this worth looking at - yet they looked at similar training and experience issues for the aircrew. Related to this, there is no assessment of the engineering publications for the Mk2, and whether there were any issues with the standard of these publications (as there were with the aircrew publications). (And, as David Hill uncovered in 2010, the Director of Flight Safety had already notified the Assistant Chief of the Air Staff of his concern over Chinook groundcrew having to use Argentinian publications captured in 1982, as they were better than the RAF's).

The Board does not ask if all relevant maintenance and engineering documentation was available to the Aldergrove detachment for the Mk2. There is no attempt, for example, to call the Engineering Records personnel at RAF Aldergrove to give evidence.

Although the 7 Squadron detachment was operating on the Engineering Order Book (EOB) of RAF Odiham, not RAF Aldergrove, this is not mentioned by the Board. No attempt is made to ensure that the EOB is correct, relevant and has been implemented. OC Engineering Wing at Odiham, the officer responsible for the airworthiness of the aircraft within RAF Odiham's chain of command, is not even called as a witness.

The Board finds what, in normal circumstances, would be a major breach of engineering regulations, i.e. the carrying out of work on the aircraft without the audit trail of a Maintenance Work Order. (Discussed further below). Only one of the Reviewing Officers (Station Commander RAF Aldergrove) comments on this; starting with the assumption that the maintenance errors were of a 'minor' nature and did not contribute to the accident. Again, as a professional RAF engineer, I cannot agree with this statement. Such slack maintenance procedures are unacceptable in peacetime operations; albeit it is also my experience that a detachment does lend itself to this approach.

However, when the flight following these problems leads to tragedy, there is no excuse for not investigating the standards of maintenance and supervision, or the full implications of the faults and defects that went uninvestigated. It is quite possible that these maintenance errors, coupled with a failure to investigate the pilots' concerns, and then the lack of a full assessment of the problems against the history of the aircraft, could have left the aircraft the victim of the wiring defect in the engine control system.

This, as well as other <u>known</u> faults such as a control jam, could definitely be the cause of an accident, not just a 'distraction'.

(At Annex N to his Chinook Airworthiness Review Team report in 1992, the Director of Flight Safety noted that RNAY Fleetlands had *'commented on the significantly high number of chafed pipes, wiring looms and fairings found during Pre-Major survey'* and that their observations *'appeared not to be acted upon'*. Also prevalent was hose chafing in the forward pylon area, and loose hydraulic pipe unions in the aft pylon area).

*

Witness 2 was Squadron Leader Peter Gregory, 2IC of 230 Squadron (Puma) and responsible for the administration of the Chinook Detachment. In his statement he said:

'During Tapper's tour as senior pilot the attachment was running smoothly despite the difficulties associated with the introduction of the Chinook HC Mk2, and Flight Lieutenant Tapper was proving to be a good senior pilot'.

This begs the obvious question as to what the witness, an outsider to the Chinook detachment but a qualified and theatre current helicopter pilot, saw as 'the difficulties'. This question was not asked. Why not?

A similar comment applies to Witness 15, Squadron Leader Barry North, OC Special Forces Flight 7 Squadron, who stated:

'However, he (Tapper) was frustrated by its (the HC Mk2's) limited CA Release, and he shared the commonly held feelings with respect to the seemingly confused manner in which the Mk2 had been introduced into RAF service'.

Again, this very serious comment regarding airworthiness is not followed up. Why not, especially given this witness was one of the most qualified people to answer it?

The Board does ascertain from Witness 4, Squadron Leader Michael Lee of 230 Squadron, that the Senior Engineering Officer 230 (Puma) Squadron, and not the Chinook Detachment Commander (Tapper), was responsible for the engineering supervision of the attached Chinook aircraft and personnel. However, no attempt is made to find out how this responsibility was being discharged or how such a major breach of engineering regulations, of which he should have been aware, was ignored. And, most importantly, how, as the front line link in the airworthiness chain, he was *'satisfied that ZD576 was serviceable for its final flight'*. Given the history of the aircraft, and the faults of the previous 24 hours, this seems an even bigger leap of faith than the Board's balance of probabilities of pilot error. However, the basis on which the witness makes this statement is not questioned at all by the Board. This also links with my previous comments on the remarks of the Station Commander RAF Aldergrove.

*

The Board makes only a superficial attempt to investigate the maintenance and fault history of the aircraft, and the wider issues of the engineering/equipment technical problems of the new Mk2 fleet - a major omission in any accident Inquiry, let alone such a high profile one as this. In particular, the Board does not question why, given its recent history, 7 Squadron - presumably the Senior Engineering Officer - chose ZD576 to go to Northern Ireland on 31 May.

Similarly, the Board does not question OC Engineering Wing RAF Odiham on how he, as the senior engineer in the front line airworthiness chain, discharged his overall responsibilities for the Aldergrove detachment. Not just for the airworthiness of the aircraft, but also for the engineering standards of the detachment.

The Board claims to have reviewed the servicing history of the aircraft in full, and includes some of the maintenance records of ZD576. But it does not make use of the information these records provide; either in their own findings, or to follow up what results had been obtained from the fault investigations on the components, including two Engine Change Units removed from the aircraft.

There were two entries in the Supplementary Flight Servicing Register that had potential relevance as a cause or contributory factor:

- Serial 2, Servicing Instruction/CHK 57 relating to the security of the DECU connectors, and;
- Serial 4, a special check on the security of the Collective Balance Spring Bracket Mount, called for by Senior Engineering Officer 7 Squadron following an incident on ZD576 on 10 May 1994.

Although the Board included the Supplementary Flight Servicing Register in Annex AK 'Extracts from ZD576 F700 and Maintenance Work Order', they did not include the Supplementary Flight Servicing Certificate (eventually supplied by MoD in 2001). However, they did confirm that no Servicing Instructions had been carried out on ZD576.

*

The Board does not seem to have sought any maintenance or engineering advice from Boscombe Down (who had so little confidence in the FADEC software that they were no longer test flying the aircraft), or made any attempt to assess the relevance of the Wilmington incident; even though the Board was aware of both issues. The fact that such basics were ignored is yet another indication that the Board were neither seriously considering this area as a potential cause, nor doing a thorough job in those maintenance/engineering areas that they *were* looking at.

Related to this, as the Board does not mention 'airworthiness' at all, it is unlikely Boscombe were given the formal opportunity to state the aircraft was not airworthy, and why. This obviously quite deliberate exclusion of Boscombe is a major indicator of the direction the Board was sent in.

The Board does not make any attempt to look at the history of the modifications to the aircraft, either from a general programme point of view, the integrity of the FADEC software development, or for the individual aircraft ZD576. No attempt is made to assess whether there were any shortfalls in the Mk1 to Mk2 programme, and whether there were any flaws in the introduction to service of the Mk2 from either a development or a production point of view. In fact, as Boscombe had not completed their assessments of installed performance, from which Release to Service limitations are derived, the Board would have been faced with a scarcity of information. Again illustrating the immaturity of the entire Introduction to Service process.

The above factors are relevant to the depth, breadth and competence of the Board's investigations. Also, to the central question that the Board does not seem to have considered at all, i.e. whether, as a result of the Release to Service process and/or the fault/defect history of the aircraft, the airworthiness chain was still intact for ZD576. In my view there is clear evidence that it was not.

*

On the operational side, the Board misrepresented the Air Accidents Investigation Branch and Boeing simulation reports, and made poor assumptions about the weather, authorisation, supervision, human-factors and flight planning. Worse, their 'cruise climb' hypothesis, that the pilots selected an inappropriate rate of climb to clear the Mull - somewhere they did not plan to fly over - is unsupported by any evidence. One of my more experienced aircrew colleagues describes this finding as *'farcical'*.

Within my own area of expertise (the airworthiness/introduction to service and engineering/maintenance sides) it appears to be more of a case of going through the motions. Some very significant and potentially relevant issues, even where they are obvious from the witnesses' evidence, have been totally ignored. Thus, the Board leaves a great deal of unused evidence in its wake, and in my view was heavily flawed in both the scope and methods of its investigations, and their subsequent analyses.

However, even with these flaws the Board did not, of course, find any evidence of negligence - let alone gross negligence.

Maintenance/engineering issues

It is impossible from the Board related documents alone to determine the fault history of ZD576. Or, indeed, the general history of the still new Mk2 fleet. Apart from an acceptance that there was a fleet-wide issue with false warnings (which continued long after the accident and was highlighted in the US Army Release to Service in late 1995) there is no evidence that the Board looked at these two areas. These omissions, particularly the former, are in my view a major failing by the Board and the Review process.

It is also interesting that neither Wratten nor Day give any consideration to either the errors that the Board *did* identify with the supervision and standards of maintenance, or the fault/defect history of the aircraft. Air Vice Marshal Day (as he then was) talked of a *'thorough review of aircrew training and standards within the Support Helicopter Force'* having *'revealed no deficiencies which might have a bearing on the accident'*. Where is the similar review on the maintenance side, where there was such clear evidence of deficiencies that even a Board that does not seem to have been looking for them found some? In his evidence to the House of Lords, Day talked of basing his hypotheses only on *'facts'* (a position shown to be false by their Lordships). Given his disposition to only use 'facts' it is amazing he was so selective in ignoring the real facts on the maintenance and engineering aspects. The limited paperwork should have set alarm bells ringing.

*

It is worth repeating the contents of the Maintenance Work Orders (MWOs) and Incident Signals for ZD576 to get a feel these issues. (There are records of many similar incidents on the engine systems of other Chinook HC Mk2s, but which I have not included here):

On 21 April 1994, an MWO was raised for the following symptom:

'Both Engine Condition Levers Flight Idle - no torque indications on either side. No.1 engine running high at Flight Idle, No.2 engine nominal. N1 - 82%, PTIT - 550°C, Fuel Flow 450. DECU Built-in Test checks satisfactory throughout'.

As a result, the No.1 Engine (Engine Change Unit) was replaced, and the subsequent omnibus Fault Report gives a slightly fuller picture:

'Chinook HC Mk2 ZD576. Power Plant Magnetostrictive Torquemeter System. Lycoming T55 L712F (the Engine Change Unit) torquemeter junction box. Post

Mid-Life Update Chinook HC Mk2 acceptance. Initially with both Engine Condition Levers at Flight Idle there were no indications to either engine. No.1 engine running high and No.2 normal. DECU Built-in Test checks satisfactory throughout. On subsequent ground runs a torque mismatch revealed No.1 ECU reading 20% and No.2 reading 37%. Both 1 and 2 RPDS's transposed and electrical resistance checks to each torque head windings - fault still apparent. Left hand ECU (No.1) replaced'.

I merely note that torquemeter failure can cause wild fluctuations in engine speed.

Although not linked to the FADEC system, on 10 May 1994 the aircraft had another airborne incident, which in turn led to the requirement for Supplementary Flight Servicing Checks:

'During sortie collective control heavy. Aircraft Returned to Base'.

The bonding had failed on the inserts that held the Collective Balance Spring to its bracket on the Thrust/Yaw Pallet Assembly. The pallet was replaced and a serious fault signal raised. It is interesting to note that, using RAF maintenance procedures available at the time, the aircraft could not be confirmed as serviceable and was eventually signed off to a Boeing procedure - an indication of the state of the maintenance documentation (a key element of the airworthiness chain).

Although the Air Accidents Investigation Branch (AAIB) found that post-crash most of the attachment brackets were detached from the control pallets, the Board decided this was likely to have occurred during the post-impact break-up of the aircraft. Thus, the Board considered any pre-impact control malfunction as *'highly unlikely'*. This is a remarkably 'brave' conclusion given they had clear evidence of a fault that was still the subject of a serious fault signal investigation at the time of the accident. The Board said they based their decision on the AAIB report, but Mr Cable's evidence to the House of Lords did not support such a positive conclusion:

'He (Mr Cable) further explained that the detachment of the pallet inserts and the components carried by them could possibly cause a restriction or jam. "It would be very difficult - impossible - to dismiss the possibility that there had been a restriction and evidence had not been found". This explanation is readily understandable given the crowded equipment in the broom cupboard'.

The evidence of the RAF Odiham Unit Test Pilot, Squadron Leader Robert Burke, to the House of Lords, is also relevant in this area:

'In relation to possible jams Squadron Leader Burke explained that, due to the complexity of the control system, a jam caused by a loose article such as the balance spring in one of the three axes, pitch, yaw or roll, could lead to quite random

results in all three axes sometimes, and certainly in two of them. He had personal experience while lifting off from the ground of a jam in one axis affecting the other two. He also referred to the problems of DASH runaways in Chinooks of both marks causing temporary loss of control of aircraft'.

In his critique of the second (2002) Boeing 'simulation', Squadron Leader Burke commented:

'It has been a bedrock of the MoD position that the Chinook was under the full control of the pilots before the crash. Boeing was not asked to look at the effects of control malfunctions in the second simulation. However, in a remarkably frank and detailed paragraph, Boeing admits its concern that the bank angle they postulate for the last instant of flight is not consistent with evidence from the wreckage. Boeing is not able to explain a slight turn to the right and draws attention to the highly unusual position of the left rudder pedal. To me, as a highly experienced professional helicopter pilot, and a helicopter test pilot with probably as much experience as anyone of control malfunctions in helicopters, this paragraph shouts out "possible control malfunction". The first simulation mentions nothing like this'.

(Initially, it was thought that a slight right turn was made, suggested by initial impact being to the right of their assumed previous track).

Clearly, this is compatible with the original problems leading to the serious fault signal. Such a flying control malfunction, and a consequential partial or full loss of control, could, for example, mean the pilot's only option was to try to gain sufficient height to clear the high ground with an aircraft that could not be fully controlled.

*

On 17 May 1994, a Maintenance Work Order (MWO) was raised for the following symptom:

'No.1 ECU PTIT rises (undemanded) to transient 950°C for about one second then resumes normal temperature'.

As a result, the No.1 Engine Change Unit and its DEU were replaced *'as a precautionary measure'*. The replacements were not bay serviced but were robbed from another aircraft, ZA704. In another major omission, the Board made no attempt to check the fault history of these robbed items. They should have done, as an incident on the No.2 engine of ZA704 on 8 March had been one of the four which Boscombe claimed had *'particularly serious implications'*, as it had been 'No Fault Found'. We do not know which engine was robbed from ZA704, but if it was the No.2 this should certainly have been identified and fully investigated by the Board.

On 26 May 1994, ZA704 made a precautionary diversion and landing at Luton Airport. The incident signal reads:

'In transit Master Caution and No.2 Engine Fail captions illuminated with no abnormal No.2 Engine indications. Master Caution cancelled "Eng fail" caption went out after 10 seconds. (An eternity in the context of the approach to the Mull). Assumed spurious in accordance with RAF HANSQUADRON Signal dated 01/02/94. Aircraft precautionary diversion to Luton Airport without further incident. Engineering advice sought. Crew recommended to continue task as DECUs indicated 88'. (Considered a 'soft' fault code that could be safely ignored - although the US Army Release to Service required it to be reported).

As a result of this incident an investigation was stated to be underway at Boeing and Textron.

On 1 June 1994, ZD576 suffered a 'lag' in the response of the No.1 engine Power Turbine Inlet Temperature (PTIT) gauge on increase of power. No MWO was raised and a technician at RAF Aldergrove transposed the No.1 and No.2 PTIT gauges and the fault did not recur.

On 2 June 1994, the day of the accident, ZD576 experienced a No.2 engine PTIT gauge failure. The fault was confirmed to be similar to the fault on the No.1 engine PTIT gauge the day before. (Which, on the face of it, would indicate a gauging problem, as it was the same gauge). But, again, no MWO was raised and no detailed investigation carried out.

There is therefore no independent evidence that the fault on 2 June was on the No.2 engine. In such a diagnosis, done 'on the fly' with no proper debrief, it is all too easy to assume the same problem as the previous day.

The fact that it was the No.2 Engine also helps when giving post-crash evidence in an area where the witnesses would have been well aware that they had broken the rules. Certainly, if it had been the No.1 engine again it would have been a very different story. The Board's investigation in this area was again superficial, and their criticism of what was a significant breach of engineering regulations which, if it were indicative of the detachment engineering standards at RAF Aldergrove, would have been a major issue, could hardly have been milder. Only one Reviewing Officer commented on this issue, and then only to 'put it under the table'.

Witness 21, Chief Technician David Carruthers of RAF Odiham, quite rightly told the Board that, as there was no feedback from the PTIT gauge to the DECU, a lagging PTIT gauge could not affect the DECU. However, he also pointed out that the PTIT thermocouple signal is routed through the DECU where it is split. Nobody on the Board then asked the obvious questions on whether problems within the DECU or the DECU connectors could have caused the gauge to lag. For example, a high resistance connection could have the same impact.

An intermittent wiring fault in the engine control system must be a distinct possibility, MoD admitting this was a serious and extant defect in Chinook Mk2 DECUs on 2 June 1994. In simply swapping the gauges without carrying out any form of system fault investigation, the 7 Squadron maintenance personnel (with the backing they should, but may not, have had from RAF Odiham) were either out of their depth in terms of their knowledge of the aircraft's fault history and system architecture, or they took the easy way out - perhaps as a result of the operational pressures that the detachment was under. Either way the Board's failure to investigate and report fully on this area was, in my view, negligence.

*

To summarise. Given the fault history of the ZD576 as a Mk2, and the known design defects across the Mk2 fleet, I would have expected any engine system problems to have generated more than a passing interest. Not just for the Board's investigations, but for the engineering staff at Aldergrove and Odiham (who were presumably informed on a regular basis of the serviceability problems on the Aldergrove detachment, and definitely knew of the ongoing airworthiness issues at Boscombe).

I am even more surprised that, as the Board did not report until 3 February 1995, eight months after the accident, they did not follow up on the outcome of the ongoing fault investigations. Firm results from these investigations could have helped understanding.

Wiring problems are an all too common occurrence, particularly on modified aircraft. I have been able to discuss the Chinook problems at Aldergrove with one tradesman. One comment he made was interesting:

'In one instance on a Chinook Mk2 that had numerous reported defects, it was found eventually that the main engine electrical connector pins had not been fastened on the cables, causing the intermittent indications'.

Such Quality Control failures had occurred during Mk1 production. That is, crucial aspects of the ZD576 case were known recurrences. MoD should know the history of electrical problems on the Mk2 during the conversion programme. It would be interesting to see it.

On 26 October 1993 Boscombe had warned that the Auxiliary Power Unit generator, used during an emergency, was rated at 20kVA but the load drawn was 24kVA. Boeing's response was that it could sustain a load of 30kVA for five minutes, a frightening view. Also, the battery buses were continually connected to the battery even when the battery switch was

OFF, meaning the battery would quickly discharge. (And the battery switch was not illuminated and difficult to see). It remains unclear what action was taken, but it would be impossible to correct these design defects between notification (26 October 1993) and issuing the Release to Service (22 November 1993).

RAF Release to Service Limitations

As is often the case when a new aircraft or aircraft version enters service, the Chinook HC Mk2 Release contained limitations affecting the flight regime and operating capabilities.

The underlying reason for the weight limitations was to cater for the relatively high probability of FADEC malfunction, including spurious warnings, either causing an engine failure or the crew to shut an engine down. This would not satisfy normal civil clearances for passenger operation, where the possibility of an engine shut down in flight must be assessed as remote before certification is given; and that assessment later verified through use.

However, these flight limitations would not provide full protection against an uncommanded engine run-up. Such a situation was known and was identified by Witness 20, Squadron Leader David Morgan, as being one of the *'flight critical'* unforeseen malfunctions (which were mainly on the FADEC system). Even the Board, at paragraph 35d, use his evidence in their assessment of the problems of the Mk2 in RAF Service. Interestingly, though, they omit the words 'flight critical' - one has to wonder why.

Uncommanded engine run-up

The time taken to manage an uncommanded engine run-up is (in accident timescales) significant. First the aircraft must be brought back under control from what may have become a dangerous and difficult to recover from flight regime. The problem must then be identified (Squadron Leader Morgan and the Board commented on the *'misleading and confusing cockpit engine malfunctions'*). Corrective action must be taken. (Again, both commented on the lack of clear FADEC emergency drills in the Flight Reference Cards). Finally, the chosen action must take effect, safely.

Did this happen in the case of ZD576? I do not, of course, know. However, I suggest that such a potential scenario, like a loss of control discussed earlier, is another one that would fit the known facts better than a *'decision by the pilots to enter cloud covered high ground at an inappropriate speed and with an inappropriate rate of climb'.*

Indeed, my own experience, and that of every pilot I have spoken to, indicates that by selecting the next waypoint whilst still well clear of the Mull, the pilots had decided to turn away from the high ground at a safe distance; and that at this point a major system or control malfunction occurred (or manifested itself) leading them to being distracted or, worse, losing control of the aircraft until a point at which the situation was irrecoverable. Sadly, many military and civil accident reports contain examples of such occurrences.

The Board, and the Reviewing Officers, seem to rely heavily on the 'fact' that the engines were operating 'normally' at the time of the impact as their main justification for dismissing these 'flight critical' engine malfunctions. They claim this is based on the evidence of another truly expert witness, the AAIB's Tony Cable. It is interesting to note what he *really* said, to the House of Lords Select Committee:

'Mr Cable in evidence stressed that throughout the investigation the evidence was "remarkably thin". While the evidence available to him pointed strongly to the engines operating normally, i.e. without distress, at the point of initial impact, he conceded that this did not necessarily mean that this was in accordance with pilot commands. He further explained that the possibility of an intermittent fault prior to impact could not be dismissed'.

Thus, nothing that is said would militate against the known 'flight critical' malfunction of an uncommanded engine run-up having occurred shortly before impact. If one then accepts the possibility that ZD576 had an intermittent wiring problem - a known design defect in the DECU connectors - such a scenario has a much higher probability of occurrence. And criticality, given the DECUs host safety critical software.

Again, Squadron Leader Burke's comments on the Boeing simulations are of interest:

'The Board of Inquiry mooted that the engines were at roughly matched power settings at a <u>mid-range</u>. This suggested a likely "cruise-climb" (a steady, gradual climb while maintaining the same forward speed) prior to the impact. In order to explain the major non-correlation between engine power/rotor rpm/thrust lever position postulated in the first simulation, and the physical evidence in the wreckage, the second simulation suggested a complex chain of events, which might have happened between the initial impact and the end of the progressive crash. If Boeing's explanation is correct, it means the engines were <u>at least at full power and probably at emergency power</u> before impact. If this was the case it directly conflicts with the cruise climb theory of the Board/MoD. Indeed, it actually means

that nobody knows what the engines were doing before impact'.

Given the evidence concerning the crew's training, and their positive attitude towards obeying regulations and Release to Service limitations, a control malfunction leading to a loss or restriction of control, or engine run-up, which could not be identified and corrected in the time available, is more likely than pilot error. What I find incredible is that the Board and the Reviewing Officers had all these facts before them, yet made no serious attempt to see if a technical problem could have fitted the accident scenario.

MoD and 'economies with the truth'

One of the concerns in all that has gone on in the various Inquiries, and the many questions in Parliament and elsewhere, must be that MoD does not appear to have carried out any form of serious review of the issues being raised. Everything in this review is in the public domain - MoD would have the advantage of having a lot more information to either support or disprove the comments being made. Instead, they have hidden behind the flag of 'no new evidence' (although if they looked they would see plenty of unused evidence), and have continued to ignore or even obfuscate those facts and questions that they do not like. A classic example of this relates to the Flight Reference Cards (FRCs):

Witness 20, Squadron Leader David Morgan, was asked:

(Q) 'Were these malfunctions covered by drills in the Chinook HC Mk2 FRCs?'

(A) 'No, the Chinook HC Mk2 FRC were based primarily on the Chinook D Model, which is not fitted with FADEC. Drills relating to FADEC were based on the best information on how the system would respond during certain malfunctions'.

(Q) 'Were there any areas where the Chinook HC Mk2 FRCs, valid on 2 June 94, were confusing?'.

(A) 'Yes, a number of emergency drills, in particular electrical and hydraulic, were poorly laid out and required the crew to be familiar with the drill to avoid confusion. The shortfall in the Chinook HC Mk2 FRCs was discussed with crews during their conversion courses'.

In their findings the Board, at paragraphs 46c and 70a, commented:

'The relative inexperience of the crew on the Chinook HC Mk2 could have amplified the degree of distraction created by even a relatively minor technical occurrence. Any distraction could have been further amplified by the poor guidance provided by the Chinook HC Mk2 Flight Reference Cards'.

In fact, some were completely blank, marked *'To Be Issued'*!

Even though the Board has identified the FRCs as an issue (and their place in the airworthiness chain is a key one) this is not explored.

The 'relative inexperience' of the crew raises the issue of why the Chinook HC Mk2 was chosen for such a high-profile passenger sortie - this is not followed up at all by the Board. It is interesting to note that the Mk2 was used despite a request from Flight Lieutenant Tapper to retain an extra Mk1 in Northern Ireland *'because of the limited operational capabilities of the HC Mk2'* - statement by witness 11, Squadron Leader David Prowse, 7 Squadron.

The same witness also confirms that he was happy with Flight Lieutenant Tapper's ability to operate the Mk2, *inter alia 'because he knew his way around the Chinook HC Mk2 Flight Reference Cards, which are particularly confusing'*. Hardly a ringing endorsement for the suitability of the Mk2 for passenger operations, although further confirmation that Flight Lieutenant Tapper was taking the problems seriously.

It is also interesting that the Board, and despite the clear implications of statements such as those from Squadron Leader Morgan, made no attempt to assess the completeness and effectiveness of the rest of the Air Publications system - nor did their Terms of Reference ask them to.

Of further interest is that MoD officials seem to have deliberately misinformed Ministers, and they in turn Parliament, about the true situation with the FRCs. Tom Brake MP, on 13 June 2000:

'To ask the Secretary of State for Defence if his Department requires manufacturers to provide complete flight reference cards prior to releasing an aircraft into operational service; if the Chinook Mk2 had a complete set of cards at the time of the fatal crash of ZD576 in June 1994, and if these included drills covering the possibility of FADEC malfunctions'.

In reply, John Spellar MP, Minister of State for the Armed Forces, said:

'All manufacturers of new Ministry of Defence aircraft are contractually required to provide full aircrew documentation prior to release to operational service. This documentation includes both Aircrew Manual and Flight Reference Cards. The Chinook Mk2 had a complete set of Flight Reference Cards in June 1994. This contained all the normal and emergency operating drills in force at that time, including drills for a possible FADEC malfunction'.

These words do not reflect the facts or the Board's findings. One has to wonder why the RAF chose to offer this lie and cause a Minister to mislead Parliament. Too late, they were re-issued in July 1994.

Conclusions

In his 22 July 2002 statement to the House of Commons on their Lordships' findings, Secretary of State for Defence Geoff Hoon MP said:

'It follows from this strict standard of proof that if there is another plausible explanation for what took place other than the one accepted by the Board of Inquiry, its conclusion cannot be allowed to stand. The reviewing officers in this case were required to be in no doubt whatsoever that the pilots' negligence was a cause - <u>although not necessarily the sole cause</u> - of the accident'.

The Reviewing Officers claimed the pilots' actions were the sole cause. Other causes had never been mooted before. This statement highlights the fact that the negligence of others more senior was ignored.

Others have demonstrated that the Reviewing Officers' finding of gross negligence is not only lacking in plausibility, but in direct contradiction to the then MoD regulations. I do not propose to go further in repeating these arguments, but they are totally valid and supported by this review. Instead, I would offer the following additional conclusions:

- The failure to show the Board the Boscombe Down letter of 6 June 1994 (reiterating that the aircraft was not airworthy) is inexcusable, and seems to indicate that the Board was being 'manipulated'.
- The cause of the incident of 19 May 1994 was still under investigation at the time of the accident (and had not been given to the Board even six months later). From the Board's comments, the engineers at Aldergrove probably had no realisation they were working on a system which had caused this major incident only two weeks earlier - one of four in-service (not flight trials related) that finally caused Boscombe Down to stop their trials flying. That none of this was brought to the attention of the Board, and a proper assessment not made of ZD576's fitness for purpose, is a case of negligence in its own right, and a clear failure of MoD's duty of care to both passengers and crew.
- The airworthiness of the Chinook HC Mk2, and the serviceability of ZD576 for this flight, were both assumed. The Board and the Review process seems to have spent its energy intent on finding aircrew error, and no other finding would be appreciated or indeed accepted.
- The Board failed to interview relevant key witnesses. In particular, Boscombe's staff, who knew most about the engineering and airworthiness issues.
- The Reviewing Officers failed to look at airworthiness, maintenance or engineering issues, and hence did not raise any of the obvious questions

that had been missed by the Board. To do so would have been questioning the RAF Command chain, as well as the introduction to service process in which they were, themselves, key players.

- Far from there being no other plausible explanation for the accident, a review of the aircraft and fleet history, coupled with the Release to Service and Development Phase problems, would have shown that (e.g.) an intermittent fault in the engine control system was more plausible (by the number of facts supporting it) than an aircrew error accident.

- Squadron Leader Robert Burke's analysis of the second Boeing 'simulation' raises the possibly, even probability, of a control malfunction - another even more plausible reason for the accident. This is supported by the Special Flying Instruction uncovered by David Hill, warning of Undemanded Flight Control Movements.

- Despite the clear evidence that technical factors could have been a primary cause, the Board made no attempt to assess any technical scenarios to see if they would also fit the accident scene. Nor was any simulation of potential flight critical incidents carried out.

- During the Board of Inquiry's deliberations, and those of the Reviewing Officers, there was ample 'new' (or rather unused) evidence that should have thrown severe doubt even on a 'balance of probabilities aircrew error' finding, let alone beyond any doubt whatsoever.

*

We have seen how a letter as vital to the investigation as the Boscombe one of 6 June 1994, together with a proper interpretation of the AAIB report on control pallet insert bonding, and a Servicing Instruction (issued within 30 days of the accident), could be totally ignored not just by the Board, but also the review process. This failure would appear to be down to the engineering staff in Group, Command and MoD, who do not seem to have carried out any review of the Board's findings.

I believe it reasonable to assume that these shortcomings by the Board, and other 'open' engineering and airworthiness issues, were drawn to the Senior Reviewing Officers' attention. The latest information, almost certainly released inadvertently by MoD and again identified by David Hill, speaking of *'positively dangerous'* safety critical software implementation and ongoing systemic airworthiness failures, reinforces my view that it may well have suited the overall MoD position to let such shortcomings lie and not open Pandora's Box.

The general airworthiness issues, and specifically the aircraft carrying an intermittent fault in the DECU connectors, perhaps causing a control malfunction in flight, should have raised serious questions regarding acceptance of the Chinook HC Mk2 into service.

I would also question why the RAF provided an aircraft with such flight limitations and unknown history (in terms of conclusions to ongoing fault investigations) for such a high-profile task. Such questions, rather than leading to findings on the pilots' error or negligence, should have led not just to another plausible explanation for the accident, but to a similar conclusion on negligence and inadequate procedures applying elsewhere in the Command and Release to Service chains. Something which, clearly, would be a major embarrassment to the RAF, as shown by the 2008/9 Nimrod Review in a very similar situation, following the September 2006 crash in Afghanistan.

John Blakeley

(Original dated 2 November 2003, updated January 2011, with minor edits February 2020).

Author's note

Private individuals can only go so far. I lack the authority to compel the release of suppressed evidence. I cannot order a police investigation or legal review. But the fresh evidence I have set out here serves to signpost the way for future action. It is the role of Ministers to correct these wrongs, and require these bodies to meet their legal obligations. The only way to break free of MoD's compartmentalisation of the issues is to order a Public Inquiry into why the systemic failures reiterated in the Nimrod and Mull of Kintyre Reviews were encouraged - in fact, directed - and have not been addressed. No government will contemplate such a thing, so it is left to the public to record the truth, in books such as this.

I hope, therefore, it has given you food for thought. While I have concentrated on ZD576, precisely the same failings occurred in many other fatal aircraft accidents. Primarily, refusal to implement mandated airworthiness regulations, followed by lies and obfuscation to protect the guilty, while blaming the innocent. MoD has sought to present subsequent accidents, among them Nimrod XV230, Hercules XV179, Hawk XX177 and Tornado ZG710, as isolated cases. They were recurrences, the lead anomaly the same in each case.

Bibliography

Aircraft Data Set

1. INTERIM Controller Aircraft Release at Amendment 1, March 1994.
2. Release to Service at Amendment 1, March 1994.
3. Chinook HC Mk1 Release to Service at Issue 2, Amendment 17, July 1987, and current as of 2 June 1994.

MoD Standards and policy directives

4. Controller Aircraft Instructions (Replaced AvP 88).
5. JSP553 - Military Airworthiness Regulations.
6. Defence Standard 00-970 - Design and Airworthiness Requirements for Service Aircraft.
7. Defence Standard 05-125/2 - Technical Procedures for Post Design Services, incorporating PDS Specifications 1-20.
8. DUS(DP)/924/11/2/9, 14 December 1989 - Joint MoD(PE) / Industry Computing Policy for Military Operational Systems.

Boscombe Down letters and reports

9. A&AEE PE/Chinook/40 APF/246/011/1, July 1993 - Chinook HC Mk1- Assessment of T55-L-712F FADEC.
10. A&AEE AEN/58/119(H), 18 August 1993 - Chinook HC Mk2 - Status of Engine FADEC Software.
11. A&AEE AEN/58/119(H), 27 August 1993 -Task E1536 - Chinook HC Mk2 - CA Release Trials.
12. A&AEE Letter Report TM 2174, incorporating Letter Report E989 and PE/Chinook/40, September 1993 - Chinook HC Mk1 Assessment of T55-L-712F FADEC.
13. A&AEE AEN/58/119(H), 30 September 1993 - Chinook Mk2 - T55 Engine FADEC Software.
14. A&AEE AAD/308/04, 12 October 1993 - Chinook Mk2 - CA Release for T55 FADEC.
15. A&AEE Letter Report PE/Chinook/41, APF/247/Annex, 22 October 1993 - Chinook HC Mk2 - INTERIM CA Release Recommendations.
16. A&AEE AEN 58/012, 26 October 1993 - Engineering Systems Division

Letter Report E1109 Chinook HC Mk2 - INTERIM CA Release.

17. A&AEE - Annex A to Letter Report TM2210, 26 October 1993 - Chinook HC Mk2 - Document in the form of an INTERIM CA Release.

Government reports

18. National Audit Office report 'Accepting Equipment Off-Contract and Into Service', 11 February 2000.
19. The Nimrod Review (2009).
20. The Mull of Kintyre Review (2011).

Independent reports

21. The Macdonald Report (Captains Ron Macdonald, Dick Hadlow and Ralph Kohn, Fellows of the Royal Aeronautical Society, 2000) & Technical Addendum (David Hill, 2009).
22. Mull of Kintyre Group Legal Review (Dr Michael Powers QC, 2007).
23. Submission to the Mull of Kintyre Review - A report discussing systemic airworthiness failings in the Ministry of Defence and how this affected the Chinook HC Mk2 in 1993/94 (David Hill, 2011).

Recommended reading:

Chinook ZD576 - A Professional Pilot's Assessment (Michael Russell, 2001)

Lying in State (Tim Slessor, 2004)

The Crash of Nimrod XV230 (Trish Knight, 2012)

The Crash Detectives (Christine Negroni, 2016)

Glossary of Terms and Abbreviations

AAIB	Air Accidents Investigation Branch
ACAS	Assistant Chief of the Air Staff
AD/HP1	Assistant Director, Helicopter Projects 1, MoD(PE)
ADA	Aircraft Design Authority
ADR	Accident Data Recorder
AFCS	Automatic/Advanced Flight Control System
ARI	Airborne Radio Installation
ASaC	Airborne Surveillance and Control
CAS	Chief of the Air Staff
C/A	Coarse Acquisition
CECO	Chandler Evans Corporation
CHART	Chinook Airworthiness Review Team (and its report)
CPLS	Covert Personnel Locator System
CPSU	Control Power Supply Unit (part of ALQ-157)
DASH	Differential Airspeed Hold
DECU	EMC-32T Digital Engine Control Unit, part of FADEC
EMI	Electro-Magnetic Interference
FADEC	Full Authority Digital Engine Control
FRC	Flight Reference Cards
GMT	Greenwich Mean Time
GPS	Global Positioning System
HaveQuick II	A frequency hopping anti-jamming system for UHF radios, providing Transmission Security (TRANSEC).
HF	High Frequency
HSDE	Hawker Siddeley Dynamics Engineering
JSP	Joint Service Publication
LCTA	Longitudinal Cyclic Trim Actuator
MADGE	Microwave Assisted Digital Guidance Equipment
MALPAS	Malvern Program Analysis Suite, developed at RSRE Malvern
MLU	Mid-Life Upgrade

MoD(PE)	Ministry of Defence (Procurement Executive)
MSA	Minimum Safe Altitude
MWO	Maintenance Work Order
Nr	% rotational speed of the rotor
PDS	Post Design Services
PM	Project Manager or Programme Manager
PSNI	Police Service of Northern Ireland (incorporating the Royal Ulster Constabulary George Cross)
PTIT	Power Turbine Inlet Temperature
RAF	Royal Air Force
RF	Radio Frequency
RIM	Radio Installation Memorandum
RN	Royal Navy
RNS	Racal Navigation System (as in RNS252 SuperTANS)
RPM	Revolutions Per Minute
RTS	Release to Service (The Master Airworthiness Reference)
RUC	Royal Ulster Constabulary (Following the collective award of the George Cross in 2000, the RUC was known as RUC GC).
SCDA	System Co-ordinating Design Authority
SEM	Service Engineered Modification
SFI	Special Flying Instruction
SI	Servicing Instruction
SPADE	Southampton Program Analysis and Development Environment, developed by Southampton University
STF	Special Trials Fit
TACAN	Tactical Air Navigation
TANS	Tactical Navigation System ('Air' is often included).
UFCM	Undemanded Flight Control Movement
UHF	Ultra High Frequency
UTC	Co-ordinated Universal Time
Validation	'Have we built the right system?'
Verification	'Have we built the system right?'
VHF	Very High Frequency

Printed in Great Britain
by Amazon